DRIED
FLOWER
GARDENING

DRIED FLOWER GARDENING

Joanna Sheen
Caroline Alexander

WARD LOCK

To our children:
Pippa
Lorna, Thomas and Crispin

First published 1991 by Ward Lock
Villiers House, 41/47 Strand, London WC2N 5JE, England

A Cassell imprint

© Text and illustrations Ward Lock Limited 1991

Reprinted 1991, 1992, 1993

Photography by Mike Evans
Illustrations by Tony Randell

Typeset in Goudy Old Style 11/12½ point
by Columns of Reading

Printed and bound in Singapore by Kyodo Printing Co Ltd

British Library Cataloguing in Publication Data
Sheen, Joanna
   Dried flower gardening.
   1. Gardens. Ornamental flowering plants. Cultivation
   I. Title   II. Alexander, Caroline
   635.9

   ISBN 0–7063–6955–6 Cased
        0–7063–7085–6 Paperback

*Frontispiece: Air-drying can be a very
decorative method of preserving flowers.*

CONTENTS

INTRODUCTION

Traditionally, dried flowers have been associated with autumnal and winter flower arrangements, to replace the fresh flowers of summer as they become less easily available. One often saw displays in muted shades of orange and brown, with some sun-bleached wheat or corn giving an overall effect of a faded, lifeless arrangement. Standards have changed dramatically in the last few years. Drying techniques have improved, the colours have become more vibrant and the choice much wider, and so the popularity of dried flowers has increased.

Commercially dried flowers are often dyed a range of bright and unnatural colours and are usually fairly expensive. The alternative, of growing and drying flowers at home, is far less intricate than one might have thought, and excellent results can be achieved by following the simple guidelines and harvesting information given in the following chapters. Many of the most expensive varieties in the shops are, in fact, the easiest to grow in your own garden, and very reliable to dry, so large savings can be made very quickly. What's more, a tremendous amount of satisfaction can be gained by growing the flowers from seed or a cutting, then harvesting and drying them for a finished arrangement in the home.

Many of the varieties mentioned in the A–Z section of this book may well be plants that are already established in your garden, or annuals that you have grown before, so you will quickly be able to start experimenting. Do take careful note of the instructions in the A–Z section, as there is a vast difference between a good specimen picked at the right time and dried in the correct manner, and a piece of plant material picked at random and abandoned to dry out! Once you have achieved the high standards that can be gained with a little care, your enthusiasm will soon increase. Then you will have to beware the 'drying bug' that can take over and make every available spot in the house overflow with plants and flowers of every description!

A bouquet of dried flowers, with such vibrant hues they could almost have been freshly picked from the garden.

Planning Your Crop

Many of the varieties that can be successfully dried are already popular garden choices, such as hydrangeas, eucalyptus, Chinese lanterns or peonies, and they may already be growing in your garden. There are several ways to tackle growing plants for drying purposes: you can harvest the plants you are already growing, plan a special area within the garden in which you will solely grow plants for drying, or combine the two by placing suitable plants throughout the garden, so the gaps created by the picked flowers are less obvious.

By taking note of when a plant is to be harvested, you can plan the more visible areas of your garden to house such plants as poppies, love-in-a-mist and honesty, all of which are picked at the seed pod stage and therefore give maximum enjoyment before they are removed from the garden and dried. Many species, such as *Achillea ptarmica*, can be harvested in small amounts as they flower, thereby leaving other flowers to develop on the plant. There are others that would be suitable for fairly prominent positions, such as hydrangeas and *A. filipendulina*, that are harvested late in flowering and so give a good show before they are removed! Obviously any plants that need cutting very early in the flowering stage, such as *Helichrysum* and golden rod, *Solidago*, should be sited in an inconspicuous spot as they will never look their best.

Apart from planning the visual aspects of the garden, you also need to choose which flowers you wish to grow and which ones may be better left off your list, and instead bought either ready dried or in fresh bunches from a florist so you can dry them yourself. Although old-fashioned roses dry beautifully and are an important asset to any arranger's collection, if you want to use a reasonably large amount of roses it is far better to buy bunches of fresh roses when they are at their cheapest and dry them for use later. Commercially grown roses usually have small heads but far longer stems, and so are useful in large arrangements.

Dried roses are a marvellous asset, when you are arranging your collection of dried flowers and foliages. Really generous amounts of roses used in an arrangement look very effective, and have good strong colour and shape.

Growing background material

Where possible you should try to grow plant material of as many shapes and sizes as possible. Background material, such as foliage for glycerining, grasses or less spectacular items, which provide blocks of colour, are just as important as prize specimens for the centre of the arrangement! As seasoned dried flower arrangers will appreciate, it takes quite a large quantity of material to fill an arrangement, and so stocks of good-quality background material or fillers, such as sea lavender, *Alchemilla*, *Achillea* 'Cerise Queen' or hydrangea heads, are a tremendous help when you come to making up your arrangements. Remember, too, the scale of plant material you are preserving: if the vast majority is ideal for miniature flower arrangements, apart from one or two hydrangea heads and a giant *Allium* head, then it is unlikely that you will use the larger material, such as *Allium* heads and *Moluccella*, at all. So balance the size of material you grow and aim towards a good spread of flowers and leaves, so you will have plenty of flexibility and scope when you come to arrange your harvest.

Other background items that are particularly helpful for filling out arrangements include lavender (the larger headed varieties and darker colourings are preferable), Carthamus, a strong thistle shape which has a soft green colouring when picked in bud, and *Achillea ptarmica* (The Pearl), which usually keeps its good clear white and is very useful for lightening dark or drab arrangements.

Growing requirements

Soil types must also come into your calculations. If a particular plant needs soil that differs from that in your garden it is unlikely to prosper, so concentrate on growing more tolerant plants or those that are ideally suited to the soil conditions that you have. Generally speaking, your soil type does not need to be good as many varieties flower happily on poorer or slightly impoverished soils, but rainfall or irrigation is essential for many varieties to achieve good stem length and, of course, the acidity of the soil is critical for some species and also influences the colour of hydrangea heads. (Alkaline soils produce pink flower heads and acid soils produce blue ones.) These guidelines also apply to problems with varieties that are sensitive to climatic conditions and have special drying requirements: it is far better to ignore these varieties unless you have the correct conditions to produce quality specimens. Consider carefully where you are going to display your dried flowers and avoid damp atmospheres or bright sunlight. *Helichrysum bracteatum* and *Limonium sinuatum* hold their colour better than most varieties in direct light. Some varieties mentioned in the A–Z section, particularly *Helichrysum*, are more likely to re-absorb moisture than others and will have to be wired to ensure they don't droop once in an arrangement, so if you prefer not to fiddle with wires you should not grow such plants.

ANNUALS

Annuals can be a very satisfying group of plants to grow in the garden, as they are relatively easy to raise and success is probably assured. They are ready to harvest within the same season and so help overcome one's impatience to see instant results. There are many sources for seeds, both by mail order and from shops and garden centres, and a large and useful crop can be raised from a reasonably small outlay on seeds.

Annuals can be sown to infill spaces within a flowerbed or can be given their own area. In a few months you can have a riot of colour, which can all be directed towards drying and preserving, or some plants can be grown for colour and some for cutting. Wonderful colour schemes can be created with annuals so rapidly, you can have broad strokes of warm reds with deep greens or lime greens. The pinks always blend beautifully with the silvers and greys but try adding dark blue and purple for a stunning effect.

As you can see from the collection shown here, there is a multitude of colours and shapes and sizes available, so the only constraint is time and space for drying.

A brilliantly-coloured array of annual plants that dry well and can be grown quickly.

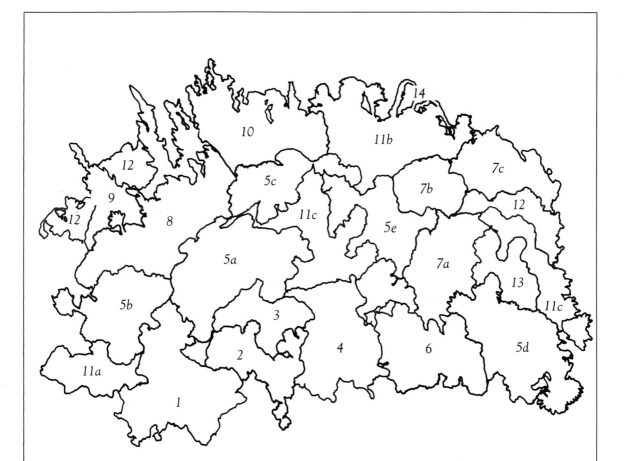

Annuals

1 *Origanum dictamnus*
2 *Ammobium alatum*
3 *Tagetes erecta*
4 *Limonium suworowii*
5a *Helichrysum bracteatum monstrosum* (salmon)
5b *Helichrysum* (lemon yellow)
5c *Helichrysum* (silver rose)
5d *Helichrysum* (cream)
5e *Helichrysum* (purple)
6 *Lonas inodora*
7a *Limonium sinuatum* (pink)

7b *Limonium sinuatum* (apricot)
7c *Limonium sinuatum* (mixed)
8 *Xeranthemum annuum*
9 *Amaranthus paniculatus* (red)
10 *Delphinium elatum*
11a *Carthamus tinctorius* (closed bud stage)
11b *Carthamus tinctorius* (orange)
11c *Carthamus tinctorius* (cream)
12 *Acroclinium roseum*
13 *Aster* sp.
14 *Ambrosinia mexicana*

Colour schemes

Colour should be another consideration when choosing plants: if you know you will want a particular colour bias then you should incorporate it into your planting scheme. Later in this chapter you will find several planting schemes that are planned around various colours, and they may form a useful basis for your own decisions. Once your enthusiasm has grown then you may wish to grow everything you can, but if space or time is limited it seems logical to concentrate on particular flowers or colours that will be of most use. Contrasts are just as important as co-ordinating colours. For example, even if your interior colours have a very strong pink, cream or peach colour theme, do allocate some space to plants with stronger, deeper colours, such as *Amaranthus*, as the strong dark red shows off the paler colours very effectively and you will have a far more stunning arrangement if you can include some darker colours as well. Clashing colours can also give a vibrant effect – for instance, red roses against a pink background – and remember that using bright greens in arrangements always helps them to look fresh.

GROWING ANNUALS

Annuals are a useful choice for drying as they are fast-growing and, if you are impatient as most of us are, then you will be pleased at the quick results that can be harvested and used within a single season. Do remember, however, that many annuals have a fairly critical picking time, so you must be prepared to watch them closely to ensure best results. Another problem can be rain that falls just when a crop is ready to pick, and this can often seriously damage its quality. One way round this problem is to stagger the sowing of annuals so that, with luck, some will escape any weather problems. When choosing varieties to sow, pick types with the maximum amount of flowers on a spike or flower head. The plants with closely spaced or double flowers are more suitable than sparser varieties. Depth or strength of colour is also important as many colours will intensify with drying but do eventually fade.

Many varieties can be sown direct into the garden, but some, such as *Craspedia* and *Gomphrena* need to be raised in trays and planted out. This system can also be useful for establishing popular plants, such as *Helichrysum* as early as possible so as to achieve an extended harvesting period later in the year.

Should your enthusiasm grow to the point where you want larger quantities of your particular favourite, then a separate area could be laid out much like a vegetable garden. This is also a help where plants may need staking or support,

such as cornflower or Bells of Ireland. In such plots, facilities for watering during establishment will probably be necessary and weed control will be a continual problem. The only viable solution is to sow the seeds into as clean a seed-bed as possible and to keep the area hand-weeded or hoed at regular intervals throughout the growing season.

Helichrysum and Statice

The ever-popular *Helichrysum* and Statice (*Limonium sinuatum*) are both fast-growing annuals. They have traditionally formed the basis for many arrangements and can be grown in a wide range of long-lasting colours. Both bloom successfully over a long period, but whereas *Helichrysum* is picked at an early stage and is probably best suited to an inconspicuous plot of its own, Statice is not harvested until it has reached full flower and so can make a valuable contribution to the flower border. The deep purple *Helichrysum* shown in the photograph on page 10 is a wonderful foil to the apricot and pink Statice, especially when arranged in small bunches rather than single stems.

Larkspur

Whatever your particular choice of colour, *Delphinium consolida*, or larkspur, is a must. Larkspur looks attractive growing as a traditional cottage garden plant and dries beautifully. You can grow plants in several shades of pink running into mauves and lilacs, pale blues, striking deep blues and white. It is easy to grow and even after the main stems have been harvested, the side shoots will provide a supply of shorter flower heads ideal for smaller arrangements.

Herbs

It is worth experimenting with all sorts of aromatic plants but, of the annual herbs, *Origanum dictamnus* and dill are among the most useful for arrangements. Oregano is a useful filler, being a soft sage-green colour, and dill has a delicate flower head.

Nigella

Of the various annuals grown for their seed heads, *Nigella* or Love-in-a-mist is one of the most popular. With its delicate form and interesting green and dark red markings, it blends with most colour schemes and is very versatile in its use. Both the flowers and the seed pods are equally attractive in the garden and then it self-seeds readily for the following year!

GROWING PERENNIALS

Perennials are a worthwhile investment in any garden, though the initial outlay may be higher on purchasing plants, rather than seeds. Patience is needed as it may take several years for plants to flower in harvestable quantities.

Sea Lavender

Two types of sea lavender are shown in the photograph on pages 16–17 — *Limonium tartaricum dumosa*, familiar to all flower arrangers as an excellent filler, and the finer *Limonium latifolium*. The quality of sea lavender can easily be marred by crushing when packed; the home-grown bunches can be allowed to retain their natural spreading form and thus will be very attractive to use.

The *Achillea* Family

The *Achillea* family provides several useful flower types. The yellow *A. filipendulina* is easy to grow, long-lasting in flower and sturdy to use. *A. millefolium* 'Cerise Queen' and the more recently introduced 'Summer Pastels' are excellent plants to off-set stronger or brighter colours, and *A. ptarmica*, 'The Pearl', is worth growing for its masses of creamy-white flowers on tall strong stems.

Peonies, Globe thistles and Delphiniums

Peonies are a wonderful asset in the garden because the flowers are expensive to buy and not readily available. They can give a glorious touch of distinction as focal points in dried arrangements. Globe thistles, *Echinops*, are also worthy of cultivation but need gentle handling. They are a wonderful steely blue and have a distinctive textural feel. Dried delphiniums are rarely available commercially; the sparkling dark blue spikes and even the paler blues dry well and are very useful in large arrangements.

Lavender and Herbs

Lavender is a plant that no dried flower enthusiast should be without as there are so many uses for it, whether in pot pourri, scented sachets or as bunches in displays. Other scented plants, particularly herbs, are increasing in popularity and many can be glycerined as well as air-dried. Perennial marjoram has a marvellous pink or dark purple colour, thymes and mints have a pleasant fragrance, bay leaves are useful in small wreaths or table centre decorations and the delicate spires of *Ambrosinia* have a lemony scent that can pervade a whole

(continued on p. 18)

15

PERENNIALS

The perennials illustrated are a colourful array, ranging from humble chives to sophisticated peonies and from tiny *Gypsophila* flowers to large hydrangea heads.

Many perennial plants are magnificent centrepieces for your arrangements as well as useful padding, which may not be such a starring role but is of equal importance. Structural and textural material is essential as components in a dried flower basket.

All varieties of *Achillea* are useful, mainly as fillers or background material. The *filipendulina* form is a strong yellow that makes a good contrast to royal purples and mauves, heather for example. The dark pink 'Cerise Queen' is excellent with all the pinks, and blues. The green *Agastache* has insignificant white flowers which shrivel to leave a soft mid-green that mixes with the majority of colour themes. *Agastache* also smells deliciously minty.

Hydrangeas and peonies whether they are fresh or dried look magnificent and cannot be too highly recommended. The pink variety of peonies in the photograph is 'Sarah Bernhardt', which holds its colour very well. Hydrangeas are relatively easy to grow and the colour can be manipulated, if necessary.

Wonderful colours and shapes are available in this selection of perennial plants.

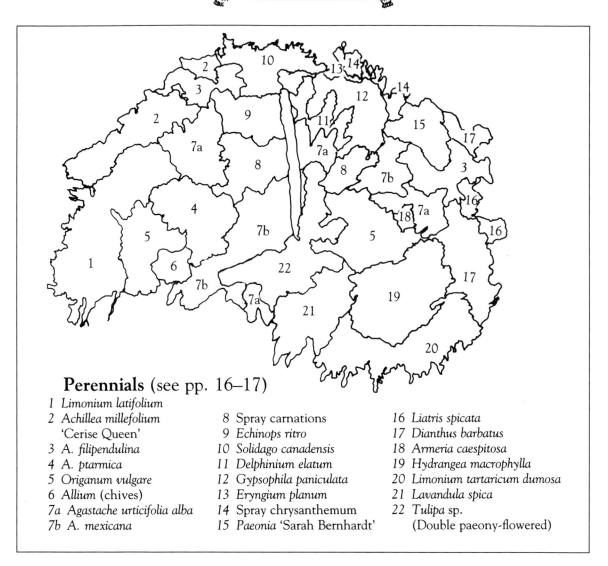

Perennials (see pp. 16–17)

1 Limonium latifolium
2 Achillea millefolium
  'Cerise Queen'
3 A. filipendulina
4 A. ptarmica
5 Origanum vulgare
6 Allium (chives)
7a Agastache urticifolia alba
7b A. mexicana

8 Spray carnations
9 Echinops ritro
10 Solidago canadensis
11 Delphinium elatum
12 Gypsophila paniculata
13 Eryngium planum
14 Spray chrysanthemum
15 Paeonia 'Sarah Bernhardt'

16 Liatris spicata
17 Dianthus barbatus
18 Armeria caespitosa
19 Hydrangea macrophylla
20 Limonium tartaricum dumosa
21 Lavandula spica
22 Tulipa sp.
  (Double paeony-flowered)

room when touched. Two more unusual plants to be recommended are *Agastache mexicana* with its blue-flowered spike and *A. urticifolia alba* which has a white flower, but dries to give a pale green spike. Both are aromatic and the subtle colourings extremely useful. The leaves can be used in pot pourri (see the recipes at the end of the book). *Helichrysum italicum* or *H. angustifolium*, otherwise known as the curry plant (for obvious reasons if one smells the foliage) is a particular favourite as the silver foliage gives a visual lift to an arrangement and is so dainty. The flowers are also useful and the shrub is evergreen so adds colour to the garden when it needs it most.

Sage, fennel, dill, rosemary and many others all have their contribution to make, and it is worth remembering that if a plant has a lovely scent, it does not matter if its appearance is somewhat dull. It can be tucked into the back or sides of a container, out of sight, but still appreciated!

GARDEN FLOWERS

This display of garden flowers includes a range of annuals, perennials and herbs, all of which can be grown and dried at home, but many of which are not readily available to purchase commercially. Textures range from the delicate green Alchemilla and white Matricaria through to the strong, dramatic forms of the yellow Craspedia (drumsticks) and Centaurea (Knapweed) and the red Celosia (Cockscomb) and peonies. Hops and Euphorbia provide a useful source of green, instead of grasses, and the leaves of peonies and roses should always be kept as background filler material. The grey leaves of Senecio are attractive, even though they tend to curl up when dried, and the small white and yellow flowers of Anaphalis are delightfully soft and delicate to use. Unusual pastel shades can be provided by stocks and asters, which can add colour to arrangements.

SEED HEADS

Some of the most beautiful plant forms to dry are the various seed heads and similar items that fall into this category. This is an obvious bonus in the garden as you can enjoy the plants for longer before they have to be harvested, but also the seed heads give texture and interest to arrangements. There are many sizes and types from which to choose and as you can see from the photograph opposite, the strength and variety of colour is amazing.

Poppy heads are very attractive and also useful as their colour ranges from slate blue to grey, green and beige. Another really dramatic head to use is the globe artichoke, *Cynara scolymus*, particularly when it is fully open, as seen in the central example in the picture. It gives a strong focal point to any design. Chinese lanterns, *Physalis franchettii*, are another very popular choice. Their orange colouring is very vivid and gives a warm glow to arrangements.

All the seed heads, such as linseed and, in particular, *Allium christophii*, look wonderful sprayed with metallic paints for festive arrangements at Christmas. Whatever shade you use, the effect is very beautiful and so simply achieved. Obviously within this group one can also include all the cones, which can be wired to use in arrangements or displayed decoratively in bowls, perhaps with pot pourri (see pp. 114–17).

Seed Heads

 1 *Typha latifolia*
 2 *Allium* sp. (Leek flower heads)
 3 *Cynara scolymus*
 4 *Cynara cardunculus*
 5 *Acanthus mollis*
 6 *Physalis franchettii*
 7 *Papaver somniferum*
 8 *Allium christophii*
 9 *Linum usitatissium*
10 *Nigella damascena*
11 *Eucalyptus gunnii*
12 *Centaurea macrocephala*
13 *Phlomis* 'Edward Bowles'
14 *Aquilegia hybrida*
15 *Sedum spectabile*
16 *Alnus glutinosa*
17 *Papaver* sp.
18 *Lunaria biennis*
19 *Iris foetidissima*
20 *Dipsacus fullonum*
21 *Fagus sylvatica*
22 *Lepidium ruderale*
23 *Anethum graveolens*

Seed heads can range from small and nondescript to the more exotic artichokes and Allium heads.

ROSES AND PEONIES

Although many forms of rose dry well, there are several varieties that lose their colour quite quickly, such as the pale yellow and pale pink forms. Reds darken dramatically during drying but then hold their colour well. You will need to experiment with your garden varieties to see which work best for you. The photograph opposite includes the commercial rose varieties 'Gerdo', 'Bridal Pink' and 'Porcelina', as well as the garden favourites 'Schoolgirl', 'Blue Moon', 'Iceberg' and many other garden varieties. In order to get the stem length for larger arrangements, give garden varieties false wire stems covered with green florist's tape.

Also shown in the photograph opposite are red, cream and pink peonies. Peonies are among the most attractive flowers to dry, and although the drying process makes them shrink, they can still have fabulous large heads and make any arrangement very special. Do take careful note of the details in the A–Z section regarding combating insect damage as it can be extremely disappointing to lose your best specimens in this way after they have dried out. If you have trouble mastering the technique of drying peonies, any fallen petals that result can easily be used in pot pourri or wedding confetti (see pp. 116–17 and p. 118).

Roses are fairly easy to dry and garden varieties can give excellent results.

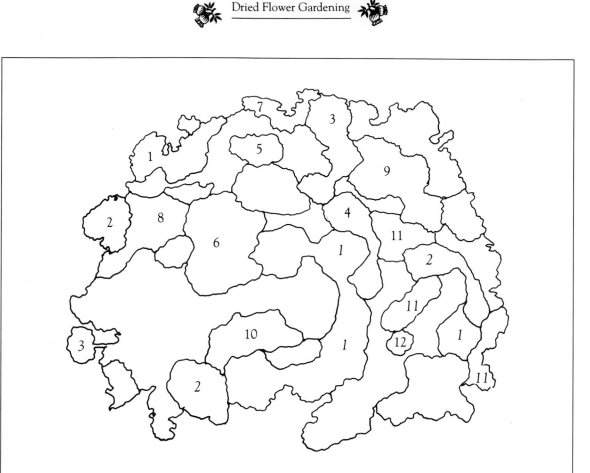

Roses and Peonies

1 *Paeonia* 'Sarah Bernhardt'
2 *Paeonia officinalis*
3 *Paeonia* 'Duchesse de Nemours'
4 *Rosa* 'Porcelina'
5 *Rosa* 'Golden Times'
6 *Rosa* 'Tamara'
7 *Rosa* 'Mercedes'
8 *Rosa* 'Jaguar'
9 *Rosa* 'Bridal Pink'
10 *Rosa* 'Minuet'
11 *Rosa* 'Gerdo'
12 *Rosa* 'Blue Moon'
plus a selection of garden roses

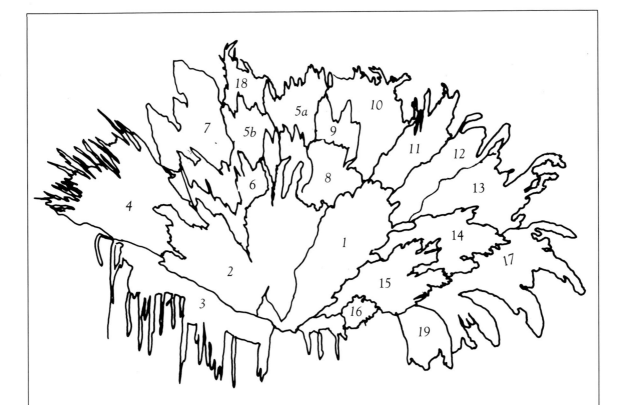

Grasses

1 *Lagurus ovatus*
2 *Zea mays*
3 *Carex pendula*
4 *Triticale*
5a *Triticum (early harvest)*
5b *Triticum (late harvest)*
6 *Phleum pratense*
7 *Cortaderia selloana*
8 *Festuca ovina*
9 *Hordeum*
10 *Avena sativa*
11 *Setaria italica*
12 *Phalaris canariensis*
13 *Cynosurus cristata*
14 *Bromus macrostachys*
15 *Poa annua*
16 *Briza maxima*
17 *Panicum miliaceum*
18 *Dactylis glomerata*
19 *Bromus sterilis*

GRASSES

Grasses are among the easiest plants to obtain for drying, although some of the showier specimens will need special cultivation. There are a great many varieties to choose from. Cereal crops such as wheat and oats have distinctive heads and can add impact to an arrangement, particularly if used in large clumps rather than inserted stem by stem. Fescue or quaking grass give a much daintier effect.

Millet has a variety of shapes, sizes and colours, some upright and some in a pendulous form, and a range of colours from gold through to green. Pampas grass has also always been a favourite but it can be very overwhelming unless used subtly in large arrangements.

Grasses are not expensive to buy ready-dried but are, surprisingly, one of the most difficult items to dry successfully at home since their all-important greenness is only retained by fast drying. Only a minimum amount of space should be allocated to growing the common varieties in the garden. On the other hand, certain ornamental varieties make interesting contrasts as clumps in the herbaceous border. Rather than just sowing one or two types of grass, mixed packets of flower arrangers' grasses are available, which give a better breadth of choice.

There are enormous numbers of grasses, both wild and cultivated, which add a feathery touch to any arrangement.

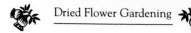

IDEAS FOR PLANTING SCHEMES

Having decided to incorporate flowers and plants for drying in your garden plan, there are several ways in which this can be done. One of the most interesting is to plant in colour themes, which provides a good colour co-ordinated selection of dried flowers to work with as well as giving pleasure while the plants are growing. There are several ideas in the following pages which can either be followed exactly or taken as a base for using some of the plants you may have already and adding some new ideas.

A theme which would be fun to work on would be a wild garden. It should not be so wild that the plants within it are allowed to take over, but rather is an apparently unstructured garden.

Plants chosen for a wild or woodland garden need to be those that flourish well with little or no interference. Avoid any that need staking or tying up. There should be a minimum of annual replanting so as to disturb the soil as little as possible.

Plants can happily be grown in tubs and containers as well as in beds. The following list does not place emphasis on any particular colour, but all the plants are very useful for drying, as well as being attractive in their own right. The list includes scented and evergreen plants and herbs (also grown for their culinary use), as well as plants that are harvested late in the flowering season or at seed-head stage and which can therefore be enjoyed to the full in the garden.

Suitable plants for patios and smaller gardens

Acroclinium roseum (Sunray)
Alchemilla mollis (Lady's mantle)
Aquilegia hybrida
Calendula officinalis (Pot marigold)
Centaurea cyanus (Cornflower)
Clematis tangutica
Dahlia sp.
Helichrysum angustifolium
   (Curry plant)
Hydrangea sp.
Lavandula spica (Lavender)

Limonium sinuatum (Statice)
Limonium tartaricum dumosa
Nigella damascena
Origanum vulgare (Pot marjoram)
Thymus (Thyme)
Xeranthemum annuum

Pink, Green and White

Here the many varied tones of pink are complemented by the mauves and blues of *Liatris*, cornflower and larkspur. The clumps of grasses provide a different texture and the white *Achillea* and sea lavender give useful highlights. The overall effect can be a beautiful swathe of subtle shades which would look restful as well as being a lovely garden feature.

PERENNIAL

1 *Achillea ptarmica*
2 *Achillea millefolium*
3 *Aster novae-belgii* (purple)
4 *Liatris spicata*
5 *Dianthus barbatus*
6 *Dianthus x. allwoodii*
7 *Gypsophila paniculata*
8 *Limonium tartaricum dumosa*
9 *Alchemilla molis*
10 *Paeonia lactiflora* 'Sarah Bernhardt'
11 *P. officinalis* (cerise)
12 *Limonium sinuatum* (pink, white, blue)
13 *Rosa* sp. (shrub, double pink)
14 *Sedum spectabile*

ANNUAL

15 *Acroclinium roseum* (white/pink)
16 *Amaranthus*
17 *Aster* (mixed pink/cerise)
18 *Centaurea cyanus* — mixed (pink, purple, blue)
19 *Delphinium consolida* (pink and blue)
20 *Gomphrena globosa* (purple)
21 *Helichrysum bracteatum monstrosum* (pink, purple and light pink)
22 *Limonium suworowii*
23 *Nigella damascena*
24 *Salvia horminum*
25 *Xeranthemum annuum* (white and purple)

GRASSES

26 *Phalaris canariensis*
27 *Miscanthus sinensis*

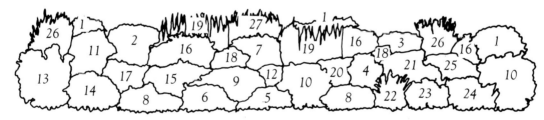

Red, Green, White

Several of the plants recommended in this scheme could be used in locations with light shade — in particular the *Euphorbia*, hellebores, hydrangeas and *Astrantia*. The bright reds are best contrasted with light greens and the scheme needs the highlights of *Achillea ptarmica*, clematis and chrysanthemum to provide interest.

PERENNIAL

 1 *Acanthus mollis* or *A. spinosus*
 2 *Achillea ptarmica*
 3 *Alchemilla mollis*
 4 *Aquilegia hybrida*
 5 *Astilbe arendsii*
 6 *Astrantia major*
 7 *Hydrangea* sp.
*8 *Chrysanthemum* sp. (orange/yellow)
*9 *Clematis tangutica* or *C. orientalis*
10 *Corylus avellana contorta*
11 *Cotinus coggygria*
12 *Dianthus barbatus*

13 *Eucalyptus gunnii*
14 *Euphorbia polychroma*
15 *Helleborus corsicus*
16 *Hydrangea macrophylla*
17 *Hydrangea paniculatum* 'Grandiflora'
18 *Iris foetidissima*
19 *Lunaria biennis*
20 *Paeonia officinalis*
21 *Physalis franchettii*
22 *Rosa* sp. ('Variegati di Bologna')
23 *Rosa* sp. (double red rambler type)

* For contrast

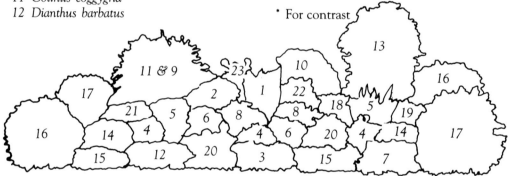

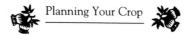

Orange, Yellow, White and Green

Strong oranges and yellows always look particularly good with deep reds and dark foliage. Here the rosemary, *Moluccella* and hellebores, plus the *Cotinus* and *Amaranthus* all work as background or contrast colours to what could be a dramatic scheme. The bright, warm colours could give life to an otherwise dull part of the garden.

PERENNIAL

1 *Alchemilla mollis*
2 *Achillea filipendulina*
3 *Centaurea macrocephala*
4 *Hydrangea paniculata* 'Grandiflora'
5 *Matricaria eximia*
6 *Phlomis* 'Edward Bowles'
7 *Physalis franchettii*
8 *Rosa* sp. (rambler, cream, double-flowered)
9 *Clematis tangutica* or *Clematis orientalis*
10 *Helleborus corsicus*
11 *Solidago canadensis*
12 *Kerria japonica*
13 *Agastache urticifolia alba*
14 *Cotinus coggygria* 'Foliis purpureis'
15 *Rosmarinus officinalis*
16 *Amaranthus* (dark red)

ANNUAL

17 *Carthamus tinctorius* (orange)
18 *Craspedia globosa*
19 *Helichrysum bracteatum monstrosum*
20 *Linum usitatissium*
21 *Lonas inodora*
22 *Tagetes erecta* (orange/yellow)
23 *Moluccella laevis*
24 *Delphinium consolida* (white)
25 *Ammobium alatum*

GRASS

26 *Panicum miliaceum*

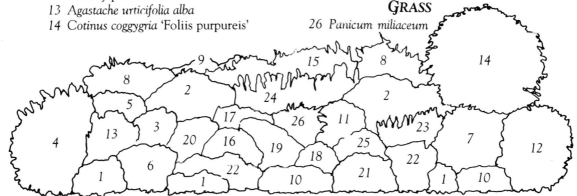

Blue, Cream, Grey, Purple and Silver

The cool, restful blues and greys of this scheme are given a touch of warmth by the flowers of the artichokes and honesty, and highlighted in summer by the soft yellow of the *Phlomis* and curry plant. *Ceonothus impressus* would make a lovely background to the scheme or, alternatively, *Eleagnus* x. *ebbingei* in exposed sites.

PERENNIAL

1 *Agastache mexicana*
2 *Acanthus mollis*
3 *Anaphalis margaritacea*
4 *Campanula glomerata*
5 *Delphinium elatum* (dark and pale blues)
6 *Echinops ritro*
7 *Eryngium planum*
8 *Eucalyptus gunnii* (pruned to form a shrub)
9 *Helichrysum angustifolium*
10 *Lavandula spica*
11 *Limonium latifolium*
12 *Lunaria biennis*
13 *Paeonia lactiflora* 'Duchesse de Nemours'
14 *Phlomis fruticosa*
15 *Rosmarinus officinalis*
16 *Rosa* sp. (rambler, double-flowered)
17 *Salvia officinalis* (and *Salvia officinalis* 'Tricolor')
18 *Senecio greyi*
19 *Hydrangea*
24 *Eleagnus* x. *ebbingei* (in exposed locations) or *Ceanothus impressus*
25 *Cynara cardunculus*

ANNUAL

20 *Papaver somniferum*
21 *Scabiosa stellata*
22 *Xeranthemum annuum*

GRASS

23 *Setaria italica*

A dozen of the best

It is not always possible to give space to every plant you would like to grow and decisions always have to be made — which plant should you leave out and which ones must be given space at all costs? If you are short of space or spoilt for choice this scheme would provide a good basic collection of plants and plenty of versatile material (and could, if needed, be supplemented by commercially dried flowers). Once you have become proficient at growing and drying, your enthusiasm may well grow in proportion, making you determined to find more garden space for an ever-expanding collection.

PERENNIAL

1 *Hydrangea macrophylla* (pink/blue)
   Hydrangea paniculata 'Grandiflora' (white)
2 *Paeonia lactiflora* (cream, pink)
   Paeonia officinalis (red, cerise)
3 *Rose sp.* (rambler, double-flowered)
4 *Lavandula spica* (dark blue)
5 *Achillea ptarmica* 'The Pearl'
6 *Gypsophila paniculata*
7 *Limonium tartaricum dumosa*

ANNUAL

8 *Nigella damascena*
9 *Delphinium consolida* (white, pink, blue)
10 *Helichrysum bracteatum monstrosum* (mixed)
11 *Limonium sinuatum* (mixed)

GRASS

12 *Phalaris canariensis*

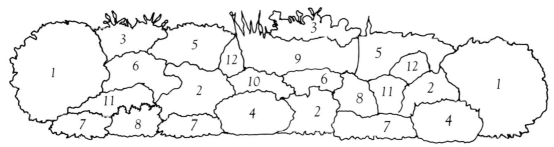

HARVESTING AND DRYING

Harvesting should take place at the correct time for the plant in question (see the A–Z section). Timing the picking is very important for top-quality results — it is critical to within hours when drying peonies, within a day for *Helichrysum*, within a day or two for *Carthamus* and within a few days for grasses. There are also other problems to beset you, such as a sudden shower of rain just when you had planned to pick something, that may ruin the petal colour of your crop. However, taking care to pick at the best moment will prevent petal drop and keep the colours at their peak. All plant material should be picked on a dry day after any dew has evaporated. The stalks should be cut cleanly with secateurs or a sharp knife and medium-thick rubber bands used to hold the stems together. If a plant has woody stems that are unlikely to shrink then raffia or string can be used to tie them up. Any leaves around the base should be stripped off and the rubber band placed near the base of the stalk so the flower heads are not crushed together. The stems shrink considerably during drying so the bands need to be tight initially. Bunches should be kept small to help the drying process, especially if the drying conditions are slow or the stems very thick or fleshy.

Drying techniques

There are several ways to preserve the material you have painstakingly grown and picked, and the method used will depend on the particular plant with which you are working and your own resources. The A–Z section concentrates on plants which can be successfully air-dried, but there is also an appendix at the back of the book listing additional items which are suitable for glycerining and drying by the silica gel method.

Air-drying is by far the easiest and cheapest method of preserving plants. It produces material that can be fragile, but which, if handled with care, easily makes up into large and impressive displays in fireplaces or into delicate

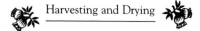

arrangements in small containers such as tea cups.

Glycerining produces robust and pliable material that can be handled many times and, indeed, can be wiped with a damp cloth should it become dusty. However, the process itself does not always have a 100 per cent success rate and often causes colour loss, so beginners may find it safer to start with air-drying and become proficient in this before progressing on to the glycerine treatment.

Silica gel is the third preserving method discussed in this book and produces a very different effect. The flowers are large and perfect, in fact some look good enough to be fresh, but they are extremely brittle and have to be dried on wired stems, so this method is not as useful for those who wish to make large arrangements. However, if miniature arranging is more appealing to you then drying with silica gel may be the answer. It certainly produces a superior result to air-drying, as can be seen on p. 38. However, this method takes up a lot of time and space and it may not be possible to produce the quantity of dried material that you would like.

AIR-DRYING

Providing a few basic rules are followed with air-drying, it is a very straightforward method of preserving flowers and you should achieve a very high success rate. Before picking anything it is important to decide where your drying area is going to be. The worst possible locations are by windows or in a greenhouse or garden shed because dampness and sunlight will spoil the colours. Ideally you should choose somewhere dry, dark and well-ventilated, with heat available. The perfect place would be a capacious boiler cupboard or an empty airing cupboard. Other possibilities include a spot over or near hot water pipes or over radiators and, if you happen to have an Aga cooker or something similar, then bunches hanging over and near it not only look decorative but also dry beautifully. In all cases the bunches should be hung away from any steam or damp air, both of which will defeat the object of the exercise, and they should never be left in places where they might constitute a fire hazard. They can be suspended on hooks, canes or lengths of strong wire. You can buy a reproduction of an old-fashioned laundry airer which can be pulleyed up and down from the ceiling, and this would make an excellent area for drying or storing dried flowers, assuming the room is not too light and sunny.

Heat is not always essential, but in many cases it can spell the difference between a resounding success and a rather mediocre result. If you have room in an airing cupboard and wish to raise the temperature a little, the lagging can be temporarily removed from the tank. Should you be lucky enough to live in a hot dry climate then heat may not be needed at all, but darkness and good ventilation will be important. The humidity of the drying area should be

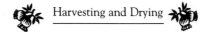

watched, and if necessary, air circulation improved or a dehumidifier installed to speed up the process. Dehumidifiers are also invaluable during storage — it is surprising how fast dried flowers reabsorb atmospheric moisture.

The bunches should then be hung upside down in the dark as soon as possible. Ensure they are hanging completely vertical or they will dry crooked and bent. The rate of drying varies with each variety, bunch size, atmospheric conditions, temperature and so on, but it is important to be able to assess when the material is thoroughly dry. This is when the densest part of each flower head is dry and stems beneath the rubber band snap when bent. It is worthwhile destroying a few specimens in order to confirm that they are completely dry, otherwise mould or general deterioration will appear later.

There are several varieties which dry very happily standing upright. Many of the plants picked at the seed pod or seed head stage, such as Chinese lanterns, come into this category, but it also applies to sturdy stemmed items such as artichokes and gypsophila, some foliage and, of course, hydrangeas. For exact details and drying instructions, please refer to the details under the relevant heading of the A–Z section, beginning on p. 45.

USING SILICA AND OTHER DRYING AGENTS

An alternative method to air-drying is to use a desiccant — sand, borax or silica gel crystals. The end results are sometimes quite stunning and it is certainly worth experimenting with this method to see if it appeals to you or not. To work successfully with silica or other drying agents you must be patient and have very nimble fingers, because the dried material can be extremely brittle and therefore easily damaged.

Without doubt, the best desiccant to use is silica gel crystals, as the other possibilities such as sand and borax can be too coarse and leave marks on the flower petals. Silica gel is, however, fairly expensive but with careful use can last for many years and be reused endlessly. Many brands of silica gel crystals are sold in a plastic container, making them very convenient to use. If you purchase some without such a container then either use a half-gallon ice cream container or an old biscuit tin.

Bearing in mind the higher cost of this method of drying, there seems no point in drying plants in this way when you have perfectly satisfactory results with air-drying. Instead, concentrate on such plants as lilies, freesias, single

A warm spot in the kitchen, away from steam or moisture, can be ideal for drying bunches of flowers.

roses, garden roses and other flowers which can look significantly better with this method. (See Appendix VI for flowers that are suggested as suitable for this treatment.)

First check that your crystals are completely dry. In many cases they are sold with an in-built colour indicator, and are a strong blue colour when completely dry. Once they start to absorb moisture they gradually turn pink. If the crystals need drying, spread them on a shallow oven tray and place in the oven on a medium to low heat for about 45 minutes.

Using silica gel crystals

Any flowers you are planning to dry in this way should be as fresh as possible, so do not waste space on blemished or eaten specimens. Stalks or stems do not dry well with desiccants and so need to be trimmed to about 1 in (2.5 cm) long or less. Ideally, flowers should be wired while they are fresh, as this is far easier than trying to insert wires in brittle desiccant-dried material. A short stub wire can be pushed up the stalk while the flower is fresh, and then the required length of wire can be added once the drying has taken place.

Silica gel can produce very dramatic results, as shown by these 'Handel' roses.

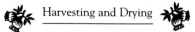

The equipment you will need is as follows:
A plastic or tin container of silica gel crystals
A second container of approximately the same size
A child's small paintbrush
A teaspoon

First place a bed of crystals approximately 1 in (2.5 cm) deep in the empty container and then position the flowers so that they rest on the crystals but do not touch each other. Then carefully spoon in more crystals beneath, around and inside each flower, taking care to maintain the basic shape and support the flower heads. Once the flowers are completely buried, replace the lid of the container and store in a warm place (if possible) for approximately 48 hours. Some materials, such as daisies and smaller items, may take a little less time, and some slightly longer.

Check the flowers as soon as possible after the 48 hours have elapsed, as material left in the desiccant for too long can become over-brittle and fall to pieces. Take great care when unearthing the flowers as they will be very fragile — it is best done with the paintbrush, very gently. Any sudden gouging with the spoon or any other weapon may well cause irreparable damage. Once you have gently extricated the flower check to see if it is completely dry or whether it requires a little longer, in which case the process must be repeated but this time leaving the flower for 24 hours instead of 48.

Having ascertained that the flowers are completely dry you should apply a light coat of matt varnish to prevent any reabsorption of moisture. Many varieties can manage well without this but a beginner would do better to assume that most varieties will reabsorb moisture and then to gradually experiment with and without varnish.

The finished flowers must be stored in an airtight container and, as a precaution, it is wise to add a small amount of silica gel crystals to the base of the container to keep any moisture to a minimum. Stems can then be lengthened with wires to fit into the desired arrangement. An ideal way to use desiccant-dried material is to display it under a glass dome, which shows off the beauty of the flowers but offers protection to their fragile condition.

GLYCERINING

Another method of preserving plant material is to replace the plant's own moisture with a glycerine and water solution. Although this is a rather unpredictable method of preserving plants, it is worth mastering for the unusual items that you can add to your collection that cannot be preserved in any other way.

It is essential to harvest material intended for glycerine treatment when it is fully mature, as glycerine is not happily absorbed by either immature or over-ripe plants. New growth does not accept the glycerine at all, so no matter how wonderful a bright green new shoot looks, don't try to pick it as it will only go limp and fail. Mid-season is the best time to pick anything destined for the glycerine treatment as it will be well matured but not past its best.

Suitable plants

There are many plants mentioned in the main A–Z section as being suitable for glycerine treatment, but the most successful are both deciduous and evergreen foliage. The leaves shown in the photograph are *Choisya* and *Helleborus corsicus* and *H. foetidus*. Many others are popular choices, such as beech, holly, ivy, laurel and magnolia, but it's fascinating to experiment and find something unusual that comes out well.

The process is fairly straightforward. Make a mixture of approximately 50 per cent boiling water and 50 per cent glycerine and pour it into a fairly tall narrow container. The ends of woody stems should be well battered with a hammer to help absorption. Stand the foliage in the mixture so that at least 3–4 in (7.5–10 cm) of each stem is below the surface. Then leave the plant material and glycerine mixture in a dark place and wait for the absorption to take place. It usually happens after about a week but some things take longer, and many items take two or even three weeks. You can tell when the leaves are ready as there will be some colour change and the leaves will feel smooth and pliable.

If small beads of glycerine appear on the surface of a leaf then remove that piece of foliage from the solution immediately. Dry off the beads of glycerine with a tissue and store in an even temperature away from strong light. It's interesting to treat the same type of foliage in two jars, placing one in sunlight and the other in darkness. Generally, one gets better colour by glycerining in the dark but a paler colour can make a lovely contrast and add to the interest of the arrangement.

One of the joys of glycerined material is that it gives you some leaves to work with, as most do not air-dry and therefore you can be left with a definite preponderance of flowers and very little foliage. This is especially so when you're trying to make a larger arrangement, as then leaves are very effective for both bulk and shape.

It is also useful to glycerine individual leaves as they can be used in smaller work. In this case, it is easier to use a shallow container and immerse the entire leaf in the glycerine solution. Again the mixture should be equal measures of glycerine and water and the process will take about the same length of time, sometimes a little less.

Whether working with large or small foliage, don't let the level of the glycerine and water mixture drop too low or dry out during the treatment but keep topping it up to the recommended depth, and don't discard the left-over liquid after you remove the plant material, as it can be reused next time.

Glycerine is very useful for preserving foliages that do not dry well by the air-drying method.

Using antifreeze

Another alternative to glycerine is to use car antifreeze. The main objection to glycerine is usually its cost, and antifreeze is considerably cheaper. Again, it is best to mix equal quantities of antifreeze and boiling water. Although this method is less expensive, experience has proved that better results have been achieved more consistently with glycerine, and some plants don't seem willing to absorb the antifreeze at all. Having said that, other foliage takes up the antifreeze and not glycerine so, again, experiment with pieces from the garden. I haven't found any problems with the blue colouring of antifreeze coming through into the foliage but some people say the colour has dyed their plant material a light blue shade, so do bear this in mind.

While we are on the subject of colouring and dyes, it is very easy to alter or just boost the colour of your material you are treating by adding a water-based dye to the original mixture. Sometimes natural material can be dyed subtly, and one should aim at enhancing the natural colour rather than creating a totally new false colour.

Storing dried material

Once you have gathered your plants and dried them successfully, your enthusiasm may lead you to drying many more bunches than you can use immediately. Much drying obviously takes place in the summer months, and the resulting material may well not be used until later in the year. Having spent a lot of time and effort on the drying technique, it is extremely important to store material carefully so that no deterioration occurs before you use it.

If you are using a dark dry area to dry flowers and you have unlimited space, then the bunches can just be stored where they were dried. Most people, however, are constantly short of drying space and need to clear it as soon as possible to make room for more pickings! If this is the case then sturdy cardboard boxes are probably the answer. The majority of florists are only too happy to let you have a couple of flower boxes in which they collected their stock from market that morning, and the shape and size of these boxes is ideal.

Ensure that the box is completely dry and has no holes in it — even the carrying holes on each end of some boxes should be sealed over as they make excellent doorways for insects or mice! Lay the bunches carefully in the box, making sure you don't bend any delicate stems against the end of the box. Once you have laid a layer of, say, five bunches at one end of the box, cover with tissue paper as shown in the photograph. Another layer can then be laid over the original one. Take care never to store material dried in different ways in the same box, e.g. keep air-dried and glycerined material apart, and glycerined material separate from silica-dried flowers.

It is recommended that you seal the boxes well as that will help minimize insect damage and also entry by any members of the rodent family. Boxes of dried material not only provide very edible seed heads but also beautifully colour co-ordinated mouse bedding! The boxes should be stored in a dry place, free of mice. Some lofts may be ideal, but not if they are uninsulated as some dampness may well be present. This also applies to garages and sheds.

Insect damage

If you should come across bunches where petals are disintegrating on to the floor, or where the base of the petals is being eaten away, then this is very likely to be caused by insect damage. Throw away any bunches that are badly damaged. If, however, the damage is only slight at that point, or if you want to play safe, place the bunch in the deep freeze for 24–48 hours and then hang up to dry again. This treatment seems to effectively eradicate any insect problems.

It seems obvious, but efficient labelling can save many minutes of frenzied hunting through boxes for a certain bunch you are trying to locate. It is useful to mark each box with a date as well as a list of its contents so the dried material can be used in rotation.

Flowers should be carefully stored between layers of tissue paper in a warm, dry place.

THE A–Z OF RECOMMENDED PLANTS

Introduction

This A–Z section includes a wide range of flowers which can be dried. It is by no means an exhaustive list — there are many other flowers, foliage and seeds worthy of experimentation!

Some of the plants listed are ideal for beginners — easy to grow and virtually dry by the time they are harvested. Others are more difficult and have specific requirements for harvesting and drying. Many of the flowers are familiar to gardeners, but the list also includes grasses and cereal crops which dried flower arrangers frequently use and may, therefore, consider to be worthwhile growing in small plots.

The growing hints should be referred to as general introductory guidelines and more detailed cultural advice sought where necessary.

The harvesting and drying recommendations should be read in conjunction with the relevant chapter in this book and it is to be assumed, unless otherwise stated, that flowers should be placed in the dark and the drying process started as soon as possible after cutting.

Papaver somniferum

ACACIA *decurrens dealbata*

MIMOSA

Deciduous Shrub

Mimosa bears clusters of small, round, yellow flowers which are strongly fragrant. The fern-like leaves are light green and feathery.

GROWING HINTS

Being frost tender, mimosa should only be established as a wall plant in warm locations. It will not grow well on lime.

HARVESTING AND DRYING

The flowers are produced from late winter into early spring. Cut when in full flower. Do not strip the leaves as they are also attractive to use. Air-dry hanging upside down.

ACANTHUS *mollis*

A. *spinosus*

BEAR'S BREECHES

Deciduous Perennial

Acanthus is a dramatic perennial, useful in the garden for its large, glossy, green ornamental leaves which inspired decorative patterns used in Greek Corinthian architecture. In summer it produces a 4–5 ft (1.2–1.5 m) tall distinctive white and purple flower spike which can be easily dried for use in large, extravagant arrangements.

GROWING HINTS

Acanthus can be grown from seed, but since only a few may be required to give an effect in the garden, it is probably best purchased as a small plant which will flower the following summer. It will grow in full shade but flowers best in full sun. The flowers of *Acanthus spinosus* are equally effective, though shorter — 3–4 ft (1–1.2 m). *Acanthus* can become invasive.

HARVESTING AND DRYING

Harvest in late summer when as much of the spike as possible is in full flower, but before the colour fades. Although sturdy it is best hung upside down to dry to prevent the tip bending over. Make sure the thick stems are fully dry before storage or use.

ACHILLEA *filipendulina*

var. 'Gold Plate' and others

YARROW

Deciduous Perennial

This is a popular and familiar plant of herbaceous borders, easy to dry and sturdy to use. The distinctive flat-topped yellow heads, measuring 3–4 in (7.5–10 cm) across, are formed on strong erect stems 3–4 ft (1–1.2 m) long. They are invaluable in indoor arrangements of all but the smallest size and look especially good with green millet or wheat, the warm orange of *Helichrysum* and *Carthamus* and clear bright yellow statice.

GROWING HINTS

Achillea filipendulina is tolerant of most soil types but enjoys full sun. It will eventually form a large clump, and the bright yellow flowers stand out best against a background of dark green or purple foliage. Tall varieties need staking or other forms of support.

HARVESTING AND DRYING

The exact timing of harvest in late summer is not very critical but, ideally, the stems should be cut when the individual florets are fully open and the flower head as a whole feels firm to the touch. The bunches will air-dry easily.

When drying or storing the bunches, make sure the heads are not crushed together as their shape is all-important. Do not, however, discard good flowers formed on bent or twisted stems as these can be used to artistic effect!

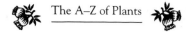

ACHILLEA *millefolium*

var. 'Cerise Queen' and others

YARROW

Deciduous Perennial

The common white yarrow is frequently found on road verges but, for the garden, several pink and pastel-coloured varieties

Achillea millefolium 'Summer Pastels'

are now available. Because of its soft colouring its use in dried arrangements tends to be as a filler or background shade to offset other bright flowers. For instance, the 'Cerise Queen' variety works well with pink *Helichrysum*, roses or peonies.

It may be worthwhile selecting strong-coloured varieties for planting since the colours tend to change during drying — for instance, from cerise to more dusky shades of plum. It can be used in arrangements of all sizes.

GROWING HINTS
Achillea millefolium is tolerant of most soils and prefers full sun. If sown in late spring it will flower the following year in summer. Though similar in form to *A. filipendulina*, it is shorter, flowering on stems 2–2½ ft (60–75 cm) high, so needs to be nearer the front of the border. The stems also tend to be weaker, so some support may be necessary at flowering time.

HARVESTING AND DRYING
Harvest in late summer, waiting until the flowers are in full colour. The small stems within the flower head need time to strengthen and firm up — if picked too early they remain limp and make the flower less strong for dried use.

The branches should be air-dried, hanging upside down. They must be fully dry before use.

ACHILLEA *ptarmica*

var. 'The Pearl'

SNEEZEWORT

Deciduous Perennial

'The Pearl' is a popular and easily-grown plant of great value to gardeners and flower arrangers. The small white double flowers are borne in profusion on long, 2–3 ft (60–100 cm), stems throughout the summer. 'The Pearl' is useful with any garden colour schemes and in arrangements provides a good highlight to offset other colours. It can be used in small-scale arrangements, but its long stems make it valuable when grouped in combination with taller flowers, especially larkspur and peonies. It is a good all-rounder.

GROWING HINTS
It is important to select a consistent double-flowering variety. Sow in late spring to flower the following year. *A. ptarmica* spreads rapidly so needs to be given space in the middle or back of the border. It likes sun or partial shade. Treatment for mildew on the leaves may be necessary during the summer. Dead stems should be cut back to ground level in the autumn.

HARVESTING AND DRYING
Cut when the flowers are well open but before the oldest flowers on the stem start to show signs of browning. Rain can easily damage the quality of the flowers so, if necessary, cut back poor quality stems and wait for a second flush of flowers to appear.

Hang the bunches upside down. It is important that the whiteness of the flowers is retained. Drying too fast at a high temperature can cause browning of the petals, while drying too slowly may result in colour loss on the stems and leaves and give a less fresh appearance. Ideally *Achillea* should be dried in a warm current of air.

ACROCLINIUM *roseum*

SUNRAY

Annual

One of the traditional everlasting flowers, *Acroclinium* is an annual with daisy-like flowers on fine stems. A range of colours is available — white, pinks and reds with yellow or black centres — all of which hold their colour well during drying. They can be used singly in small arrangements or bunched in mass as strong focal points in others.

GROWING HINTS
Sow under glass in early spring or outdoors in late spring, to flower in the summer. Use as a front of border plant or in locations where space is limited.

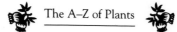

HARVESTING AND DRYING

Harvest before the flowers are completely open as they will develop further during drying. Hang the bunches upside down. *Acroclinium* air-dries easily.

AGASTACHE *mexicana*

A. *urticifolia alba*

AGASTACHE

Deciduous Perennial

Agastache looks very similar to mint, with 2–3 ft (60–100 cm) long spikes of either blue (A. *mexicana*) or white (A. *urticifolia alba*) flowers and nettle-like leaves. The plants have aromatic leaves, smelling of mint or lemon. The blue variety is useful as a background to bright pinks. The white flowers, however, become less significant when dried, leaving a light green spike particularly effective in contrast to bright reds.

GROWING HINTS

Agastache is not a common garden variety, so the seed or plants may be difficult to obtain.

If sown in early spring, it should flower in late summer in its first year and in mid-summer in following years. It grows well in full sun and is attractive to bees. Cut back in autumn.

HARVESTING AND DRYING

Wait until it is fully in flower and the spikes are 2–3 in (5–7.5 cm) long. The stem needs to have time to firm up before cutting otherwise, once dried, it will tend to become limp if exposed to damp atmospheres. It is better to pick too late than too early. However, do not allow the white flowers to discolour to brown as this will impair the appearance after drying.

After the leading stems have been cut, lateral branches will develop, allowing a second harvest.

Strip unnecessary leaves from the base of the stems before drying. These can be dried separately for use in pot pourri. Hang upside down to air-dry but ensure the stems are fully dry before using in arrangements.

ALCHEMILLA *mollis*

LADY'S MANTLE

Deciduous Perennial

The mass of minute lime-green flowers produced in summer are useful when dried as a delicate filler in small basket arrangements. In the garden *Alchemilla* is equally valuable as an edging plant or for planting under dark green or purple leaved shrubs.

GROWING HINTS

If purchased as seed, it must be sown in the autumn to germinate in the spring. Once established it seeds freely and grows best in a moist soil.

HARVESTING AND DRYING

Timing of cutting is not too critical but it must be while the flower mass retains its fresh green appearance and has not begun to deteriorate to yellowish brown. Being such a small, delicate flower head it dries easily, and faster drying with warm air will help to maintain the fresh colour.

ALLIUM sp.

ONION, LEEK, CHIVE, ETC.

Bulb

Leaving the remains of the vegetable crop to go to seed can provide some useful additions to a collection of dried flowers but be warned — they never completely lose their smell!

The various ornamental onions available for the flower garden can be chosen to flower throughout the summer and most are pink, mauve or white. They

range from small rockery varieties to the large *A. aflatunense* which can grow up to 5 ft (1.5 m) in height. Generally, those with denser flower heads will dry best, though the rather different, spear-shaped head of *A. siculum* is excellent for drying.

GROWING HINTS
Most of the onion family enjoy a sunny position and can spread freely if allowed to seed.

HARVESTING AND DRYING
The flowers can be cut as the buds start to open or left until the seed heads have developed. The stems are very fleshy and so it is best to band only two or three together, hang them upside down, and allow them a long time to dry. Drying too slowly can cause deterioration and discoloration of the stems, so choose a warm place where the smell will not give offence!

ALLIUM *christophii*

syn. *A. albopilosum*

CHRISTOPHII
Bulb

This distinctive variety deserves a special mention because of its dramatic seed head resembling an exploding firework, which can easily measure 7 in (17.5 cm) across.

GROWING HINTS
The flowering stems are short so the plant should be established near the front of the border or alongside a patio, where it can enjoy a sunny position. The flowers are mauve and complement white and pink colours in the garden. Seeds should be sown in the autumn but establishment is not reliable and propagation by division is more successful. Once established, *Allium christophii* spreads naturally.

HARVESTING AND DRYING
A. christophii flowers in late spring or summer and the flower heads can be left until they have dried on the plant. Cut with as long a stem as possible and store in an airy place, preferably by hanging or standing them individually to prevent damage.

ALNUS *glutinosa*
COMMON ALDER
Deciduous Tree

The common alder is a tree frequently found adjacent to water or in damp locations. The alder's main value to the dried flower arranger lies in its small cones which are popular for small arrangements such as wreaths and in Christmas decorations.

GROWING HINTS
The trees are cheap to buy, especially when small. The upright habit of the common alder and the larger Italian alder, *Alnus cordata* (which has bigger fruits), and their growth rate make them suitable for screen planting or shelter belts.

HARVESTING AND DRYING
The cones can be cut when green in late summer and dried slowly or left until the autumn when they have turned dark brown.

AMARANTHUS *paniculatus*

A. caudatus

LOVE-LIES-BLEEDING
Hardy Annual

Amaranthus caudatus is best known as 'Love-lies-bleeding' because of its long trailing crimson tassels, on stems which

Amaranthus paniculatus

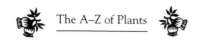

can be 3–4 ft (1–1.2 m) tall. It can be dried and used to good effect, but it is the shorter growing form, A. *paniculatus*, that is more popular with dried flower arrangers. It has dense erect plumes in either light green or dark red. The latter are especially valuable in dried arrangements as a dense, rich background to light pink larkspur or *Helichrysum*.

Do not confuse either form with A. *tricolor*, which is a foliage pot plant.

GROWING HINTS
Sow in late spring to flower in mid to late summer. *Amaranthus* likes an open position and its erect form is best used in more formal garden schemes.

HARVESTING AND DRYING
Wait until the whole plant is in full flower and the yellow stamens have just started to appear. Pick the entire stalk and dry as a whole. The leaves can be removed later, if necessary, but can usefully be retained in view of the flower's value as a filler in arrangements. Side shoots will provide a second crop.

Dry A. *caudatus* upright to retain the trailing effect. Dry A. *paniculatus* upside down to retain the erect plumes. To prevent the flowers developing beyond their prime, dry at warm/hot temperatures. The stems can be quite dense so ensure they are fully dry before use.

AMBROSINIA *mexicana*
AMBROSINIA
Annual

Ambrosinia has a tall, delicate, finely-pointed green flower spike with a fragrance similar to lemon balm. 'Green Magic' is a good variety for drying, growing to about 2 ft (60 cm) tall.

GROWING HINTS
The seed may be difficult to obtain. Sow in late spring, in an open position, to flower in late summer.

HARVESTING AND DRYING
The harvesting time is not critical. Cut when mature and air-dry quickly to retain the best colour.

It is essential that Ambrosinia is thoroughly dried upside down before use and subsequently not exposed to a damp atmosphere otherwise the tips will become limp and curl over.

AMMOBIUM *alatum* 'Grandiflorum'
WINGED EVERLASTING FLOWER
Annual

Ammobium flowers are best described as being like tiny pure white *Helichrysum*, but with daisy-like yellow centres when fully open. They are most useful in small arrangements or wreaths, with clusters of the flowers wired together.

GROWING HINTS
A native to Australia, *Ammobium* thrives in light, dry soils. It can be rather thin and ragged in form, so is perhaps best grown in a separate plot. Sown in spring, it will flower successively through the summer if continuously cut, the small flowers appearing at the end of green, winged stems 1–2 ft (30–60 cm) high.

HARVESTING AND DRYING
Harvest the stems selectively, choosing flowers that are half open. They will develop further during drying and may then display their yellow centres. If harvested too late the yellow centres will discolour.

The winged stems shrink dramatically during drying. What looked like a large fresh bunch may be rather small and bedraggled when dried, so be sure to pick enough. The bunches must be hung upside down as soon as possible after cutting and dried reasonably quickly to hold the pure whiteness of the flowers.

The stems always remain weak and

will rapidly absorb moisture again, causing the flower heads to droop. *Ammobium* must therefore be kept in a constantly dry atmosphere and may, even then, need support for the flower heads.

ANAPHALIS *margaritacea*

A. *yedoensis*
PEARL EVERLASTING
Deciduous Perennial

This delightful grey foliage plant is very effective in summer with its clusters of everlasting white flowers. The individual flowers are similar to *Ammobium* — opening to show a yellow centre.

GROWING HINTS
Anaphalis is probably easiest to obtain as a small plant. It spreads to form a clump enjoying full sun and a well-drained soil. A. *yedoensis* will also grow successfully in dry shady places. Growing to about 18 in (45 cm) high, *Anaphalis* is an ideal plant for the front of the border.

HARVESTING AND DRYING
Anaphalis flowers in late summer. Allow the leaves to remain on the stem when cutting, and air-dry hanging or upright. If dried too slowly the flowers will mature and go to seed. This can look attractive but will be too delicate for successful use.

ANETHUM *graveolens*
DILL
Annual/Herb

Dill is a valuable herb to have in any garden. It can also be left to flower and the dried seed head will retain some of its distinctive scent. The heads are similar in form to the delicate wild umbellifers such as cow parsley, but with yellowy-green flowers.

Anethum graveolens

GROWING HINTS
Dill can be sown from spring to early summer and will flower about ten weeks later. It will survive in any soil but will not flourish if too dry.

HARVESTING AND DRYING
The head, with as long a stem as possible, can be harvested at the flowering or seed stage and should be hung upside down to dry.

53

AQUILEGIA hybrida

COLUMBINE or GRANNY'S BONNET

Deciduous Perennial

The delicate columbine is a true cottage garden plant — a reliable perennial available in a range of soft shades of cream, pinks and blues. It flowers in late spring on stems 2 ft (60 cm) high.

GROWING HINTS

Sow in open ground so that the plants form small groups in the herbaceous borders. Once established they will seed freely. *Aquilegia* will tolerate most soil types but prefers sun or light shade and not too dry a soil.

HARVESTING AND DRYING

The flowers can be air-dried but it is the seed heads which are most useful. Pick them in early summer, while they are still a fresh green, and stand upright to air-dry. (They can be hung upside down but will shed seeds!)

In arrangements with other seed heads, the bright green is a lovely contrast to the orange of *Physalis franchettii*, Chinese lanterns, and the grey of poppy heads.

ARMERIA caespitosa

A. maritima

THRIFT or SEA PINK

Evergreen Perennial

Armeria is a low-growing perennial, forming dense green cushions with bright pink flowers growing to 6–12 in (15–30 cm) tall. It is an ideal plant for the rockery, flourishing in a sunny, well-drained position.

The bright pink flowers, on short stalks, appear in late spring or early summer. They should be picked in full flower and hung upside down to air-dry.

Their size makes them useful in small dainty arrangements. The colour changes to mauve during drying.

ASTER sp.

ASTER

Annual

The annual asters, which can be grown from seed, are deservedly popular as late-flowering bedding or edging plants and as cut flowers. Some of the larger double-flowered varieties, such as 'Milady' and 'Duchess', can provide unusual and strong colours for dried flower arrangements, though it is difficult to dry them successfully without petal loss. Cut the flowers just before they are fully open and hang up to dry quickly.

ASTER novae-belgii

MICHELMAS DAISY

Deciduous Perennial

Michelmas daisies can vary in height from dwarf varieties of less than 12 in (30 cm) up to more than 5 ft (1.5 m) tall. Some of the *Aster novae-belgii* hybrids which have a more double flower can be successfully dried. The tall dark-rose, crimson or red colours are probably the most useful.

GROWING HINTS

The perennial asters prefer a sunny, open position which is not too dry. Flowering in late summer or autumn, they make a valuable contribution to any garden.

HARVESTING AND DRYING

Harvest when the flowers are fully open and dry quickly to prevent them maturing too far. The petals will shrivel and curl but an effect will be achieved by the overall mass of flowers.

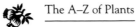

ASTILBE *arendsii*
FALSE GOAT'S BEARD
Hardy Perennial

The *Astilbe arendsii* hybrids are plants growing to 2–3 ft (60–100 cm) high with delicate flowering plumes, in colours from creamy-white to pink and dark red. The dark-leaved varieties can be used to contrast with light green foliage plants near the front of a border. (The white flowered *Astilbe* is difficult to dry without discoloration.)

GROWING HINTS
Astilbes are generally available for purchase as plants. They prefer partial shade and need a soil that is deep and moist. They are probably most at home near water.

HARVESTING AND DRYING
Flowering is in summer and the stems should be cut when the plant is in full flower but before it reaches maturity. Hang the stems upside down. Astilbe will air-dry easily in a warm place, but it is advisable to dry the white varieties more quickly.

ASTRANTIA *major*
MASTERWORT
Deciduous Perennial

Astrantia is a very natural cottage garden plant and looks good in well-established, rambling, herbaceous borders. It has small pinkish-white umbelliferous flowers on branching stems, growing to 2 ft (60 cm) in height.

GROWING HINTS
The seeds need to be sown in autumn so that they can overwinter before germinating. *Astrantia* enjoys full sun or partial shade but needs a moist soil. Once established, its roots will spread easily and it can be propagated by division.

HARVESTING AND DRYING
Astrantia flowers in early summer. The flowers can be successfully harvested when fully open and hung to air-dry.

ATRIPLEX *hortensis*
ORACH
Hardy Annual

Related to the dock family, *Atriplex hortensis* 'Rubra' is a crimson-leaved form, fast growing and very attractive as a contrast in herbaceous borders. Its tall seeding spike can be used in dried arrangements in a similar way to the red *Amaranthus paniculatus*. The green variety is a lovely light fresh colour.

GROWING HINTS
Sow in spring in open ground and harvest in late summer. It grows 4–5 ft (1.2–1.5 m) high.

HARVESTING AND DRYING
Cutting should be when the round flat seed pods have fully developed in size. If left too late the seeds will drop when dried. Use the dark colours to add depth to pink arrangements, or contrast strongly with yellows and light greens.

AVENA *sativa*
OATS
Hardy Annual Grass

Oats are an agricultural cereal crop, cultivated for porridge, breakfast cereals and horse feed. They grow taller than other cereals, reaching 4–5 ft (1.2–1.5 m), with seeds borne on pendulous panicles. Oats, especially when harvested green, are very useful in dried flower arrangements. They are one of the cheaper grasses to buy but, for serious growers, could be worth cultivating in a small plot.

GROWING HINTS

Different varieties are available for autumn or spring sowing. Oats require full sun and grow on a range of soil types.

HARVESTING AND DRYING

The ears emerge in late spring or early summer. Cut soon after the ear has emerged fully from the stem but while it is still bright and green. Hang upside down in the dark and dry quickly in warm air, to retain the colour. Alternatively, oats can be left to ripen naturally to their full harvest colour before cutting. At this stage additional drying is only necessary if the branches are to be stored. Late harvested oats can be dried upright.

BERGENIA hybrids

BERGENIA

Evergreen Perennial

The low-growing bergenia with its large evergreen leaves is a useful plant for the front of the border. It provides interest throughout the year and its pink flowers are particularly welcome in the garden in early spring. The best varieties for drying are those with densely-clustered flowers.

GROWING HINTS

Best purchased as plants, bergenia will spread to form a dense ground cover in ordinary soil, in sun or shade.

HARVESTING AND DRYING

At a time of year when there is little else available for drying, bergenia can be cut in full flower. The fleshy stems, which may be rather short, dry quickly in warm air and the pink flowers change to a delicate mauve. Wired in clusters, these provide an unusual touch in natural arrangements of soft pinks, green and white.

BRIZA sp.

QUAKING GRASS

Hardy Annual Grass

Quaking grass is a native of chalk grassland and is so named because of its delicate nodding seed heads, which remain long into the autumn. It has always been a popular ornamental grass and is best used in small, dainty arrangements.

GROWING HINTS

Quaking grass does not have the vigour to compete with other grasses in rich soils but will survive well on poor dry soils of low fertility, in full sun. The largest form, *Briza maxima*, will give the best effect but *B. media* and *B. minima* can also be used. Sow in spring, either in patches in the border or in plots or rows in a corner of the vegetable garden.

HARVESTING AND DRYING

Ideally, harvest in summer when the heads have developed fully but before the seeds are mature. However, timing is not critical and *Briza* can be harvested later although the colour will have faded. This grass will air-dry easily and quickly standing upright or hanging.

BROMUS sp.

B. macrostachys
B. secalinus

RYE BROME GRASS

Annual Grass

Many types of brome grass exist but *Bromus macrostachys* is worth mentioning as a distinctive full-headed variety. It is a light green grass, growing up to 2½ ft (75 cm) tall, with an open panicle form. The individual spikelets or seeds may develop a slight purple coloration with maturity. The fullness of its form makes rye brome a useful arrangement filler.

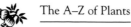

GROWING HINTS

Sow in the spring. Rye brome grows readily from seed and will thrive in poorer, drier soils in the open. It will survive mild winters and will self-seed readily. Sow in wild corners of the garden or restrict to plots.

HARVESTING AND DRYING

Wait until the branched panicle carrying all the seed heads has fully emerged from the stem. Cut while it is still green or wait (about a week) until the purple shades develop. Hang upside down. As with all grasses, the earlier the harvest and the faster the drying process, the greener the end product will remain.

CALLUNA *vulgaris*

ERICA sp.

HEATHER ('LING') or HEATHS

Evergreen Shrubs

The summer and autumn flowering heathers and the winter flowering heaths can be used as fillers in dried flower arrangements and should be cut in the early stages of flowering. They do, however, have a tendency to drop their leaves when dry, so are best used fresh and allowed to dry out *in situ* undisturbed. Alternatively, they can be sprayed with a fixative. A far superior result can be obtained using the glycerine method.

All prefer sandy, leafy, acidic soil and dislike lime.

CAMPANULA *glomerata*

CLUSTERED BELLFLOWER

Deciduous Perennial

Campanula glomerata gives reliable ground cover for the herbaceous border and, with its clusters of violet-blue flowers among bright green leaves, it provides, when dried, a natural-looking,

dark blue background filler for 'country' arrangements.

GROWING HINTS

Clustered bellflower spreads well in any soil that does not get too dry, in sun or partial shade. It flowers in early summer, on erect stems 1–2 ft (30–60 cm) high.

HARVESTING AND DRYING

The stems should be cut in full flower (but before the earliest clusters of blooms start to wither) and the leaves left on. Hang upside down to dry, fairly quickly, since retention of the green in the leaves is important.

CARLINA *acaulis caulescens*

CARLINE THISTLE

Deciduous Perennial

This is a very prickly plant to handle but well worth the effort! The carline thistle, fully mature with its silvery-white and biscuit-coloured seed heads, is an eye-catching specimen especially in autumnal arrangements.

GROWING HINTS

Sow in spring in an open sunny position on any soil. It is a stemless thistle flowering above a rosette of leaves and, once established, can tolerate dry conditions.

HARVESTING AND DRYING

The thistle flowers in summer, with heads 4–5 in (10–12.5 cm) across. Wait until the head has matured and is beginning to go to seed before harvesting.

Prolonged drying will be necessary because of the density of the head, so dry in a warm place and ensure the centre is thoroughly dry before using. The flower head will need to be wired or given a false stem before being used in arrangements.

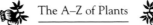

CARTHAMUS *tinctorius*

SAFFLOWER

Annual

Until recently *Carthamus* was little heard of but, commercially, is now widely grown because of its usefulness as a dried flower. It bears distinctive, thistle-like flowers on tall, strong branching stems up to 3 ft (1 m) high. Like thistles, the leaves tend to be prickly although spineless varieties are now becoming available.

The orange varieties are very striking and lovely to use in combination with the yellow *Achillea filipendulina*, linseed, wheat, millet and dark red *Helichrysum*. A cream variety is less showy, but more versatile in colour combinations.

The strength and height of *Carthamus* are assets in tall arrangements but the individual heads can also be used in small arrangements — especially if picked in the green, unopened bud stage.

The green of dried *Carthamus* is particularly prone to fading in direct sunlight.

GROWING HINTS

Sow in spring in open ground. It will benefit from a good soil and grow tall and strong, though may need treatment for blackfly.

HARVESTING AND DRYING

Carthamus flowers in mid-summer. If the green bud stage is required, allow the buds to swell fully and cut as late as possible before they burst. If harvested too early the buds will shrivel when dried.

When planning to harvest *Carthamus* in full flower, careful observation is necessary. The terminal bud (not necessarily the tallest) will open first and then the secondary flowers will follow — slowly if the weather is cold and wet, but quickly if it is hot and dry. The first

Carthamus tinctorius

flower will begin to die off. The best quality will be achieved by cutting the stem when the maximum number of flowers are fully open, but before more than one or two have over-matured. (A certain proportion will still, inevitably, be in the green bud stage.) The leaves lower down the stem should still be fresh green at this harvesting stage. Rapid air-drying in the dark is necessary as the fresh greenness is an important characteristic of the plant. To check dryness, make sure the stems snap when bent and dissect a large flower head.

CELOSIA *argentea cristata*

COCKSCOMB

Half-hardy Annual

Cockscomb is best known as a pot plant with its unusually formed bright red flower. It is not commonly seen as a dried flower but the dense, dark red head can be useful to give depth of colour to arrangements with bright greens, warm oranges and yellows.

GROWING HINTS

Celosia is usually raised in greenhouse conditions, sown in early spring and transplanted four to five weeks later. Direct sowing is, however, possible in sheltered locations.

HARVESTING AND DRYING

Harvest when in full flower and do not strip the leaves. Hang upside down and dry rapidly to maintain the best colour. Snap the stems to test dryness.

CENTAUREA *cyanus*

CORNFLOWER

Half-hardy Annual

Cornflower is available in blue, pink, mauve, purple and white but it is the blue variety which is most sought after in dried flower arrangements. It is especially useful in small decorative work such as posies or arrangements around straw hats. It can look particularly appropriate in natural combination with wheat and grasses, for instance, plaited into the ties around wheatsheaves.

GROWING HINTS

Select strong growing double-flowered varieties with good stems. Sow in full sun in spring. To produce straight upright stems the plants need support so are best grown in rows or clumps. The flowers start to bloom about 12–14 weeks after sowing.

HARVESTING AND DRYING

Regular daily cropping is necessary to obtain the best quality flowers. Select only the flowers that have *just* opened fully. If allowed to mature further, the flowers will start to fade and be prone to petal drop after drying — pick these separately for use in pot pourri. Secondary buds will continue to develop so the flowers can be cropped over several weeks.

The weakest point in the stem is just below the head, so it is imperative that the flowers are not allowed to droop, but are hung upside down immediately. Rapid drying is essential.

CENTAUREA *macrocephala*

KNAPWEED

Deciduous Perennial

Centaurea macrocephala has large golden-yellow thistle-like flowers and bright green leaves. The stems are strong and can grow to about 3 ft (1 m) high. It is a very striking herbaceous plant or dried flower, especially if used in combination with other yellows, oranges and reds and against dark green or purple backgrounds. The brown, cup-shaped remains of the seed heads are also attractive in the autumn and useful as strong focal points.

GROWING HINTS

Sow in patches in late spring in an open position. It will survive but not grow tall if in too dry a location.

HARVESTING AND DRYING

Centaurea flowers in late summer. Wait until the yellow petals have burst through from the bud stage but do not allow the plant to flower fully before cutting — it will open further during drying. Dry rapidly to retain a good colour. The centre of the flower head will be the last part to dry fully.

Once the primary flowers have been cropped, side shoots will develop so extending the harvesting period over several weeks. These later flowers will have shorter stems that may need to be extended by wiring.

If left until the autumn to go to seed fully, what will remain is a brown 'cup' made up of small feathery sepals. These will need little further drying before they can be used but some of the old seeds may have to be removed if the heads are to look their best.

Spray gold or silver for Christmas arrangements.

CHRYSANTHEMUM sp.

CHRYSANTHEMUM

Hardy Perennial

Of the numerous chrysanthemum hybrids, those with dense, double-flowering heads dry best and some subtle colours can be obtained. They should be cut just before the flowers reach maturity and dried quickly to prevent the petals dropping. The petals shrivel during drying so the head size shrinks considerably.

The flowers are rarely suitable as focal points but make adequate additions to a colour scheme. Dark purple spray chrysanthemums are especially useful to give depth of colour to tall arrangements.

Centaurea cyanus

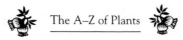

CLEMATIS sp.

CLEMATIS

Deciduous Perennial Climber

The clematis plants — including the common *Clematis vitalba* (Old Man's Beard) provide a source of decorative fluffy seed heads in the later summer and autumn. The stems can also be used as the basis for wreaths. The yellow flowering *C. tangutica* and *C. orientalis* can be particularly recommended.

GROWING HINTS

Clematis likes its roots to be in the shade, where the soil does not dry out too much, but the growing shoots to be in the sun. This makes it an ideal plant to use as a climber through other shrubs and trees. It benefits from periodic thinning out or pruning in spring. Specific cultural details should be noted for individual varieties.

HARVESTING AND DRYING

The harvesting stage of the seed heads is not critical, though quality may be damaged by wet weather later in the year. Once cut, they can be left to air-dry naturally. Later, the plants' stems can be cut back, trimmed and wound into circlets or heart shapes while still supple. They can be decorated immediately or left to dry out for later use as the basis for wall displays or table centres.

CORTADERIA selloana

PAMPAS GRASS

Perennial Grass

The giant plumes of pampas grass, rising out of large clumps of reed-like leaves, are unmistakable in any garden. Indoors they should only be used in large-scale arrangements.

GROWING HINTS

Pampas grass requires lots of space and a deep, good soil in a sunny position.

HARVESTING AND DRYING

The flowering heads appear in late summer and remain well into the autumn. The cream or pinkish plumes should be harvested when they have emerged fully but before they become mature, otherwise during drying they will become too fluffy as the seeds develop. If picked at the right stage, they can be stood upright to air-dry naturally and need not be confined to the dark.

CORYLUS avellana contorta

CORKSCREW HAZEL

Deciduous Shrub

This deciduous shrub or small, multi-stemmed tree is an ornamental addition to the garden because of its twisted branches and catkins in spring.

GROWING HINTS

The corkscrew hazel grows to about 10 ft (3 m) in height in all except very acid soils. Straight stems shooting from the base should be cut back each winter to favour the contorted ones.

HARVESTING AND DRYING

The branches are unusual enough to be used on their own or in very simple arrangements in vases or jugs. Select the most interesting shapes and cut when the branches are bare. They do not need to be dried before use. At Christmas they can be painted (with white, silver or gold) and hung with decorations.

Salix matsudana, the corkscrew willow, is a small fast-growing tree, easily rooted from cuttings. It also has twisted branches, though the contortions are less extreme.

COTINUS coggygria 'Foliis purpureis'

C. coggygria 'Royal Purple'

SMOKE TREE

Deciduous Shrub

The round dark purple leaves of these varieties of *Cotinus* are marvellous as background colouring in the garden and the fine feathery flowers on mature shrubs give the impression of smoke — hence the name. Both flowers and leaves can be dried, but it is the latter which will provide the most striking feature.

GROWING HINTS

Cotinus grows to about 10 ft (3 m) tall and thrives in any soil. It can feature as a specimen or be at the back of the border but will not look its best in shade. Place it in contrast to silver or bright green foliage plants or as a background to yellows (such as *Achillea filipendulina*), warm oranges or bright, light blues. The flowers are produced more profusely on mature and unpruned or lightly pruned plants.

HARVESTING AND DRYING

Pick the flowers in late summer and hang to air-dry. The leaves too should be left until late summer and can be pressed, dried slowly like eucalyptus or glycerined.

CRASPEDIA globosa

DRUMSTICK

Annual/biennial

The tiny yellow flowers of *Craspedia* are packed in a tight ball on the end of a long, clean, strong stem, thus resembling a drumstick. They last well as cut flowers and are also popular dried, forming a strong focal point in arrangements. Their distinctive shape is well illustrated in the display of garden flowers on page 19.

GROWING HINTS

The seeds should be sown early in spring under glass, pricked out four to six weeks later and planted out in late spring. *Craspedia* grows up to 3 ft (1 m) in height and support may be needed to ensure good straight stems.

HARVESTING AND DRYING

Craspedia flowers from late summer into the autumn and should be picked just as (or just before) the flowers reach their prime. The stems will stand upright but should not be dried too slowly or the flowers will deteriorate.

Craspedia globosa

CUCURBITA *pepo*

GOURD

Half-hardy Annual Fruit

These ornamental (but inedible) fruits can be grown in green, yellow, white or orange combinations of colours. They provide interesting ornaments for the winter.

GROWING HINTS

Like pumpkins or marrows, gourds are rambling plants and best allocated to a corner of the vegetable plot. They like a sunny position in any soil. Sow in spring under glass and plant out in early summer.

HARVESTING AND DRYING

Harvest when the fruits have developed to full size, about 4 in (10 cm) in diameter, and are ripe. Allow them to dry naturally at room temperature over a period of several weeks and then apply varnish to retain the bright colours.

CYNARA *cardunculus*

CARDOON

Deciduous Half-hardy Perennial

The cardoon is similar to the artichoke but not edible! It is taller but has a smaller, more thistle-like head with mauve-purple flowers that retain their colour well during drying. It branches more freely but has similarly architectural grey-green foliage and is a very attractive garden plant.

Growing, harvesting and drying rules are the same as for artichokes.

CYNARA *scolymus*

GLOBE ARTICHOKE

Deciduous Half-hardy Perennial

If the gastronomic delights of artichokes are forgone they can develop into dra-matic flowers and be picked at various stages of their development for different effects. The large, mauve flower heads are held on thick, sometimes branched, stems 3 ft (1 m) or more high above decorative silver grey leaves.

The outer bracts of the heads are a greeny-grey colour, often with a dark purple tinge. If cut when small and closed they can be used as solid elements in arrangements with, for instance, dark red hydrangeas, bright red roses, *Nigella* and cocksfoot grass. If left longer and dried, so that they are captured in full flower, a group of stems on their own in an earthenware pot make an eye-catching feature. If the flower matures further towards seeding the colour fades and eventually the centre turns to a pale biscuity colour, surrounded by silvery white.

GROWING HINTS

Artichokes need a good moist soil and will benefit from mulching. Sow direct into open ground in spring, spaced 2 ft (60 cm) or more apart. If established early, flowers will develop in the first autumn. Subsequently, flowering will begin in summer. Their attractive foliage makes them equally suitable for corners of the flower border or the vegetable garden. Not all plants will survive a hard winter but those that do will grow to a significant size — 5 ft (1.5 m) in height and spread, and the mature flowering heads can measure 6 in (15 cm) across.

To be enjoyed as a vegetable, the heads need to be picked much earlier than for drying — while the globe is still tightly closed and before the tips of the edible outer bracts have developed sharp spines.

HARVESTING AND DRYING

As indicated above, the artichokes can be cut at different stages. The young unopened artichokes can be selected at various sizes and cutting these early in

Cynara scolymus

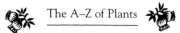

the season will encourage further buds to develop.

Drying an artichoke, so that its full flowering glory is captured, is more difficult. The head contains a reserve of moisture and continues to mature while drying, and the rate of development will vary according to the speed of drying. Cutting when the mauve flower petals just start to appear in the centre of the head usually results in the flower drying in its prime.

If the artichokes are allowed to flower naturally on the plant, the tufted seeds will eventually develop. This is also a very attractive stage at which to cut and dry the heads. Any parts of the centre discoloured by rain or dead petals can be gently pulled out. (This can be a prickly job!)

Artichokes need a *very* long time to dry. They can be hung upside down, stood upright or laid down. They must be in as warm a location as possible, but not necessarily in the dark. To test for dryness push a skewer into the densest underpart of the head at the top of the stem. If still soft, leave it longer to dry and harden, otherwise mould will ultimately develop.

DACTYLIS *glomerata*
COCKSFOOT GRASS
Perennial Grass

Cocksfoot is a perennial grass, historically important agriculturally in pastures and meadows and often found on road verges. Because it is indigenous and exists naturally in many larger gardens it is probably not worthy of special cultivation. However, it is valuable for use in 'natural' arrangements. The head is a dark, dull, green but with a purple tinge which makes it an ideal complement to flowering artichokes and red hydrangeas.

GROWING HINTS
Sown in late summer, cocksfoot will flower the following year in late spring. In its leaf stage cocksfoot is short, but in fertile sites the flowering stems can reach 4–5 ft (1.2–1.5 m) tall.

HARVESTING AND DRYING
Cut when the branched flower head, with its tightly packed spikelets (the individual flowers), has fully emerged. At first green, the purple coloration develops quickly after the head emerges. Harvest before the tiny yellow anthers can be seen hanging from the flower heads. Hang in bunches upside down and air-dry quickly to retain the colour. Ensure the parts of the stems under the rubber band are fully dry and brittle before storing.

DAHLIA sp.
DAHLIA
Half-hardy Annual (Tuberous)

The small double or pompom varieties of dahlia can be successfully air-dried and are available in a wide range of colours. (The richer colours are likely to be more successful.) They are by no means as spectacular when dried as they are fresh, but can nevertheless be useful for their colour and form.

GROWING HINTS
Dahlias grow easily from seed, cuttings or division of tubers. They can be planted out in any soil in a sunny position and will flower reliably in late summer. In a mild climate dahlias will overwinter.

HARVESTING AND DRYING
Pick in the early stages of full flowering and hang up to air-dry relatively quickly to prevent the flower overmaturing and losing petals.

DELPHINIUM *consolida*

LARKSPUR
Annual

Larkspur is indispensable as a dried flower and well worth growing in the garden. It is available in a variety of colours — pale and dark blues, pinks, mauves and white — and the flower

Delphinium consolida

spikes grow to about 3 ft (1 m) in height. It can be used in basket displays or arranged naturally, like a fresh flower, in a vase with grasses (such as *Setaria*), peonies and *Achillea ptarmica*.

GROWING HINTS
Select double-flowering types that have

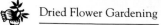

large individual florets densely packed up the stem (*Delphinium ajocis* is not suitable). Sow in spring in any soil, in a sunny position. Do not transplant.

HARVESTING AND DRYING
As a fresh flower larkspur is usually cut when 50 per cent of the flowers are in bloom. Drying it at this stage retains the greenish buds at the tip of the stem and can give a fresh look to a display. However, larkspur is generally cut for drying when it is 90 per cent in flower. Cutting later than this or drying too slowly makes it susceptible to petal drop. It dries easily but should be dried fairly quickly hanging upside down.

A second crop of shorter stems may be obtained from side shoots after the leaders have been cut.

If storing in a box, make sure the tips are not bent against the box ends. However, if the blooms become crushed during storage, they can be opened out by holding the stems over steam for a short while.

DELPHINIUM *elatum*
DELPHINIUM
Deciduous Perennial

Though more difficult to dry successfully than larkspur, the tall hybrid delphiniums — growing up to 6 ft (2 m) tall — are useful for big arrangements. The large flowered and dark blue varieties can be particularly striking especially when used with bright greens and creamy whites. (The smaller *Delphinium belladonna*, with branched heads, is not so suitable for drying.)

GROWING HINTS
Plant in full sun, in the middle or back of the border, in rich, well drained soil. Take precautions against slugs which are attracted to the young shoots. The tall delphiniums are susceptible to wind damage, so provide support if necessary.

HARVESTING AND DRYING
Cut when the plant is 90 per cent in flower and air-dry fairly quickly, hanging upside down.

DIANTHUS *barbatus*
SWEET WILLIAM
Hardy Biennial

Sweet Williams are not an obvious choice for drying but they can provide a welcome splash of colour in the garden as well as being very useful background fillers to cover oasis in small arrangements. They are available in crimson, pink, white or variegated colours and should be grown at the front of herbaceous borders.

GROWING HINTS
Sow outdoors in late spring or early summer, thinning or transplanting as necessary. Flowers will appear in the late spring of the following year.

HARVESTING AND DRYING
Cut and bunch when in full flower and air-dry quickly. The petals will shrivel and become flecks of colour against the green or plum colouring of the bulk of the flower head. If the dried Sweet Williams are exposed to moisture in the air, they will rapidly deteriorate in quality. The greenness is also prone to rapid fading in bright sunlight.

DIANTHUS *caryophyllus*
D. x. *allwoodii*
CARNATION
PINK
Half-hardy Annual/Biennial
Hardy Perennial

The large double 'button-hole' type of carnation can be successfully dried. Though available in a range of colours, it is the strong reds which hold their colour best and can be most successfully used in dried arrangements.

The smaller perennial pinks also dry well and again it is the stronger darker colours which are to be recommended. The single flowers shrivel but the closed buds are decorative in small posy arrangements, though their greenness tends to fade rapidly in daylight.

GROWING HINTS

Carnations should be sown under glass in late winter or outdoors in late spring. They like a sunny position in fertile soil and will flower in late summer. Pinks are easily propagated from cuttings.

HARVESTING AND DRYING

Cut pinks and carnations when they are just in full flower and air-dry quickly, hanging upside down. The stems under the carnation heads may be weak and have to be wired.

DIPSACUS *fullonum*
COMMON TEASEL
Biennial

The common teasel has always been a favourite element in dried flower decorations, picked when it has turned brown in the autumn. But instead, try cutting it just as, or after, it bears its ring of mauve flowers and it will then retain its greenness when dried and thus look fresher and be more versatile in use.

Teasels are frequently found on road verges, stream banks and waste ground. Seeds can be collected in the autumn and if sown then will produce a large rosette of leaves in the first year, followed by tall flowering stems in the second.

Dipsacus fullonum

ECHINOPS *ritro*
GLOBE THISTLE
Deciduous Perennial

Globe thistles do not thrive in dry locations but, given the right combination of having their heads in the sun and their roots in moist soil, they will grow vigorously up to 6 ft (2 m) tall without needing food. The prickly grey leaves and steely-blue flower heads look good with delicate white and pale pink colourings or strong creams and fresh greens. The distinctive globe shape of the flowers, which grow up to 1½ in (3.5 cm) in diameter, give form and focus to arrangements, though they need careful handling as the heads will easily break off if knocked.

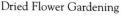

GROWING HINTS

Sow in late spring, to flower in late summer. Locate in the middle or back of a herbaceous border and allow plenty of space for each plant. The tall, rather soft stems may need support during the growing season.

HARVESTING AND DRYING

The cutting of globe thistles for drying needs careful timing. As the heads develop in size they change from grey-green towards lavender blue when the individual florets are about to break bud. The secret is to cut them at this stage before the florets open.

Hang upside down to air-dry. Once dry they need to be handled with great care — not only because they are very prickly but because the heads can be easily damaged or broken off.

If allowed to flower fully before cutting the dried heads will look untidy and be even more fragile.

ERICA sp.

HEATH

Evergreen Shrub

See *Calluna vulgaris*.

ERYNGIUM sp.

SEA HOLLY

Perennial

The sea hollies are all sturdy plants with silvery grey leaves and foliage and distinctive clusters of steely-blue flowers on branched stems. The biennial *E. giganteum* has large flower heads whereas the flowers of *E. alpinum* are smaller and bluer. They look good planted in borders with white or deep blues and purples but, being prickly, should not be too close to well-used paths!

Eryngium has very strong stems when dry. The tall branching stems of *E.*

planum (which may also be a pronounced blue in colour) can be used in big arrangements or the smaller heads arranged individually in posies. It is equally versatile with a range of colours — in combination with pink larkspur, dark blue lavender, cream *Helichrysum*, fresh green grasses or apricot statice.

GROWING HINTS

The seeds need to overwinter and germination can be slow but, once established, *Eryngium* likes full sun and will grow well in a dry, well drained soil or through gravel.

HARVESTING AND DRYING

The harvesting stage is not as critical as with *Echinops*. Wait until the flower heads have developed fully in size and start to turn blue. Air-dry hanging or standing.

EUCALYPTUS sp.

GUM TREE

Evergreen Tree

The silvery or grey-green leaves of eucalyptus are justifiably popular for fresh and dried flower arrangements. They are fast growing trees; many are frost tender but *E. gunnii*, the cider gum, is one of the hardiest. They are fairly tolerant of all soil types but, with the exception of *E. parvifolia*, dislike shallow chalk soils.

The foliage generally used by flower arrangers is the juvenile leaves, which can be distinctly different from those produced by the adult tree. However, eucalyptus responds well to hard pruning, which stimulates the continued production of juvenile leaves.

GROWING HINTS

If eucalyptus is being grown for its foliage rather than as a specimen tree it is best purchased as a small pot-grown tree and pruned to develop a shrub-like form.

HARVESTING AND DRYING

Eucalyptus can be used fresh in arrangements and allowed to dry in place naturally, or it can be bunched and hung upside down. It is important to dry eucalyptus slowly to prevent the leaves curling and becoming brittle and to hold the distinctive and attractive colour of grey-leaved varieties. Ideally, hang it somewhere in the house where its wonderful aroma can be enjoyed!

Eucalyptus can be preserved with glycerine. This process tends to turn the leaves a dark green.

EUPHORBIA polychroma

syn. *E. epithymoides*

CUSHION SPURGE
Perennial

Euphorbia polychroma spreads easily to form dark, green-leaved clumps. It flowers in spring, the flowers being insignificant but contained in bright yellow-green bracts on stems 18 in (45 cm) high. This fresh colouring stands out especially well against dark backgrounds and lasts a long time.

GROWING HINTS

Spurge can be propagated by cuttings, division or by seed sown in the autumn. The plants like sun or partial shade.

HARVESTING AND DRYING

The stems exude a milky sap which is poisonous and can be an irritant, so take care when cutting and handling. Harvest when the bracts have opened fully but before they start to lose their fresh colour. The cut ends of the stems can be sealed by placing them for a few seconds on a hot oven plate or in hot water. The bunches should then be hung upside down and dried slowly. Fast drying will cause shrivelling.

FAGUS sylvatica

F. sylvatica purpurea

BEECH
Deciduous Tree

It is a natural tendency of beech to hold much of its juvenile foliage during winter — a characteristic that makes it particularly valuable as a hedging plant. These dry light brown/bronze winter leaves can be used in their natural state or can be glycerined and dyed. The purple-leaved beech is particularly dramatic.

Beech mast — the seed pods — can be collected as they fall, or picked when closed, so that they open while drying. They are ideal for use in wreaths and Christmas decorations.

FESTUCA sp.

FESCUE GRASS
Perennial Grass

The fescues are a large family of grasses possessing very fine, delicate flowers on branched stems. Their fine form makes them suitable for delicate arrangements though, if cut in full flower, they are not to be recommended for use by hayfever sufferers! *Festuca ovina* (Sheep's fescue) is often included in lawn seed mixes and *F. glauca* (Blue fescue) forms clumps and is useful as a rockery or edging plant.

F. longifolia is one of the tallest species in this family, which generally have rather delicate seed heads. Fescues are tolerant of most soils and are drought-resistant.

GROWING HINTS

Sow in late summer, to flower in early summer the following year. Alternatively, simply allow selected areas of lawn grass to grow and flower, under trees for instance, and take a crop of whichever attractive species appear. With so many species and hybrids, it would need a skilled botanist to identify specimens which might be found naturally in larger gardens.

HARVESTING AND DRYING

Cut in the early stages of flowering, after the heads have emerged fully but before the anthers (and pollen) appear. Dry by hanging in warm air.

GOMPHRENA globosa

GLOBE AMARANTH

Half-hardy Annual

The globe amaranth is not a well-known garden plant but, like *Carthamus*, is becoming more widespread in popularity because of its everlasting qualities. It grows to 1 ft (30 cm) in height and has clover-like flowers in white, rose or purple. The latter is particularly distinctive. *G. haageana* has pastel orange flowers and is a little taller. All are useful in small arrangements both as fresh or dried flowers.

GROWING HINTS

Sow under glass in early spring and transplant out four to six weeks later. It flowers from early summer onwards and is a reliable plant for the front of the border.

HARVESTING AND DRYING

Cut when the flowers are completely open. They are naturally papery and will air-dry easily, hanging upside down.

GRAMINEAE sp.

GRASSES

Annual/Perennial Grasses

Grass species are numerous, varying in size and flower form. Certain types have attractive foliage so are suitable for inclusion in flower borders. Others are best grown in selected corners since it is only the flower head which is of interest

to the dried flower gardener. Select ornamental grass seed mixtures if establishing afresh, but don't forget the rougher corners and garden boundaries which will often yield a surprising variety of grass heads during spring and summer, without any establishment being necessary.

Specially seeded 'wild' garden areas have gained in popularity recently. Establishing wild flower, herb and grass gardens help to preserve native flora, as well as providing food for butterflies, bees and other insects. Choose seed mixtures with a good range of wild grass species if interested in harvesting for drying. The most important grasses for drying are listed separately in this A–Z (see Appendix III).

Listed below are other grasses which also dry well. Each will establish if sown in moist fine seed beds in spring, but many have minute seeds and will not tolerate very dry conditions until well-rooted. Harvest as soon as the flower heads have fully emerged to retain the freshest green colour. Hang upside down in a warm, airy, dark position. Most are fine-stemmed types, so dry easily.

ANNUAL

Agrostis nebulosa	Cloud grass
Aira elegans	Hair grass
Pennisetum villosum	Feathertop grass
Poa annua	Meadow grass
Polypogan monspeliensis	Beard grass

PERENNIAL

Deschampsia flexuosa	Wavy hair grass
Deschampsia caespitosa	Tufted hair grass
Pennisetum setaceum	Fountain grass
Stipa pennata	Feather grass

Hay fever sufferers are advised to cut grasses especially early and to be wary of working with grasses cut when in full flower, or which develop into full flower while drying.

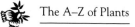

GYPSOPHILA *paniculata*

var. 'Bristol Fairy'

BABY'S BREATH

Hardy Perennial

Gypsophila is a delightful flower to grace the garden and is invaluable in fresh and dried displays. A combination of dried roses and *Gypsophila* with green millet or *Agastache urticifolia* can be easily arranged in a vase as if they were fresh. *Gypsophila* is a wonderful filler for large arrangements, and a delicate and essential addition to any small wedding posies or head-dresses. For drying it is important to select a double-flowered variety which will give a frothy mass of tiny white flowers.

GROWING HINTS

Sow under grass in early spring and plant out into a sunny position in the middle of a border. *Gypsophila* prefers chalky, well-drained soils.

HARVESTING AND DRYING

Cut when it is in full flower. This is important as the flowers are so tiny and they need to be fully open to give the maximum effect. *Gypsophila* should be hung upside down with the bunches well separated from one another so they do not tangle. It will air-dry quickly and easily this way. Drying fast in heat will make the fine stems brittle and possibly discolour them. If storing in boxes, put tissue paper between the layers to prevent tangling and pack lightly to prevent crushing.

HELICHRYSUM *angustifolium*

syn. *H. italicum*

CURRY PLANT

Evergreen Shrub

The curry plant has narrow, silvery-green leaves that are strongly aromatic, and clusters of small yellow flowers in summer. Both flowers and foliage can be readily dried but the latter is probably most useful for texture and colour as a filler in arrangements.

GROWING HINTS

Whether in the herb or the herbaceous garden, the curry plant looks good in a front of border position in full sun. It likes a dry soil. It can be pruned to keep a neat rounded appearance, growing to about 1 ft (30 cm) high.

HARVESTING AND DRYING

The flowers should be harvested just before they reach maturity and hung up to air-dry. The foliage can be used fresh in arrangements and allowed to dry out naturally, or hung up to air-dry.

HELICHRYSUM *bracteatum*

monstrosum

STRAW FLOWER

Half-hardy Annual

Helichrysum is one of the best known species of everlasting flower. It is easy to grow and dry, available in a range of colours, and deservedly popular with beginners and experienced flower arrangers alike. It holds its colour well after drying.

Helichrysum can grow to 3 ft (1 m) high but dwarf 12–15 in (30–37.5 cm) varieties are available and especially useful where growing space is limited. Select the double-flowered varieties.

Many colours are available: golden yellow, lemon yellow, white, orange, purple, red, light pink, dark pink and salmon. The light pink is deservedly popular in wedding arrangements. The dark purple is marvellous at giving visual depth to complement lighter colours. Red is, of course, ideal for Christmas decorations.

Before selecting the colours to grow, consider the colouring of other flowers

that you intend to dry. For instance, choose dark pink *Helichrysum* to contrast with light pink larkspur, salmon with green grasses, lemon with pale blue statice, etc.

GROWING HINTS
Sow under glass in early spring or in the open in late spring. An ideal spacing for the larger plants is 6–10 in (15–25 cm) apart. *Helichrysum* like full sun and a well-drained soil. The problem with establishing them in a flower garden is

Helichrysum bracteatum

that they need to be picked in bud so their colour outdoors cannot be fully enjoyed. If intensive cropping is envisaged sow them in a separate plot, perhaps in the vegetable garden.

HARVESTING AND DRYING
Beginners invariably harvest *Helichrysum* too late, waiting until the flowers are fully open, so that by the time they are dry they have over-matured. It is best to

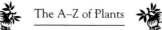
pick them in the morning when the buds have just started to open, i.e. the outer layer of petals has opened but the centre is still a 'bud' shape. If cut when the central part of the flower is visible it will develop quickly and may open too far while drying and not look so attractive. Once the main flower has been picked, side shoots will develop, providing an extended harvesting period.

If the flowers have strong stems they can be bunched and hung up to dry and then used in arrangements as they are, provided they will not be placed in a damp atmosphere. If *Helichrysum* is allowed to reabsorb moisture after drying, the stems become too weak to support the heads, which will droop. For this reason, and because some stems are naturally weak, many people wire *Helichrysum* when they are fresh and then let them dry. Wiring later can be tedious as the centre of the flower becomes very hard. At the end of the season any tiny flowering heads remaining can be used in pot pourri.

If some of the flowers open out fully during drying and others remain in tight bud, try placing the large open flowers lower down and the small buds higher in an arrangement, thus giving a very natural progression of form.

HELICHRYSUM *subulifolium*

HELICHRYSUM

This variety of *Helichrysum* does not have the double flower of *H. bracteatum* but is a bright yellow against light green foliage.

Growing to about 12–15 in (30–37.5 cm) tall, it flowers throughout the summer and can be used as a fresh or dried flower, harvested just as it reaches full flowering.

HELLEBORUS *corsicus*

CORSICAN HELLEBORE

Evergreen Perennial

Helleborus corsicus is a very valuable edging and ground cover plant for shaded borders. It has dark green, leathery, prickly edged leaves. In winter and spring it carries large clusters of cup-shaped, pale green long-lasting flowers, growing to 1–2 ft (30–60 cm) in height.

GROWING HINTS
The hellebore is best purchased as a plant and located in good well-drained soil in a shady sheltered position. Once established it will grow quickly and seed freely, so give it plenty of room.

HARVESTING AND DRYING
Cut in late spring and hang up to air-dry very slowly. The petals will shrivel somewhat while drying but the flower head will, nevertheless, remain a fresh green and be useful as a background filler in arrangements.

HORDEUM *vulgare*

BARLEY

Annual Grass

Barley is an annual agricultural cereal grass, produced for the malting industry and as a livestock feed. It has long distinctive whiskers, or awns, on the ear which, as it matures, arches over. Most barley crops are 'two-rowed' — having two rows of seed in each ear or flower — but the 'six-rowed' varieties have fuller, more attractive ears for flower arranging.

GROWING HINTS
Barley would only be worth growing if in a small separate plot in the garden. When buying seed, check whether it is an autumn or spring sown type. (Six-row varieties generally require autumn sowing.)

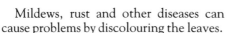

Mildews, rust and other diseases can cause problems by discolouring the leaves.

HARVESTING AND DRYING

Barley is one of the first grasses to come into ear in late spring. Wait until the whiskery head has fully emerged beyond the leaves, but cut before the anthers emerge and the pollen is released if you want to capture the fresh green colour.

Alternatively, leave the head to mature and arch over and harvest in summer when it is naturally golden. This latter stage is most appropriate for harvest festival decorations.

In the green stage, fast drying is necessary to hold the colour, and it is wise to ensure the bunches are not too large. Hang upside down to dry and make sure the awns are not bent. Once dry, the awns become brittle. Bunches harvested when mature and golden will naturally be more dry and can be finished off slowly, standing upright.

HUMULUS *lupulus*

HOP

Deciduous Perennial Climber

The hop is a vigorous climber growing up to 20 ft (6 m) in summer and dying back below the ground in winter. It is dioecious — bearing male and female flowers on separate plants. It is only the females that bear the attractive cone-like flowers. These contain essential oils and bittering acids used in brewing beer. Hops are traditionally associated with herbal remedies for insomnia — hence hop pillows! The clusters of flowers are very pretty and natural-looking in arrangements and can be used in bridal head-dresses and posies in the early autumn. The commerically produced full length 'bines', about 10 ft (3 m) long, are popular as wedding or party decorations wound around marquee poles, columns or over church doors. In the house they can be hung along old beams, unsightly pipework, over fireplaces (providing they are not close enough to become a fire hazard), above old dressers or along the top of kitchen units. For festive occasions they can be made into colourful swags by tying in bunches of other dried flowers.

GROWING HINTS

Hops prefer a deep rich soil to give them vigour, and must be given a structure to climb up. Commercially they are grown up coir strings, with two or three young shoots encouraged to twine up each string and the others removed. In the garden they will scramble up through trees or over a trellis. The golden hop, *H. lupulus* 'Aureas', can be very effective as contrast foliage. Cut back to ground level in late autumn and feed well in spring. Hops are susceptible to aphids

Humulus lupulus

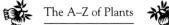

and certain mildew diseases which may affect the foliage colour in some seasons.

HARVESTING AND DRYING

The flowers start to show in mid-summer, but it is necessary to wait until they are fully developed in late summer or early autumn before cutting otherwise they will shrivel during drying.

The hop flowers are produced on side branches, or laterals, up to 18 in (45 cm) long. These sprigs can be picked and dried, or used fresh in arrangements and allowed to dry out naturally. The characteristic scent of hops can be quite strong for a few weeks after picking. Similarly, the full-length bines can be hung in position when fresh or semi-dried. Once fully dry the flowers become very brittle and should not be disturbed.

HYDRANGEA *macrophylla*
MOP-HEAD HYDRANGEA
Deciduous Shrub

Hydrangeas are frequently and easily grown in gardens, yet are not commercially grown in sufficient quantity to make them readily available for purchase as dried flowers. As a garden plant or dried flower they are invaluable. The colours of the fresh flowers vary from whites and pinks to blues, the difference being caused primarily by the nature of the soil — pink on alkaline or lime soils and blue on acid or clay ones. Flowers in shade tend to be green. The intensity of the colours deepens as the flowers reach maturity and when dried can make a wonderful display on their own or be an excellent background filler.

GROWING HINTS

For drying, be sure to select the sterile mop-head 'Hortensia' varieties (such as Altona, Hamburg and General Vicomtesse de Vibraye) rather than the lace-cap varieties.

Hydrangeas prefer a moist soil in a position of partial shade, but once established can grow well in full sun or in containers. During hot, dry weather keep the plants well watered. Flowers that have wilted will be of poor quality. Make sure they are in a position where their autumn colour can be appreciated.

Hydrangeas can be grown easily from cuttings. They will benefit from regular feeding and grow up to 5–6 ft (1.5–2 m) in height. A special additive composed of iron and aluminium can be bought to feed hydrangeas which, on lime soils, can suffer from mineral deficiencies. This additive alters the flower colouring from pinks towards blues.

HARVESTING AND DRYING

Timing the picking of hydrangeas correctly needs experience plus an awareness of changes in the weather. Hydrangeas picked too early will shrivel. Leave them too late and they will be ruined by the first frost or by wet weather.

As the hydrangea heads mature in the autumn, they gradually change and intensify in colour. To the touch they change from feeling soft, damp and cold to firm, dry and papery. Pick them at this stage and hang or stand them up to dry slowly. Fast drying will shrivel the petals. It will take several weeks to dry out the stems completely but, once dry, the flowers will hold their form and colour well as long as they are not in sunlight.

If early frosts threaten, pick the heads even if they are not quite ready, then stand them in a little water in a vase and leave them to dry out slowly.

Hydrangeas are sensitive to frost and a hard winter can damage the following year's flower buds. It is wise, therefore, to select flowers for drying with care and leave at least half of them on the bush for winter protection. Further pruning to remove dead heads can be done in the spring, as necessary, when the danger of late frosts is over.

HYDRANGEA *paniculata*

'Grandiflora'

HYDRANGEA

Deciduous Shrub

This particular variety is worth a special mention. In colour it is creamy white with a pink tinge. The form of the flower head is not globular but lilac-shaped and the individual florets are smaller than the hortensias. Both its colour and size make it particularly useful as a garden or dried flower. The full head can be used as a feature in large arrangements or small clusters of florets removed for use in daintier displays.

Harvesting and drying principles are the same as for other hydrangeas.

IRIS *foetidissima*

STINKING IRIS

Evergreen Perennial

Do not be put off by the name. The smell of stinking iris — likened to burnt rubber — is only associated with the roots or the bruised foliage. It has mauve or yellowy-green flowers but its main feature is its bright orange seeds held in the open seed pod through autumn and early winter. A bunch of these pods on their own can make an attractive display, or they can be incorporated in autumnal arrangements.

GROWING HINTS

The iris grows readily from seed and should be established in clumps in shade. It will tolerate quite heavy shade. It grows to about 1–2 ft (30–60 cm).

HARVESTING AND DRYING

Cut just after the pods have split open to reveal the shiny berries, and hang upside down to air-dry. The berries will eventually shrivel but their colours will remain strong.

KERRIA *japonica* 'Flore Pleno'

JEW'S MALLOW

Deciduous Shrub

Kerria japonica is an easily grown shrub which sends up suckers of arching green stems, soon forming a large clump about 6 ft (2 m) high. The variety 'Flore Pleno' has double yellow flowers in spring. It should be cut when the maximum number of flowers are in full bloom, bunched and hung up to air-dry.

LAGURUS *ovatus*

HARE'S TAIL GRASS

Annual Grass

Hare's tail is a popular ornamental grass, both for the garden and in dried arrangements. It has a small, soft fluffy head, growing to 1–2 ft (30–60 cm) in height. It can be dyed successfully, though it is a shame to spoil the soft grey/green colour of the best early-cut specimens. Use dyes only on the paler sun-bleached heads.

GROWING HINTS

Hare's tail can be sown in pots in early spring or in the garden a little later. Establish in clumps in a rockery or the front of a border. Being a native of Mediterranean regions it survives well in dry locations, but benefits from watering during early establishment.

HARVESTING AND DRYING

Cut when the hare's tail is full and fluffy, around flowering time. Alternatively, leave it on the plant to fade naturally in the sun if it is to be used for dyeing. The stems are very fine so bunches will be small. Hang up to air-dry, keeping the bunches separate from one another. Similarly, if boxing them for storage, separate layers of bunches with tissue paper to prevent the heads tangling.

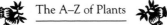

LAURUS *nobilis*

BAY

Evergreen Shrub

Bay trees, often grown as small container shrubs for the patio, provide leaves that can be dried for use either in cooking or small arrangements, such as wreaths or flat wall posies. They are best picked during the autumn or winter and will dry easily in any warm location (a kitchen is ideal).

Bay trees also make large background or screening shrubs. They are tolerant of hard pruning but are liable to frost damage in severe winters.

LAVANDULA *spica*

LAVENDER

Evergreen Shrub

A selection of lavenders is available in pink and white as well as the traditional blue. All can be used for drying in bunches or the flower heads can be harvested separately for aromatic use. When growing for arrangements choose varieties with large full buds densely packed on long flower spikes, and as dark a blue as possible (e.g. *L. spica* 'Hidcote Giant' and 'Munstead'). A big bunch of lavender can be attractive on its own as a decoration but can also be a useful contrast with larkspur, red roses, lemon-yellow *Helichrysum*, etc. Lavender is best used as clusters of stems wired together, rather than as single spikes.

GROWING HINTS
Lavender can be grown from seed, though germination may be erratic, and can easily be propagated from cuttings. It likes a well-drained soil in full sun and is best used in the front of the border or as a low hedging plant. It is ideal for patios. Do not overfeed. Hard pruning in the spring will create longer-lived, more compact plants.

HARVESTING AND DRYING
To dry bunches, the lavender needs to be cut early, just before the buds open to show the tiny flowers. Hang and dry it gently or it will become brittle. For use in pot pourri, leave it later and then the flowers can easily be stripped from the stems.

LIATRIS *spicata*

L. *callilepis*

GAYFEATHER

Deciduous Perennial

Liatris has bright purple flower spikes growing from 1–2½ ft (30–75 cm), above fine narrow leaves. Unlike most flower spikes the buds start to open from the top downwards. The strong colour and form make *Liatris* a useful plant in combination with grey foliage and white and pink flowers (especially pink larkspur).

GROWING HINTS
Liatris likes full sun and does well in poor, light soils. It can be grown from seed or propagated by division.

HARVESTING AND DRYING
Cut when about half the head is in flower but before the top flowers mature too far. If left longer they may go to seed while drying. *Liatris* has a robust stem and can be dried upright or hanging. It holds its colour well and is dry when the base of the stem snaps when bent.

LIMONIUM *latifolium*

SEA LAVENDER

Hardy Perennial

Limonium latifolium is a finer and more delicate form of *L. tartaricum dumosa*, with smaller flowers and less rigid stems. Growing conditions are the same but it

reaches about 2 ft (60 cm) and has tiny flowers with violet blue centres. *L. latifolium* should be picked when the flowers are fully open. It dries easily and quickly and is less prickly to use than *L. tartaricum dumosa*. Even when dry it can retain a strange musty smell.

Limonium sinuatum

LIMONIUM *sinuatum*

(syn. *Statice sinuata*)

STATICE
Half-hardy Annual

Statice and *Helichrysum* are the two best known everlasting flowers. Growing to

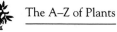

1–2 ft (30–60 cm) high, statice is available in many colours — white, pink, blue, purple, yellow and apricot (the latter can be very variable in shade, ranging from peachy yellow to raspberry pink). All the colours are bright (except the apricot) and last a long time. The white and blues tend to be the sturdiest to use and the yellow has the most brittle flower heads.

GROWING HINTS
Sow direct into open ground in late spring or raise under glass earlier. Statice is native to Mediterranean regions so tolerates full sun and dry locations, and it prefers an alkaline soil. The leading shoot can be picked out before flowering to increase the growth of side shoots. Statice can be grown either in a border where its bright colour can be appreciated or in a special plot if many plants are needed. It is well suited to locations of limited space.

HARVESTING AND DRYING
The flowers are papery and naturally dry easily, keeping their colour well. Nevertheless, it is a good idea to dry them in the dark as this retains the green stem colour and keeps them looking fresh.

Pick when all the flowers have opened and dry slowly or they will become brittle. Bunch loosely so the stems can be easily separated for use after drying, without damaging the heads. Rain tends to discolour the bright pink variety.

LIMONIUM *suworowii*
POKER STATICE
Half-Hardy Annual

Poker statice is very distinctive. It has densely packed, tiny pink flowers on a thin wavy spire that may be branched. The stems grow to about 18 in (45 cm), of which 10 in (25 cm) can be covered in flowers. They are unusual and fun to use.

GROWING HINTS
Sow in the spring in full sun. Poker statice tolerates most soil types and dry conditions, though stems will be much shorter if too dry.

HARVESTING AND DRYING
It flowers in mid to late summer and should be cut when the spike is in full colour — allowing the stem to gain as much length as possible but before the lowest flowers begin to lose their colour. Bunch and air-dry hanging upside down. The stems are fine but strong and easy to use in arrangements.

LIMONIUM *tartaricum dumosa*
SEA LAVENDER
Hardy Perennial

Sea lavender is universally popular as a background filler in dried flower arrangements. It forms a dense low mass, 1 ft (30 cm) high, of branched flowering stems above a rosette of dark green leaves. The tiny flowers are like white stars with pink centres when fully open.

GROWING HINTS
Sown in spring, it will flower in its second summer. It is a robust plant surviving in most conditions and soil types. In the garden it should be grown at the front of the border, but could also be established in gravel around patios.

HARVESTING AND DRYING
Wait until all the flowers are fully open but pick before the pink centres start to go brown and while the stems are still green. Sea lavender is the easiest of all plants to dry and in warm weather will need little help to dry out completely. Nevertheless, make sure the stems are dry before storing and do not crush the bunches at any stage or the stems will become distorted and tangled.

Sea lavender takes dye easily and the softer colours of pink, lavender blue,

pale yellow and peach are very useful in arrangements.

LINUM *usitatissium*
LINSEED
Annual

Linseed is an agricultural crop grown for its oil-rich seeds. It is closely related to flax, and grown in some regions for its tough, fibrous stems used in the production of linen. It grows to 2–3 ft (60–100 cm) tall and, in fields, is identifiable in mid-summer by its flushes of pale blue flowers which appear in the morning and last only a day, having lost their delicate petals by evening.

GROWING HINTS
When buying seed do not confuse it with other garden *Linum* species, which are unsuitable for drying. Sow in spring in open ground. In the garden allow it to establish in dense patches for the best effect.

HARVESTING AND DRYING
Linseed has quite a long harvesting period, from mid-summer, when the immature seed pods are green among a few late flowers, until late summer when all the flowers have developed into spherical pods. As the plant matures, the colour of the seed pods changes from green to yellow and eventually, by early autumn, both seed pods and stems will be brown.

The young green stage is best chosen for a fresh look. The yellow stage tones well with harvest-coloured arrangements, and the mature brown pods can be sprayed gold or silver for Christmas decorations. Take care when harvesting because a sharp knife or pair of secateurs will be needed to cut the fibrous stems.

Because the seed contains oils, drying it properly is not straightforward. An initial bout of drying in warm air is needed to hold the green colour of the stems and leaves, but then a long period of slow drying is necessary to ensure that the pods can be kept and stored successfully. If not fully dry, mould will develop. Crush individual pods and rub them between a finger and thumb to test for dryness. To assist the drying process do not pack too many stems in each bunch and, when storing, keep the bunches separate to prevent tangling. The seeds are very attractive food to mice so dry, store and display linseed in a safe place.

LONAS *inodora*
AFRICAN DAISY
Annual

Lonas grows from 12–18 in (30–45 cm) high and has clusters of bright yellow button flowers on the top of a strong stem. In colouring it is like the much larger *Achillea filipendulina*, but its scale makes it useful in small arrangements. It looks good in contrast to orange *Helichrysum* or blue statice.

GROWING HINTS
The plants enjoy a sunny position in well-drained soil. Sow in open ground in late spring.

HARVESTING AND DRYING
Lonas flowers in mid-summer and should be cut as soon as it is fully open. Hang the bunches upside down to air-dry.

LUNARIA sp.
HONESTY
Biennial/Perennial

Honesty has always been popular for winter dried flower arrangements because of its silvery white oval seed pods. In the garden it looks best in an informal situation, and either white or violet-purple flowering varieties can be used (or the type with variegated leaves). Biennial

(*L. biennis*) and perennial (*L. rediviva*) varieties are available.

GROWING HINTS
Honesty grows easily from seed and will spread freely. It prefers light shade. Sow in late spring to flower the following spring/early summer.

HARVESTING AND DRYING
The seed pods develop on stems about 2–3 ft (60–100 cm) high. These can be picked early and dried to retain their greenness. If left, their green colour gradually fades to silvery-white and the flat discs of the pods become dry and papery. Timing of picking at this stage is not critical but the seed heads are fragile and can be damaged by wind and torn if left too long. The two outer discs of the pod can be removed by rubbing the pod gently between a finger and thumb to reveal the shiny, almost translucent, inner disc. Save the flat brown seeds.

Honesty needs very little drying — only enough to make sure the lower part of the stems are brittle. Handle with care once fully dry, and store out of

Matricaria 'Snow Puffs'

reach of mice, for whom the seed heads make wonderful bedding material.

MATRICARIA *eximia*
FEVERFEW
Half-hardy Annual

Flowers in the *Matricaria* family are similar to small spray chrysanthemums in form. Dwarf varieties make good edging plants. The white, double-flowered *Matricaria* dries successfully to a form similar to *Achillea ptarmica* 'The Pearl'. The herb feverfew has small daisy-like flowers, white with a yellow centre, and can also be dried.

GROWING HINTS
Sow under glass in early spring and plant out after the late frosts. Once established, feverfew seeds freely. Plants will grow up to 3 ft (1 m) in height.

HARVESTING AND DRYING
Cut when in full flower and dry hanging upside down.

MATTHIOLA sp.

STOCK

Half-hardy Annual

The double-flowered stocks can be dried with moderate success to give an effect similar to larkspur. Pick when in full flower and dry quickly in a warm place. They hold their scent very well and produce some delightful musky colours. Unfortunately, however, they tend to absorb moisture and the stems go limp easily, so may require wiring.

MISCANTHUS sinensis

MISCANTHUS GRASS

Perennial Grass

The tall, ornamental miscanthus grasses, growing to 6 ft (2 m) tall, are useful plants for the middle or back of the border. The pinky-brown flowering plumes appear in late summer and last into the winter.

For drying, pick when the flowering plumes have fully emerged but before they are damaged by autumn weather.

MOLUCCELLA laevis

BELLS OF IRELAND

Annual

Always popular with fresh flower arrangers, Bells of Ireland can be dried successfully, though need to be handled carefully as the bells break off easily. The bells are pale green calyces, containing little white lemon-scented flowers. In the garden the colour shows up well against a dark background.

GROWING HINTS

Sow under glass in early spring or in open ground in late spring. The stems grow to 3 ft (1 m) tall and may need support. Bells of Ireland like a moist soil.

HARVESTING AND DRYING

The flowers appear in late summer and, for drying, the stems should be cut when the bells have become firm to the touch. To retain the fresh green colour it is necessary to pick before the lower bells begin to fade. Fresh young bells at the top of the stem will probably not have 'set' by this stage; they will shrivel during drying and need to be trimmed off. Alternatively, the stems can be left longer to fade and bleach naturally in the sun, though discoloration will occur from rain. Always remove the leaves before drying. Tie only a few stems in each bunch and hang to dry slowly. Handle carefully when dry, but keep any fallen bells as they can be used for interesting effect in small arrangements or collages (secured by glue). Try spraying them with gold or silver to make Christmas decorations. Bells of Ireland can also be preserved by glycerining.

NARCISSUS sp.

DAFFODIL

Bulb

Certain varieties of double-flowering daffodils can be dried successfully, such as 'Golden Ducat', but the problem with them is that the stems are very fleshy, take a long time to dry out fully and then will quickly reabsorb moisture in a damp atmosphere. Drying in silica is more successful.

NICANDRA physaloides

SHOO FLY PLANT

Hardy Annual

The value of *Nicandra* to dried flower arrangers lies in its seed, which is reminiscent of Chinese lanterns (*Physalis*

Moluccella laevis

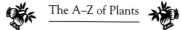

franchettii) but pale green in colour. The flowers, which appear in summer, are pale lilac-blue bells.

GROWING HINTS

Nicandra can be grown easily from seed sown in the open in spring. It has a bushy growth up to 3 ft (1 m), so needs plenty of space.

HARVESTING AND DRYING

As with most other seed pods it is necessary to let the pods mature before picking, otherwise they will shrivel when dried. They can be picked while still green or allowed to fade on the plant, and dried slowly either upright or hanging. Remove the leaves before drying.

NIGELLA *damascena*
LOVE-IN-A-MIST
Hardy Annual

Love-in-a-mist is a delightful annual with its fine leaves and delicate flowers of pink, blue or white. It can be dried in full flower but the most useful part of it is the seed pod. Picked at the right stage, the pod is green with stripes of dark maroon, surrounded by a finely-cut tracery of leaves. (The blue flowered 'Miss Jekyll' variety has a good seed pod colour.) In arrangements the dark stripe is a marvellous complement to pink or red and the head fits well into either small or large displays. It is an essential part of any dried flower garden and is

Nigella damascena

ideal where there is limited space.

More unusual, interestingly shaped seed pod varieties, such as the yellow-flowered *N. orientalis* 'Transformer', are being developed specifically for drying but seeds may be more difficult to purchase.

GROWING HINTS
Sow in autumn or spring. Germination can be very slow in dry conditions but, once established, *Nigella* will self-seed freely. It likes most soils and a position in full sun, and will flower in early to mid-summer. It grows 1½–2 ft (45–60 cm) high.

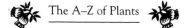
HARVESTING AND DRYING

The seed pods are at their best three to four weeks after flowering. Wait until the pods have developed to their full size but have not started to fade in colour. If picked too early, the pods will shrivel during drying.

If cut at the early flowering stage rapid drying is necessary to prevent petal drop, but if cut later the seed pods will air-dry easily (and the seeds can be collected for the next year's sowing). If left longer the pods will dry naturally on the plant but will fade considerably.

ORIGANUM *dictamnus*

syn. *O. marjorana*

SWEET or KNOTTED MARJORAM
Annual

A useful plant for the herb garden, sweet marjoram can be used in cooking and as a filler in dried flower arrangements. It grows to only 10 in (25 cm) tall and is grey-green in colour with minute white flowers forming in green bobbles up the stem (hence the 'knotted' appearance).

GROWING HINTS

Sow in late spring in open ground in full sun.

HARVESTING AND DRYING

Cut bunches of stems as low to the ground as possible and hang up to air-dry in the kitchen where the aroma will be appreciated.

ORIGANUM *vulgare*

POT MARJORAM or OREGANO
Perennial

Pot marjoram grows wild in sunny dry locations, especially on chalk. The dark pink flowers are very attractive to bees and butterflies and dry easily for use in

Origanum vulgare

small arrangements. The leaves can be used in cooking.

GROWING HINTS
The plants grow from 12–18 in (30–45 cm) tall and can be established in the herb garden or flower border. (The shorter golden-leaved variety 'Aureum' makes a bright edging plant.) Sow in spring in an open position.

HARVESTING AND DRYING
Harvest when just about to break bud or in full flower and hang up to dry. A kitchen always seems the most appropriate place for drying herbs!

PAEONIA sp.
PEONY
Deciduous Perennial

Peonies are glorious plants for the herbaceous border, flowering in late spring or early summer. They are widely used as cut flowers and though not easy to dry are magnificent when successful. When dried they can be mistaken for a full-blown English rose and, in arrangements, add a touch of great distinction.

GROWING HINTS
Peonies can be grown from seed, but since they take a few years to bloom well, they are best purchased initially as small plants and grown in rich, deep soil in sun or light shade. The flower buds can be damaged by late frosts so a sheltered position is advisable. Once established, do not transplant as the roots dislike disturbance. The double *P. officinalis* varieties, available in white, pink and crimson red, are the earliest to flower, in late spring. 'Rubra plena' dries to a magnificent rich dark red.

The double pink *P. lactiflora* 'Sarah Bernhardt' is the most popular commercially grown variety, but the double white variety 'Duchesse de Nemours' dries equally well. Both flower in late spring or early summer.

P. tenuifolia has simple red flowers with bright yellow stamens and dries very well.

HARVESTING AND DRYING
The harvesting stage is critical. Peonies open very quickly in warm sunny weather and within a day can have developed too far to dry successfully.

Double peonies As the bud swells, the outer petals open but the centre mass can still be firm and hard. These central petals then unfurl and it is important to cut the flower as soon as the centre is soft and the stamens are visible, but before it has opened enough to reveal the young seed pod at the centre. If the outer petals start to reflex the flower has matured too far and attempts to dry it will only result in a hanging stem and a heap of petals on the floor!

Single peonies Allow the flower to open fully to display the yellow anthers but cut before the petals reflex. Remove all but the top one or two leaves (to speed the drying process), tie not more than five in a bunch (or the heads may be crushed) and hang up to dry quickly in warm air. Slow drying may result in the flower maturing too far and the petals dropping during later use. Do not despair, however, if early attempts at drying fail — the petals are lovely in pot pourri!

Peonies can be prone to insect damage after drying. Eggs laid in the young flower (particularly of later flowering varieties) can survive even high-temperature drying and hatch out during storage, allowing larvae to eat away the base of the petals and making the flower eventually disintegrate. If infestation is suspected, putting the dried flowers in the deep freeze for 48 hours and then into a warm atmosphere will usually solve the problem! If the flower head becomes squashed or mis-shapen during drying or storage, holding it over the

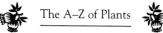

steam from a kettle for a short while will enable the petals to soften and expand.

PANICUM *miliaceum*

COMMON MILLET or BROOM-CORN MILLET

Annual Grass

Millet is an annual grass of agricultural importance grown particularly in the Far East and used in wholefoods and cage-bird seed. *Panicum miliaceum* is yellowy-green and grows 3–4 ft (1–1.2 m) high. It has a pendulous, weeping form which is not only attractive in the garden but is superb in dried arrangements. Most dried flowers are necessarily stiff in form, but this millet adds softness and movement to arrangements. *P. violaceum* is an ornamental purple-tinged form.

Papaver somniferum

GROWING HINTS
Millet requires warm, moist soil to germinate and become established so it is best sown in late spring in full sun. Cultivate it in groups in the garden.

HARVESTING AND DRYING
Wait until the loose panicle head has fully emerged from the stem and then harvest. If left too long the seeds will start to develop, colour will begin to fade and there will be a problem of the seeds being shed after drying. Tie in small bunches and hang to air-dry fairly rapidly to hold the colour. Once dry, keep millet out of the reach of mice!

PAPAVER sp.

POPPY

Annual

Papaver somniferum is available in either 'mini' or 'maxi' sizes, but it is the latter

which is most impressive and useful in arrangements. Because it is harvested at the seed pod stage its flowers can be enjoyed in the garden through the summer. The flowers are large, papery and whitish-mauve, with a dark base to the petals. They grow to about 2½ ft (75 cm) tall and the seed pods are large, round and a biscuity-grey colour. They have a strong form for use in arrangements and look particularly good in contrast to deep purple *Helichrysum* or red *Amaranthus*.

P. somniferum 'Hen and Chickens' has a curious seed pod composed of a central round pod surrounded at the base by a dense ring of smaller heads — hence the name. (In some countries it is illegal to grow *P. somniferum*.)

P. rhoeas, the common red field poppy, has small elongated seed pods which can be used in clusters in delicate arrangements. The tall and colourful double-flowered garden varieties have larger pods which are more useful.

P. nudicaule should be avoided for drying because it is poisonous.

GROWING HINTS
The tiny seeds should be sown in spring in a fine moist soil. Establish in groups in full sun against a dark background to enjoy the full benefit of the flowers.

HARVESTING AND DRYING
Drying poppies in the flowering stage is generally unsuccessful as the petals drop easily. Enjoy the display of flowers and wait for the seed pods to swell to their full size. The pods are green initially but mellow and develop a matt-grey patina with maturity. This is the best time to harvest. If picked too early the pods will shrivel when dried; if left too late they will discolour. The pod will seem almost dry by the time it is harvested but further drying is advisable to ensure that the thicker part of the stems, and the centre of the seed pod, are fully dry, otherwise mould may develop later.

Hang or stand up to air-dry —

somewhere out of reach of mice and where it does not matter if the seeds drop out.

PHALARIS *canariensis*
CANARY GRASS
Hardy Annual Grass

The short, fat, arrow-shaped heads of canary grass make it particularly useful in arrangements. Commercially it is often available in dyed colours but the natural green is very attractive. It can be tall, growing to 3–4 ft (1–1.2 m).

GROWING HINTS
Sow in spring to flower in the summer. Establishment in the autumn can result in larger flower heads but a hard winter or late frosts can kill off young plants or cause discoloration. Canary grass will self-seed if some heads are left uncut in the autumn.

HARVESTING AND DRYING
Cut soon after the heads have emerged while still tight in form. The seed head will expand as the seeds inside develop but colour loss will occur with maturity. Unwanted leaves can be stripped to reduce the bulk for drying. Air-dry upside down quickly if you want to retain the best colour.

PHLEUM *pratense*
TIMOTHY GRASS or MEADOW CAT'S TAIL
Perennial Grass

Timothy is a common perennial grass of agricultural importance in traditional hay meadows. The flower head is a thin dense cylindrical spike, and grows 3–5 ft (1–1.5 m) high. It is frequently to be found growing on road verges. Its pencil-like form can add interesting texture or give direction to arrangements.

GROWING HINTS

Sow in summer or autumn to flower the following year in early summer. The grass develops into clumps and is shallow rooting, so prefers moist soils.

HARVESTING AND DRYING

Cut as soon as the flowering spike has emerged beyond the leaves, while it is still green. Strip off any unwanted leaves. Air-dry upside down and store carefully to ensure the flower spike is not bent. Use in natural 'country' arrangements.

PHLOMIS *fructicosa*

P. 'Edward Bowles'

JERUSALEM SAGE
Evergreen Shrub

Phlomis is a shrub growing up to 4 ft (1.2 m) tall. It has soft grey-green leaves and whorls of yellow flowers. The flowering stems can be dried but it is the brown seed heads at the end of the season which have a particularly strong

Physalis franchettii

form for use in arrangements. *P.* 'Edward Bowles' is the smaller of the two varieties suggested here, growing up to 3 ft (1 m), but has larger leaves.

GROWING HINTS

Plant in a sunny position in well-drained soil. The colouring blends well with white borders.

HARVESTING AND DRYING

Cut when in full flower and hang up to dry, or leave until the seed heads have developed fully and turned brown. Picked at the later stage, the stems need very little additional drying and can be stood upright.

PHYSALIS *franchettii*

CHINESE LANTERN
Deciduous Perennial

Chinese lanterns are popular and easy to grow, but very expensive to buy because they are not widely commercially grown.

In autumn the bright orange seed heads are unmistakable. When dried, they make a lovely display just on their own or mixed with other plants of strong form such as grey eucalyptus leaves and *Allium christophii* seed heads.

GROWING HINTS
Physalis seed is readily available and should be sown under glass in early spring or in a warm place in late spring or early summer. It may take several weeks to germinate. The plants should then be grown on in a well-drained and sunny position where they have adequate space to spread. The long underground roots will rapidly help the plant form a large clump, growing to 2 ft (60 cm) in height. Propagate by division in spring.

HARVESTING AND DRYING
The insignificant white flowers appear in early summer and develop into the lantern-shaped seed pods which are green at first, later changing to orange. The stems should be cut in the autumn when as many as possible of the lanterns are orange but before the plant is damaged by frost or rain. The leaves should be removed. The bunches will air-dry easily and should be laid in open boxes. Alternatively, stand upright in a well-ventilated or warm place.

POLYGONUM *bistorta*

P. amplexicaule

KNOTWEED
Deciduous Perennial

Polygonum bistorta is a very useful ground cover plant, having leaves similar to docks (*Rumex*) but with tall, pink-flowering spikes in late spring and early summer. It grows to a height of 1½–2 ft (45–60 cm). *P. amplexicaule* is taller, growing up to 4 ft (1.2 m) high, with larger crimson spikes.

GROWING HINTS
Polygonum likes light shade with a moist soil. It is naturally invasive and will have to be kept under control where space is limited.

HARVESTING AND DRYING
Cut when in full flower and hang up to air-dry.

ROSA sp.

ROSE
Perennial Shrub/Climber

The dried roses generally available for purchase are invariably of the type grown commercially for cut flower use, with small heads. Many other types of garden roses can be successfully dried to marvellous effect and have a completely different look to the commercial roses. Often a few well-placed roses in an arrangement can be the perfect finishing touch, providing essential focal points for a colour scheme and adding a feeling of quality to a display.

So many different varieties of rose are available that it would be pointless to make specific recommendations. Besides, it is worth experimenting with all types! For small dainty arrangements, the tiny spray roses and small-headed bud roses can be used. For larger arrangements select the double flower types — preferably those that have the full-blown 'Old English' look. Garnette roses are especially recommended for drying.

Flower colours often change or intensify during drying. Red roses usually hold their colour well though some can finish very dark. Rich yellows look good initially but can go dull quickly. Peach, dark pinks and purples dry well, but some of the paler pinks can be unpredictable and fade quickly. White roses can dry surprisingly well, though very high temperatures will cause discoloration at

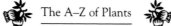

the base of the petals. However, some people like the "antique" look of faded roses!

GROWING HINTS

It is impossible to summarize in one paragraph all the intricacies of rose growing! Suffice it to say that they generally require a deep, rich soil, management to eradicate pests and diseases, and regular pruning. Further detailed cultural advice should be sought on individual varieties. The shrub and botanical species types are generally more trouble-free.

HARVESTING AND DRYING

In the garden, pick the roses as the flowers begin to open and fill out in shape, but before they reach their full flowering glory. Strip off the thorns from the base of the stem if necessary, but do not remove the leaves as these can be used as a dark green filler.

Keep the bunches small to prevent damage to the flowers and hang up to dry as quickly as possible in warm air. Once fully dry the stems can become very brittle, so roses should always be the last items added to a display so they are not accidentally damaged. The heads can, of course, be wired if necessary. Rose petals or small rose heads are lovely in pot pourri.

ROSMARINUS officinalis
ROSEMARY
Evergreen Perennial

Rosemary is a lovely scented herb to grow in the garden and use in cooking. It needs a warm sunny location and a well-drained soil. Some varieties can grow up to 6 ft (2 m) tall but the smaller ones are ideal for patios, border edges or informal hedges. The flowers — blue, white or light pink — appear in late spring.

Sprays of the foliage, with or without flowers, can be cut to hang in the kitchen for culinary purposes or to use in arrangements. The leaves are brittle when dry so it is advisable to make decorative use of the rosemary as soon as possible and let it dry fully in position without disturbance.

SALVIA horminum
syn. S. sclarea
CLARY
Hardy Annual

Clary is a small bushy border plant growing to 18 in (45 cm) high and noticeable for its brightly coloured bracts ranging from greenish-white and pink to purple. It provides a lasting splash of colour in the garden throughout the summer and can then be cut and dried. Because of this, it is a useful annual for small gardens and around patios.

GROWING HINTS

Sow outdoors from late spring onwards in clumps. Alternatively, raise under glass and transplant out in late spring to avoid frost damage. Clary needs full sun and, for drying, is best grown in a poor soil.

HARVESTING AND DRYING

Avoid the temptation to harvest too soon and wait until the coloured bracts have stiffened a little and become firm. Tie in small bunches and hang up to air-dry slowly. Fast drying can make the leaves shrivel.

SALVIA officinalis
COMMON SAGE
Evergreen Shrub

The common sage has an undramatic purple/blue flower spike and soft grey-

green leaves which are strongly aromatic and used in cooking. Small bunches of the leaves can be cut and dried in autumn for a background filler in arrangements.

GROWING HINTS
Sage needs full sun and a well-drained soil. Growth needs to be pruned back to prevent the bushes sprawling and becoming untidy.

HARVESTING AND DRYING
Cut the leaves in autumn when they are less likely to shrivel during use. Tied in small bunches, they will air-dry easily, hung in a kitchen.

SANTOLINA *chamaecyparissus*
LAVENDER COTTON
Evergreen Shrub

Santolina has dense, aromatic, silver-green foliage and yellow button-like flowers in summer. It is a useful plant for the front of the border or small hedges, but needs pruning in spring. Like the curry plant, *Helichrysum angustifolium*, both flowers and foliage can be dried.

GROWING HINTS
Plant in a warm sunny position on well-drained soil and prune hard in spring to maintain fresh young growth. *Santolina* can be propagated from cuttings.

HARVESTING AND DRYING
The flowers appear on thin stems in mid-summer. Cut when in full flower and hang up to air-dry. The foliage will dry easily hung up in small bunches or may be used fresh in arrangements and allowed to dry in place naturally.

SCABIOSA *stellata*
S. 'Paper Moon'
S. 'Satellite'
SCABIOUS
Hardy Annual

Scabious 'Paper Moon' is a hardy annual with unusual papery seed heads on long strong stems. The soft lavender blue flowers are a delight in the herbaceous border, especially in informal planting schemes, and can be enjoyed to the full since it is only the later seed heads which are cropped.

GROWING HINTS
Sow outdoors in spring in full sun or plant out seedlings 6–9 in (15–22.5 cm) apart. Scabious will grow well in ordinary well-drained soils but occurs naturally on lime. It can develop 20–30 flower stems on a single plant, growing up to 3 ft (1 m) high, so should be located in the middle of a border with adequate space to flourish.

HARVESTING AND DRYING
The seed heads develop rapidly after flowering. If harvested while still a pale green they will look better than if left to mature on the plant. Rain can quickly cause discoloration. Keep bunches small to prevent damage to the individual heads, which are very fragile and should be handled as little as possible. Very little drying is needed.

SEDUM *spectabile*
ICE PLANT
Deciduous Perennial

Many members of the *Sedum* family are low-growing plants suited to rock gardens, but the *Sedum spectabile* varieties, such as 'Autumn Joy', are taller growing, reach-

Sedum spectabile 'Autumn Joy'

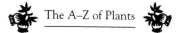

ing 1½–2 ft (45–60 cm). They make a reliable flowering contribution to the herbaceous border from late summer to mid-autumn and are popular with bees and butterflies. The leaves are fleshy and pale green and the tiny pink flowers are held in flat-topped clusters on long stems. The flowers dry to a dark dusky pink.

GROWING HINTS
Plant in a sunny well drained position near the front of the border. Once established, *Sedum* can be easily propagated by division or cuttings.

HARVESTING AND DRYING
Pick in the autumn, waiting until the flower heads have developed enough to become firm. The stems are fleshy and take a very long time to dry. Strip the leaves, tie small numbers of stems together and hang up to air-dry in a warm place. (Leaves and side shoots can still develop while the flowers are drying.) Do not store until the stems are completely dry otherwise they will go mouldy. Alternatively, the flowers can be used straightaway and left to dry naturally, provided the arrangement is to be kept in a warm, dry room.

SENECIO *greyi*

S. laxifolius

SENECIO
Evergreen Shrub

Senecio is a handsome evergreen, grey-leaved shrub with daisy-like yellow flowers in summer. It grows up to 5 ft (1.5 m) tall. Sprays of the foliage make a useful filler in flower arrangements, especially in contrast to deep pinks.

GROWING HINTS
Plant senecio in full sun in well drained soil. It is reasonably hardy but may suffer damage in severe winters. Prune hard in

spring to prevent it becoming too woody and straggly. Senecio can be easily propagated from cuttings.

HARVESTING AND DRYING
Cut sprays of foliage in the autumn or winter and hang up to dry in small bunches. The leaves will curl a little but this does not detract from their value as a soft grey filler. Alternatively, use them fresh and allow to dry naturally in position in an arrangement.

SETARIA *italica*

ITALIAN MILLET
Annual Grass

Setaria is an annual grass and there are many varieties, including S. *lutescens* which is a smaller, yellowy version. The size of the heads differs according to the variety, but the very large fat heads are commonly used as food for cage-birds. The charm of S. *italica* lies in its fresh colour, retained when dried. It looks particularly attractive with pink larkspur.

GROWING HINTS
Sow in full sun in late spring to ensure warm soil temperatures.

HARVESTING AND DRYING
Cut soon after the flower heads have emerged and developed in size, but before the colour starts to fade. Colour retention is important so hang up to dry quickly in warm air, in the dark.

SOLIDAGO *canadensis*

GOLDEN ROD
Deciduous Perennial

Golden rod is a deciduous perennial bearing plumes of bright yellow flowers over bright green foliage on stems that range from 2–6 ft (60 cm–3 m) high, depending on the variety. It can spread

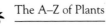

to form large clumps. Harvested at the correct stage its fresh colouring is most useful in arrangements complementing yellow roses, *Lonas* and *Achillea filipendulina*, or contrasting with pure white gypsophila and deep blue larkspur or lavender.

The taller varieties are particularly useful in large arrangements, perhaps with *Echinops* and bright green millet.

GROWING HINTS
Golden rod can be established in any soil but tolerates poor dry soil well, in sun or light shade. It can be raised from seed sown in spring or propagated by division.

HARVESTING AND DRYING
Cut the stems in summer as (or just before) the first flowers begin to open. Do not wait until they are in full flowering colour as the heads will burst into seed very quickly during drying and the fresh yellow will be lost. It is better to pick too early than too late.

Hang up to dry quickly in warm air so as to retain the greenness of the leaves and halt the development of the flowers.

TAGETES *erecta*
AFRICAN MARIGOLD
Half-hardy Annual

The large, orange and yellow double-flowered African marigolds, which make colourful bedding plants, can be easily dried. They should be picked in the early stages of full flower and hung up to air-dry. The flowers will shrink but retain their dense colour well. The base of the flower head at the top of each stem tends to be weak and wiring may be necessary. The flowers are rarely suitable as focal points, but provide strong colour.

TANACETUM *vulgare*
TANSY
Deciduous Perennial

Tansy, a herb which self-seeds freely in the garden, can be used as a dried flower.

Sprays of small neat yellow flowers can be left on their stems for tall arrangements or used separately for more delicate work, especially with fresh greens and white.

TRITICALE
BEARDED WHEAT
Annual Grass

Triticale is a hybrid between wheat (*Triticum*) and rye (*Secale*). The ears have whiskers, or awns, giving them a softer appearance than wheat, but the awns are shorter and less brittle than those of barley. It can be used in natural arrangements or to make sheaves, but the effect is generally soft and feathery whereas wheat is strong and sculptural.

Cultivation and harvesting instructions are as for wheat. It has very good natural disease resistance and is grown as an agricultural cereal where drought tolerance is necessary.

TRITICUM *aestivum*
COMMON WHEAT
Annual Grass

Wheat, grown as an agricultural crop for bread and biscuit making, is an extremely useful element in dried flower arrangements because of its strong form. It can also be used on its own to make ornamental wheatsheaves which give a 'country' feel to any decorative scheme.

GROWING HINTS

Autumn- and spring-sown varieties are available in agricultural use and should be cultivated accordingly. If wheat is to be grown in the garden it is best established in its own plot. The young plants develop grass-like tillers initially, but in late spring growth is rapid as the stem extends to 2–3 ft (60–100 cm).

HARVESTING AND DRYING

As soon as the ear of wheat appears in late spring or early summer, it starts to flower. If cut too early the bunches will have too leafy an appearance and the ears will be small, but as soon as the plant has flowered, the green colour begins to fade from the ear and leaves, to become the familiar golden harvest colour of full summer. Wheat should be cut either at flowering time (when the ear is level with the leading 'flag' leaf) for the best green colour or left until the golden stage.

At the green stage the plant contains substantial reserves of sap. It should be tied in thin bunches and hung up to dry as quickly as possible.

The golden stage requires little additional drying and the rigid stems can be stood upright. Keep dried wheat out of the reach of mice!

TULIPA sp.

TULIP
Bulb

As with daffodils, tulips are not an obvious subject for drying and are difficult to dry successfully. However, there are some colours and varieties with which it is worth experimenting. The late double peony-flowered tulips have sufficient density of petals to be effective and the darker colours will be most successful. The parrot tulips have fringed and twisted petals, some are variegated and they can all look extraordinary.

Of the single tulips the paler colours are unlikely to dry or last successfully, so choose the dark pinks, reds or, especially, the purples.

HARVESTING AND DRYING

Tulips should be cut in the early stages of flowering and hung up to dry in very warm air. The stems are fleshy and take a very long time to dry. Even after thorough drying they will readily re-absorb moisture from a damp atmosphere and go limp. Tulips should always be wired after drying to support the stems or arranged so that the heads are supported by surrounding flowers.

TYPHA latifolia

BULRUSH or REEDMACE
Deciduous Perennial

Bulrushes grow naturally beside streams and ponds and in waterlogged areas. They spread rapidly and should not be introduced into a new pond without careful thought or strict management to contain their growth. However, bulrushes that are already available in the garden can be dried to make impressive displays on their own, or with other tall seed heads such as teasel.

HARVESTING AND DRYING

The problem with bulrushes is to stop the cylindrical brown heads bursting into seed. They should therefore be cut as soon as they have turned brown, in mid-summer, and air-dried as quickly as possible. (The terminal spike above the head should be trimmed off before drying to improve the appearance.) If the leaves are to be retained the stems should be hung up to dry. If not, they can stand upright.

Bulrushes grow up to 7 ft (2.2 m) in height, so plenty of space is needed for drying and displaying.

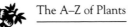

XERANTHEMUM *annuum*

EVERLASTING FLOWER
Hardy Annual

Xeranthemum has daisy-like flowers with petals that are naturally stiff and straw-like. It is available in white, dusky pink, rose pink, lilac and purple. (The white and strong pinks are very useful.) It can look delightful sown in drifts in informal garden schemes and flowers successively in summer. The flowers can be dried easily and used individually in dainty arrangements, massed in bunches in larger displays, or mixed with grasses for a very informal 'country' effect. No wiring is needed.

GROWING HINTS
Select double-flowering varieties and sow in spring in full sun. *Xeranthemum* will grow adequately on poor soils. The plants form small clumps of greeny-grey foliage. Flowering height is 1½–2 ft (45–60 cm).

HARVESTING AND DRYING
Xeranthemum flowers in late summer to early autumn. Initially, pick single stems on which the flowers have opened fully, tie in small bunches and hang up to dry. This early crop provides flowers that can be used individually.

As more buds break into flower, there will come a stage when it is worthwhile cutting handfuls of stems at a time. These bunches will include open and half-open flowers, as well as buds. This variation within a bunch gives it a very natural look but more drying is needed with the bunches hanging in warm air. (The young closed buds will always tend to absorb moisture and become limp so display these only in a dry atmosphere.)

Timing of harvesting is not very critical but as the flowers age they discolour and can be damaged by rain. Discard all such flowers as they will spoil the overall effect.

ZEA *mays*

MAIZE, SWEETCORN, CORN
Annual Grass

Maize is an annual grass of agricultural value in the production of grain, and certain types are sown as a fresh vegetable. It grows 5–7 ft (1.5–2.2 m) in height. The fruiting cob is yellow in the common edible varieties, but multi-coloured and miniature variants are also available for ornamental use.

GROWING HINTS
Sow in late spring in full sun. The large seed will easily emerge from 2–3 in (5–7.5 cm) below the soil surface, therefore sow deep enough to utilize the moisture available.

HARVESTING AND DRYING
Maize plants bear the male flowering parts, or anthers, at the top of the stem. This light, biscuit-coloured plume can be an unusual item when dried — useful as a filler or background in medium-sized or large arrangements. Remove the top 2–2½ ft (60–75 cm) of the maize plant and hang up to air-dry in warm air in the dark, so as to retain the greenness of the leaves.

Later in the autumn, the familiar cob with its tightly-packed seeds can be picked for drying. Wait until the fleshy seeds have hardened (much beyond the edible stage!) and the cob has started to dry out naturally on the plant. (This reduces the tendency of the seeds to shrink and shrivel.) Allow plenty of time for the cobs to dry out fully and, once dry, store away from mice in a dry ventilated place. The leaves around the cob can be peeled back as part of the ornamental effect.

DRIED FLOWER ARRANGING

One of the joys of growing and drying your own flowers is that there is only the cost of your own time to take into account. When buying bunches of dried flowers for a basket this size, you can easily spend large amounts of money and still not achieve the full look you wanted.

In this arrangement there are eight bunches of a peachy rose called 'Gerdo', several bunches of light and dark blue delphiniums, four bunches of white larkspur, *Achillea ptarmica*, various types of statice and some *Eryngium*, or sea holly. With a basket this size, it is very important to introduce some strong splashes of colour, which can be created by bunching several flower heads of the same type together.

Fill the basket with dry florists' foam and then a covering of *Limonium tartaricum dumosa*. This hides the rather dull-looking foam and forms a base for the arrangement. Then add the longer items, such as the delphiniums and larkspur, to create the outline shape. Once the overall outline is achieved you can fill in with clumps of the various components until the basket looks really full and impressive.

It is far better to create something very special that will be much admired than to be mean with your material and produce many small, insignificant arrangements with the absolute minimum of ingredients. As is mentioned in earlier chapters, many of the larger items you can easily grow in the garden are the most expensive to buy commercially, so make the most of your collection of flowers and create a really eye-catching display.

One of the most pleasurable points about arranging with dried flowers is that it opens up a much wider choice of containers than one would have with arrangements of fresh flowers. As there is no need for water you can make up arrangements in porous containers that leak if filled with water, or precious boxes and baskets that are too valuable to be used with water even if lined!

A lavish basket of roses and delphiniums can bring summer into the house all year round.

Florists' foam

The most popular way to arrange dried flowers is perhaps by using the grey-brown florists' foam intended specifically for dry arrangements. There is a brighter green counterpart for fresh arrangements. This foam is easily sliced and shaped to the size of container you wish to use, and holds the stems firmly in position. It can be reused. Another popular alternative is insert the stems in a ball of clay that hardens after a while. Although perfectly satisfactory, it is far harder to use than florists' foam, and cannot be reused. Squashed chicken wire is another alternative which is particularly useful for large containers and arrangements. Some very ambitious large-scale arrangements, say, in an enormous fireplace, could use up a great many blocks of foam, and so filling the container with squashed chicken wire is considerably cheaper.

Arranging without mechanics

Another possibility is demonstrated opposite — using no mechanics at all. In this terracotta container the flowers have been kept in the original bunches in which they were dried or bought. The taller bunches are placed in position first at the back of the container, and the others are grouped in tiers to show off each variety to its best advantage. Some manoeuvring can take place, with strategic bunches being made larger or smaller in order to obtain the desired effect. When the majority of the container is full, single items such as the artichokes are arranged as the bottom tier to cover any stems that might be visible.

The overall effect of an arrangement of this kind is a bold display of colours, shapes and textures, giving the eye plenty to look at. The informal nature of the arrangement particularly suits terracotta containers of this type or alternatively you could use basket-ware or other containers with a rural feel.

The actual flowers and plants used in this display include wheat, *Phlomis*, bulrushes, *Allium* heads, poppies, *Amaranthus*, *Alchemilla* and linseed, artichokes and marjoram to name but a few. The seed heads in the centre of the display are *Iris foetidissima*.

As you can see from the photograph, this type of arrangement is far from economical with flowers and materials. If you had to buy all the bunches used in this terracotta container then it would be an extremely expensive arrangement. If, however, you have had a successful year growing these plants in your garden and then drying them, it can be a pleasure to have such a splendid excuse to show off a reasonable number of bunches from your collection.

Casual arrangements can make a fantastic impact if they are strong enough and are carefully accessorized.

FIREPLACE ARRANGEMENT

Once you have mastered smaller and simpler arrangements, decorating an area like a fireplace can be a real challenge. There are many ways to tackle it. The photograph opposite shows a formal way of filling a fireplace when it is not in regular use. There are other equally effective ideas, such as an informal arrangement in a large hamper or basket, a terracotta container similar to the one shown on the previous page, or natural features such as wheat sheaves and hop bines to give a harvest atmosphere to the room.

A great many flowers went into this arrangement, but again, if the material has been home-dried you are saving a considerable amount of money. The base is a large basket which has been packed with blocks of dry florists' foam taped together to prevent them slipping. The basic shape is made with air-dried eucalyptus and *Carthamus*, then pale blue delphiniums are introduced around the edge and through the design. Apricot *Limonium sinuatum*, 'Gerdo' roses and salmon *Helichrysum* are then added to give an attractive contrast and warmth to the arrangement.

A splendid array of flowers like this can be put together without incurring a great deal of expense, if you grow the flowers yourself.

IDEAS FOR CONTAINERS

There are many attractive containers on the market today which enable you to have a refreshing change from the standard table-top arrangement. Apart from interesting shapes such as cornucopias, hampers, ducks and boxes, there are many varieties of wall-hanging containers that offer plenty of scope for unusual arrangements of your collection of dried materials.

The particular container used in the arrangement opposite has a narrow pocket into which you can place dry florists' foam ready for an arrangement. Here, a collection of cream and gold flowers and grasses has been used. They include millet, roses, *Helichrysum* and *Achillea ptarmica* 'The Pearl'. It is a very monochromatic colour scheme that provides a restful change from some of the stronger colour combinations and effects that are equally exciting. This tranquil arrangement might look attractive in a bedroom decorated in creams and pinks or peaches.

There are other shapes and styles that can be wall-hung. One that immediately springs to mind is a dried flower wreath or garland. These are somewhat trickier to make but look extremely pretty in any room in the house.

Once you have a good selection of materials to work with, your eye will automatically spot new ideas for containers, whether at jumble sales, in auction rooms or shops and markets selling modern pieces. Since they do not have to be waterproof you can let your imagination run riot.

The same rule applies to accessories. If you are making an arrangement for a bathroom, then why not include some shells, stones or pebbles? These can be attached with glue or wire around the edge of the container. Carrying a theme through an arrangement can be great fun, whether it's for a kitchen, using wooden spoons as an ingredient, or something arty in a studio including some sable brushes!

Keeping an open mind and generally being observant will bring many new ideas into view. There are plenty of lovely natural accessories to introduce into arrangements, such as mosses, cones and berries, shells, driftwood, stones and sea-washed lumps of glass. If you have no fixed view of what will and won't be suitable then all sorts of items will spring to mind. Just be prepared to have a large cupboard full of objects that are bound to be useful one day!

This gentle arrangement of colours would tone well with many colour schemes.

VICTORIAN-STYLE ARRANGEMENT

Many suitable containers may well be lurking in your cupboards. This vegetable tureen is not part of a set and is only ever used for flower arrangements. The base was filled with dry florists' foam and taped securely. The lid was then carefully stored away so that it was neither lost nor damaged while the base was in use elsewhere.

This particular arrangement has a very light, frothy effect with the mass of *Gypsophila* that has been used. The base flowers are red peonies, silver rose *Helichrysum* and pink roses, with some *Limonium sinuatum*. The arrangement could well have stood on its own without the *Gypsophila* but the delicate touch it adds is very pleasing. This particular style of display would look pretty anywhere, but perhaps a bedroom would be the best place. This type of design is also useful for wedding arrangements and displays.

If a flower arrangement looks a little strong in colour for the room in which you want to display it, then adding white can be a very quick way to lighten the colours. Either *Gypsophila* or *Achillea ptarmica* 'The Pearl' both have a similar effect. Since *Gypsophila* is so easily available and simple to dry, it can be a very easy choice for dainty displays.

This antique tureen makes a perfect container for a soft and dreamy arrangement.

ARRANGEMENTS FOR WEDDINGS

Dried flowers are becoming increasingly popular for weddings, and with good reason. Arranging the flowers, if fresh, always has to be a last-minute job, and the pressure of decorating houses or a church when one has a million other things to do as well can be tremendous. Even if a professional is doing the flowers for you, there is always the worry that they won't appear when they should! With dried flowers you can create arrangements, bouquets, pew ends — anything, in fact — many weeks beforehand and store them carefully as you finish them.

If you plan to take on the flowers for a family or friend's wedding then obviously you will have to decide what needs to be grown, and which plants will be ready to harvest and dry before you want to start work on them. The basic colour scheme is obviously the main choice to be made, plus the style of arrangements. You can plan formal arrangements like the one featured in the photograph opposite or something far more countrified, using swags of oats and other cereals, trailing hop bines, baskets and other rustic containers.

Brides and bridesmaids look very pretty with circlets of dried flowers on their heads, and if a bouquet is made from dried flowers then it can be kept forever. The most popular colour scheme for weddings of late must surely have been peaches and cream. Although this is a wonderfully subtle colouring that suits every bride, it can look far more exciting and eye-catching if stronger colours are used. In the display shown here, very strong purples are mixed with cream, gold and pink for a really stunning effect.

Many people seem to think that dried flowers are all pale colours or have an orange and beige bias to them, but this particular display proves how mistaken they can be. This selection of colours is just as bright and vibrant as a fresh arrangement would be. The flowers used were cream peonies (very rarely available commercially and so beautiful), *Limonium sinuatum*, roses (both 'Bridal Pink' and a pale pink called 'Porcelina'), millet, *Helichrysum* and pink larkspur.

There is never any need to waste anything with dried flower work, and should you have any spare petals there are plenty of ideas for using them on pp. 114–19, including a recipe for the wedding confetti.

Planning dried flowers for a wedding can be a much easier alternative to fresh flowers, as they can be arranged many weeks beforehand.

TABLE CENTRE ARRANGEMENTS

Table centres are always a very decorative way to finish a festive table. The design shown here could blend with several colour schemes and can be brought out as and when it is needed.

The base is an oval piece of cork on to which a small green plastic florists' attachment, known as a 'frog', is glued. The florists' foam is then impaled on this 'frog'. Two special candle holders are then inserted into the foam to take the candles, which are made slightly different heights by sawing off a length from the bottom of the second candle before it is used.

A wide variety of material has been used. The plant material includes eucalyptus, iris seed heads, tansy, carnations, *Celosia*, *Solidago*, *Aquilegia* seed heads, poppies, *Matricaria*, *Craspedia* and hydrangeas. The shape will partly be governed by the size of your table and the amount of space available.

If you are short of space, then instead of making a large table centre some very small posy arrangements could be placed on each side plate, or small arrangements glued to some wooden napkin rings. Narrow garlands also look stunning ranged down the centre of the table.

A long-lasting table centre made from a selection of dried garden flowers.

USING LEFT-OVER DRIED FLOWERS

If a great deal of time and effort has been expended in getting your dried flower stocks together, then you will want to waste as few of them as possible. No matter how careful you are there will always be occasions when you break a head off its stem, some petals fall out or other accidents befall you. A perfect way to use every little scrap of material is to make up bright and colourful bowls of pot pourri with any damaged or discarded pieces.

There is no limit to what you may include in your personal pot pourri mix: as long as the finished result smells beautiful and looks attractive, the ingredients are to some extent irrelevant. A number of recipes are listed here to start you off with ideas and give you a base to experiment with, but the real fun starts when you adapt recipes to suit yourself.

Home-made pot pourri is fun to make and smells wonderful.

Basic pot pourri

This basic recipe is very versatile and the ingredients can be interchanged depending on which left-overs you have available at the time. Use a measuring jug to obtain the correct volume of ingredients. Orris root powder is available from chemists or health food shops.

> *1 pint (600 ml) dried rose petals*
> *½ pint (300 ml) dried peony petals*
> *¼ pint (150 ml) dried mint leaves*
> *¼ pint (150 ml) dried geranium leaves*
> *6 tbsp (90 ml) roughly crushed cinnamon sticks*
> *5 tbsp (75 ml) dried orange and lemon peel, roughly crushed*
> *1–1½ oz (5–7.5 ml) orris root powder*
> *6 drops rose essential oil*

Mix together all the ingredients, except the essential oil, in a large dry washing up bowl or mixing bowl until they are evenly dispersed. Add the oil drop by drop. Then fill a plastic bag with the mixture and tie the top into a tight knot. Leave it in a cool dark place for about five to six weeks, giving it a vigorous shake about twice a week.

   Once the mixture is ready to use it can be displayed with some whole flower heads placed around the edge of the container or scattered on the surface of the mixture for additional decoration.

Blue Moon pot pourri

> *1 pint (600 ml) dried cornflower flowers*
> *¼ pint (150 ml) dried pale blue larkspur flowers*
> *¼ pint (150 ml) dried dark blue larkspur flowers*
> *¼ pint (150 ml) dried blue/lavender Limonium sinuatum flowers*
> *¼ pint (150 ml) dried eucalyptus leaves*
> *6 tbsp (90 ml) roughly crushed star anise, nutmeg and*
> *   ginger*
> *5 tbsp (75 ml) dried lime and grapefruit peel, roughly chopped*
> *1–1½ oz (5–7.5 ml) orris root powder*
> *6–8 drops lemon verbena or rose geranium oil*

Again, mix together all the ingredients except the oil, and then follow the instructions given in the previous recipe.

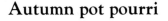

Autumn pot pourri

1 pint (600 ml) small dried orange/red Helichrysum heads
½ pint (300 ml) small cones such as larch
¼ pint (150 ml) small red/gold autumn leaves, pressed
¼ pint (150 ml) acorns
12 cinnamon sticks, cut in three
5 tbsp (75 ml) chunky-cut dried orange peel
4 drops orange essential oil
4 drops cinnamon essential oil
slices of dried apple for decoration

Again mix together all the ingredients and proceed as in the previous recipes. If you wish, you can use a little extra oil and drop it deep into the opened scales of the cones as they will retain the smell beautifully. This mixture can look lovely placed in a large basket surrounded by cones and miniature bundles of wheat and oats with dried slices of apple in between.

Cottage garden pot pourri

This recipe is perfect for using really miscellaneous left-overs. It looks best if you can get some colour co-ordination or blending, but alternatively why not go for broke and have a really brightly coloured mix!

2 pints (1.2 l) dried mixed flowers and petals
10 tbsp (150 ml) mixed chunky spices and herbs
1–1½ oz (5–7.5 ml) orris root powder
8 drops any oil of your choice!

Follow the instructions given in the previous recipes, choosing whichever ingredients you wish to use.

When using the essential oils it is sometimes more successful to use one type only at a time but you can experiment by mixing a few together, particularly if you have only a few drops left in several bottles. If you find your recipe has been a great success then do remember to write down what your proportion of ingredients and oils were as you may not remember should you wish to repeat it!

As well as using oils in pot pourri you can also sprinkle them carefully on to dried flower arrangements, fairly deep down in the display. A bowl of cones sprinkled with essential oils always looks attractive and only takes a few seconds to prepare. (The scent is stronger if you add the oil to the cones and then keep them in a bag for six weeks as mentioned in the basic pot pourri recipe). If you are arranging a hop bine as part of a room decoration then some hop flowers are bound to fall off. They make a pretty pot pourri on their own with essential oils, so they need not be wasted.

Natural confetti

Another possibility for petals, especially peony and rose petals, is to make scented or unscented natural wedding confetti. So many churches, hotels and other places are against the throwing of highly-coloured and dyed paper confetti because of the mess it creates that it seems a good alternative to return to real rose petals that will decompose naturally and look far more attractive.

For the wedding confetti, you can use any petals that blend with the overall colour scheme at which you are aiming. If you want some petals to be flat and some curled then a few fresh petals that have dropped naturally from some roses could be pressed while the fresh roses are being dried. Peony petals, in particular, are very large and have wonderfully strong colours. If you want to scent the confetti then place the collection of petals into a polythene bag and add several drops of whichever essential oil you prefer. The confetti should then be left for at least a week or two before it is used.

Many other ingredients, apart from flower heads and petals, can be included in a pot pourri mix. In the photograph on pp. 114–15 the pot pourri includes cinnamon sticks, dried apple slices, hops and pine cones. Shells look attractive mixed with flowers and there are many citrus mixes that include orange or lemon peel.

Another attractive feature is a large bowl or basket full of rose heads — perhaps using both the commercial and old-fashioned varieties, with a few miniature ones added for good measure. Dishes to hold the pot pourris or other ideas are easily made by glueing dried flowers and ribbons around a tiny basket or dish before filling it with the pot pourri.

Spring fragrance

> *1 pint (600 ml) dried narcissus heads (ideally dried in silica gel)*
> *1 pint (600 ml) dried apple blossom*
> *1 pint (600 ml) myrtle leaves*
> *1 pint (600 ml) eucalyptus leaves*
> *2 oz (50 g) orris powder*
> *10–14 drops lily of the valley oil*

Mix all ingredients as in previous recipes.

Many seed pods and cones hold essential oils very well and can be scented and displayed alone. A large basket of pine cones, scented with a suitable essential oil, looks very attractive on a large hearth.

Strawberries and cream

1 pint (600 ml) strawberry leaves dried
1 pint (600 ml) pale pink globe amaranth flowers
1 pint (600 ml) dark pink globe amaranth flowers
1 pint (600 ml) cream globe amaranth flowers
2 oz (50 g) orris powder
12 drops strawberry fragrance oil

Mix all ingredients as in previous recipes.

Traditional Christmas

1 pint (600 ml) larch cones
1 pint (600 ml) roughly snapped cinnamon sticks
½ pint (300 ml) star anise
½ pint (300 ml) allspice berries
1 pint (600 ml) dried rose hips
1 pint (600 ml) conifer or spruce leaves
3 tbsp (45 ml) dried orange peel
2–3 oz (50 g–75 g) orris root
5 drops pine essential oil
5 drops cinnamon essential oil
5 drops orange essential oil

Mix all ingredients as before. This pot pourri looks particularly attractive in a large shallow basket edged with pine cones, red and green tartan bows, spruce sprigs and miniature Christmas tree baubles. Make a Christmas feature of this pot pourri on a hall table to welcome guests with a traditional fragrance.

APPENDIX I
Flowers grouped according to their colour

All the major species in the A–Z section are listed here under the predominant flower colour. When available in two or three colours they are listed accordingly, but if more, the plant is shown as being available in a selection of colours.

Available in a selection of colours

Acroclinium roseum	Sunray	*Gomphrena globosa*	Globe amaranth
Aquilegia hybrida	Columbine	*Helichrysum bracteatum*	Straw flower
Aster sp.	Aster	*monstrosum*	
Astilbe arendsii	False goat's beard	*Hydrangea macrophylla*	Mop-head hydrangea
Centaurea cyanus	Cornflower	*Limonium sinuatum*	Statice
Chrysanthemum sp.	Chrysanthemum	*Matthiola* sp.	Stocks
Clematis sp.	Clematis	*Nigella damascena*	Love-in-a-mist
Dahlia sp.	Dahlia	*Papaver* sp.	Poppy
Delphinium consolida	Larkspur	*Rosa* sp.	Rose
Delphinium elatum	Delphinium	*Salvia horminum*	Clary
Dianthus barbatus	Sweet William	*Tulipa* sp.	Tulip
Dianthus caryophyllus	Carnation		

Blue/Mauve

Acanthus mollis	Bear's breeches	*Lavandula spica*	Lavender
Agastache mexicana	Agastache	*Limonium latifolium*	Sea lavender
Campanula glomerata	Clustered bellflower	*Linum usitatissium*	Linseed
Cynara cardunculus	Cardoon	*Nicandra physaloides*	Shoo fly plant
Cynara scolymus	Globe artichoke	*Nigella damascena*	Love-in-a-mist
Echinops ritro	Globe thistle	*Papaver somniferum*	Annual poppy
Eryngium sp.	Sea holly	*Scabiosa stellata*	Scabious

Brown

Alnus glutinosa	Common alder (cones)	*Fagus sylvatica*	Beech (leaves and seed cases)
Centaurea macrocephala	Knapweed (seed cups)	*Miscanthus sinensis*	Miscanthus grass
Corylus avellana contorta	Corkscrew hazel (stems)	*Phlomis fruticosa*	Jerusalem sage (stems)
		Typha latifolia	Bulrush

Crimson/Red

Amaranthus sp.	Love-lies-bleeding	*Celosia argentia cristata*	Cockscomb
Atriplex hortensis 'Rubra'	Orach	*Paeonia* sp.	Peony
		Polygonum amplexicaule	Knotweed

Green

Alchemilla mollis	Lady's mantle	*Festuca* sp.	Fescue grass
Amaranthus paniculatus	Love-lies-bleeding	*Helleborus corsicus*	Corsican hellebore
Ambrosinia mexicana	Ambrosinia	*Hordeum vulgare*	Barley
Aquilegia hybrida	Columbine (seed head)	*Humulus lupulus*	Hop
		Lagurus ovatus	Hare's tail grass
Astrantia major	Masterwort	*Moluccella laevis*	Bells of Ireland
Avena sativa	Oat	*Origanum dictamnus*	Sweet or knotted marjoram
Briza sp.	Quaking grass		
Bromus sp.	Rye brome grass	*Panicum miliaceum*	Common millet
Carthamus tinctorius	Safflower (bud)	*Phalaris canariensis*	Canary grass
Cucurbita pepo	Gourd (fruit)	*Phleum pratense*	Timothy grass
Dactylis glomerata	Cocksfoot grass	*Setaria italica*	Italian millet
Dipsacus fullonum	Common teasel	*Triticale*	Bearded wheat
Euphorbia polychroma	Cushion spurge	*Triticum aestivum*	Common wheat

Orange

Carthamus tinctorius	Safflower
Iris foetidissima	Stinking iris (berries)
Physalis franchettii	Chinese lantern (seed pod)
Tagetes erecta	African marigold

Pink/Purple

Achillea millefolium 'Cerise Queen'	Yarrow	*Limonium suworowii*	Poker statice
		Lunaria sp.	Honesty (flowers)
Allium sp.	Onions, leeks, chives	*Origanum vulgare*	Pot marjoram
Armeria caespitosa	Thift	*Paeonia* sp.	Peony
Bergenia sp.	Bergenia	*Polygonum bistorta*	Knotweed
Dianthus x. *allwoodii*	Pink	*Sedum spectabile*	Ice plant
Calluna vulgaris	Heather	*Xeranthemum annuum*	Everlasting flower
Erica sp.	Heath		
Liatris spicata	Gayfeather		

White (Cream)

Achillea ptarmica	Sneezewort
Agastache urticifolia 'Alba'	Agastache
Ammobium alatum	Winged everlasting flower
Anaphalis margaritacea	Pearl everlasting
Calluna vulgaris	Heather
Carlina acaulis caulescens	Carline thistle
Carthamus tinctorius	Safflower
Cortaderia selloana	Pampas grass
Erica sp.	Heath
Gypsophila paniculata	Baby's breath
Hydrangea paniculata	Hydrangea
Limonium tartaricum dumosa	Sea lavender
Lunaria sp.	Honesty (seed pods)
Matricaria sp.	Feverfew
Paeonia sp.	Peony
Xeranthemum annuum	Everlasting flower

Yellow

Acacia decurrens dealbata	Mimosa
Achillea filipendulina	Yarrow
Anethum graveolens	Dill
Centaurea macrocephala	Knapweed
Clematis orientalis	Clematis
Clematis tangutica	Clematis
Craspedia globosa	Drumstick
Euphorbia polychroma	Cushion spurge
Helichrysum angustifolium	Curry plant
Helichrysum subulifolium	Helichrysum
Kerria japonica	Jew's mallow
Lonas inodora	African daisy
Narcissus sp.	Daffodil
Nigella orientalis 'Transformer'	Love-in-a-mist
Phlomis fruticosa	Jerusalem sage
Santolina chamaecyparissus	Lavender cotton
Senecio greyi	Senecio
Solidago canadensis	Golden rod
Tagetes erecta	African marigold
Tanacetum vulgare	Tansy
Zea mays	Maize (cobs)

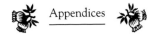

APPENDIX II

Plants useful for their foliage

Anaphalis margaritacea	Pearl everlasting
Cotinus coggygria	Smoke tree
Eucalyptus sp.	Gum tree
Fagus sylvatica	Beech
Helichrysum angustifolium	Curry plant
Laurus nobilis	Bay
Rosmarinus officinalis	Rosemary
Salvia officinalis	Common sage
Santolina chamaecyparissus	Lavender cotton
Senecio greyi	Senecio

APPENDIX III

Grasses suitable for drying

The species listed below are all grasses whose appearance and value to the dried flower arranger are described individually in the A–Z section.

Avena sativa	Oat
Briza sp.	Quaking grass
Bromus sp.	Rye brome grass
Cortaderia selloana	Pampas grass
Dactylis glomerata	Cocksfoot grass
Festuca sp.	Fescue grass
Hordeum vulgare	Barley
Lagurus ovatus	Hare's tail grass
Miscanthus sinensis	Miscanthus grass
Panicum miliaceum	Common millet
Phalaris canariensis	Canary grass
Phleum pratense	Timothy grass
Setaria italica	Italian millet
Triticale	Bearded wheat
Triticum aestivum	Common wheat
Zea mays	Sweetcorn

APPENDIX IV

Flowers which can be dried at seed head stage

Several plants can be enjoyed throughout the summer in the garden, then later cut at seed head stage, for use in dried flower arrangements. Species which fall into this category are listed below, but for further details refer to the A–Z section.

Allium sp.	Onions, leeks, chives
Alnus glutinosa	Common alder
Anethum graveolens	Dill
Aquilegia hybrida	Columbine
Atriplex hortensis	Orach
Carlina acaulis caulescens	Carline thistle
Centaurea macrocephala	Knapweed
Clematis sp.	Clematis
Cynara scolymus	Globe artichoke
Cynara cardunculus	Cardoon
Dipsacus fullonum	Common teasel
Iris foetidissima	Stinking iris
Linum usitatissium	Linseed
Lunaria sp.	Honesty
Nicandra physaloides	Shoo fly plant
Nigella damascena	Love-in-a-mist
Papaver sp.	Poppy
Physalis franchettii	Chinese lantern
Scabiosa stellata	Scabious
Zea mays	Maize/sweetcorn

APPENDIX V

Plants that dry well with the silica gel method

A great many plants dry well with this method but as this book concentrates mainly on air-drying, this is a short list of particular favourites that benefit from drying in silica gel crystals.

Anemone coronari and *A. elegans*	Anemone	*Paeony* sp.	Peony
Fuschia hybrida	Fuschia	*Rosa* sp.	Rose
Helleborus orientalis and *H. niger*			

Roses are especially successful, as are peonies. Old-fashioned roses look wonderful when dried with silica gel, but must be given false or wire stems to blend in with other large pieces of plant material that have been air-dried.

APPENDIX VI

Plants that can be preserved in glycerine

Again, this is not an exhaustive list but it gives a few favourites which can be very useful in arrangements, since air-drying does not work well for foliage.

Adiantum capillus-veneris	Maidenhair fern
Betula sp.	Birch
Buxus sempervirens	Common box
Calluna vulgaris	Heather
Choisya ternata	Mexican orange blossom
Eucalyptus sp.	Eucalyptus
Euphorbia robbiae	Spurge
Fagus sylvatica	Common beech
Garrya elliptica	Garrya
Hedera sp.	Ivy
Hosta sp.	Hosta
Moluccella laevis	Bells of Ireland
Polygonatum multiflorum	Solomon's seal
Quercus sp.	Oak
Rosa sp.	Rose

INDEX

 Index

ACKNOWLEDGEMENTS

Caroline Alexander would like to thank the following for their help in the production of this book:

William Alexander for his expertise and assistance in the preparation of the A–Z section, and for his kind permission to reproduce transparencies used to illustrate the A–Z section. Tom Wright for his horticultural advice.

Joanna Sheen would like to thank the following for their help in the production of this book:

Everyone at Joanna Sheen Ltd who helped when things got busy. Her family who as usual took all the strain. Jane Struthers for being there whenever she was needed and for helping to edit the manuscript. Ward Lock, especially Jane Donovan and Alison McWilliam, for being part of this project.

The publishers and authors would like to thank the following for their help in the production of this book:

The Hop Shop for the provision of dried flowers for the photographs. The shop is open every Saturday, and items are also available by mail order. The shop address is:

> The Hop Shop
> Castle Farm
> Shoreham
> Sevenoaks
> Kent
> TN14 7UB
> Telephone (09592) 3219

Joanna Sheen Ltd for the loan of the pot pourri, baskets, terracotta pots and other flower arranging items. The shop address is:

> Joanna Sheen Ltd
> 7 Lucius Street
> Torquay
> South Devon
> TQ2 5UW
> Telephone (0803) 201311

Suttons Seeds for kind permission to reproduce transparencies used in the A–Z section.

Mr and Mrs Gary Long for the use of their fireplace.

THE LOST YEARS OF MERLIN EPIC INCLUDES:

The Lost Years of Merlin
The Seven Songs of Merlin
The Fires of Merlin
The Mirror of Merlin
The Wings of Merlin

THE LOST YEARS OF MERLIN

*An ALA Best Book for Young Adults and
a 1997 Colorado Book Award Finalist*

"A novel rich with magic."   —*The New York Times Book Review*

"How wonderful! An extraordinary journey of mind, body, and spirit—for both Merlin and ourselves. This first book of the *Lost Years of Merlin* epic leads all of us to eagerly look forward to the rest."
—Madeleine L'Engle

"In this brilliant first volume of a trilogy, T. A. Barron has created a major addition to that body of literature, ancient and modern, dealing with the towering figure of Merlin. . . . Through the ordeals, terrors, and struggles of Merlin-to-be, we follow an intense and profoundly spiritual adventure. Barron has found Merlin's lost years for us, and a great deal more."
—Lloyd Alexander

"Using the magic of storytelling, author T. A. Barron relates the events of an equally magical childhood of the great Merlin. Barron's fans will not be disappointed with this book. It incorporates his favorite themes of love conquering evil and the nurturing power of nature with lots of fast-paced adventure all told with his masterful storytelling touch."
—*Rocky Mountain News*

continued on next page . . .

†HE SEVEΠ SOΠGS OF ΠΕRLIΠ

"This second installment of the sequence that began with *The Lost Years of Merlin* is as full of action and excitement as its predecessor, but is kinder and gentler in tone; while its origins are epic, it is foremost a tale of the heart . . . it is Merlin's inner journey that readers will cherish above all: His development is convincing and heartwarming. A rich and resonant read."   —*Kirkus Reviews*

"*The Seven Songs of Merlin* is a sparkling gem that shines with the multifaceted brilliance that is Barron's."
                                        —*Chinaberry Book Review*

"This richly layered fantasy is filled with harrowing escapades and many surprises. While readers may never doubt the outcome, they will eagerly devour the chapters to arrive at the satisfying conclusion. Arthurian legend is used as the starting point for a delightfully original story of magic and myth that retains the spirit of the classic series. . . . Readers will surely be waiting impatiently for the third part of this marvelous series."
                                        —*School Library Journal*

". . . [T]he tale is spellbinding, and readers will relish not only the action and the well-crafted setting, but also Merlin's growth from a callow youth to a wiser, more caring wizard-in-training."   —*Booklist*

THE FIRES OF MERLIN

"Barron weaves a writer's brand of magic that connects the past to the present, myth to reality and the human heart to the infinite universe."
—*Family Life*

"With each book, Barron's *Lost Years of Merlin* saga just keeps getting richer in characterization, ambience, and Celtic lore. . . . Fans will definitely be clamoring for more."
—*Booklist*

"With each book Barron refines his grasp of the very best that the genre of fantasy can offer a reader. He has woven together a thrilling tale with memorable characters, not the least of whom is a dragon hatchling. His meticulous and thorough research into Celtic, Welsh, and Arthurian lore provides the exquisite warp and woof for this richly colored tapestry of story. But Barron's understanding about human relationships and the needs of the human spirit give living substance to the literary elements so that the book glows with a true magical light."
—Barbara Kiefer, Columbia University

"Young readers with a taste for mythical adventures will devour Barron's books, perhaps without realizing the strong undergirding they give to the courage, humility, and integrity Merlin displays."
—*Book Page*

". . . [A]n exciting adventure."
—*Curriculum Administrator Magazine*

". . . [A]n excellent stimulus for the imagination."
—*Somerset (PA) Daily American*

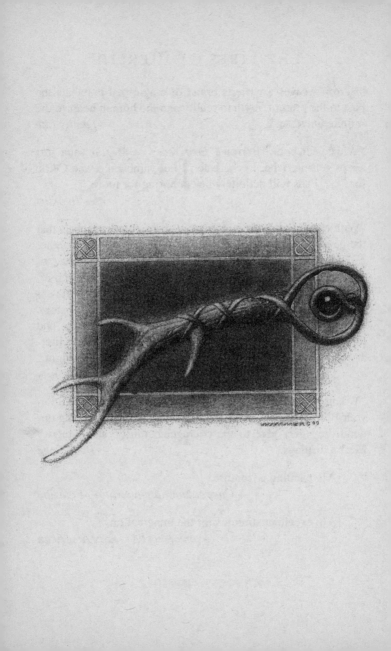

THE MIRROR OF MERLIN

Book Four of
The Lost Years of Merlin

—————————————

T. A. BARRON

ACE BOOKS, NEW YORK

THE MIRROR OF MERLIN

An Ace Book / published by arrangement with
the author

PRINTING HISTORY
Philomel hardcover edition / September 1999
Ace special sales mass-market edition / September 2001

Visit our website at www.penguinputnam.com

Check out the ACE Science Fiction & Fantasy newsletter
and much more on the Internet at Club PPI!

ACE®
Ace Books are published by The Berkley Publishing Group,
a division of Penguin Putnam Inc.,
375 Hudson Street, New York, New York 10014.
ACE and the "A" design
are trademarks belonging to Penguin Putnam Inc.

PRINTED IN THE UNITED STATES OF AMERICA

10 9 8 7 6 5 4 3 2 1

Visit T. A. Barron's website: www.tabarron.com

W E S (compass, eye)

THE LOST

be there giants?

Ruins of Varigal

Lake of the Face

dwarves last seen here

crossing

living stones   Tuatha's Grave

Crystal Cave of the Grand Elusa

orchards

THE MISTED HILLS

Cobblers' Rowan   Arbassa, Home of Rhia

The River Unceasing

DRUMA WOOD

The Last Shomorra

Tree lings once lived here

shore of the speaking shells

Trouble found here

dunes

Forgotten Island

Emrys' Landing

I. SCHOENHERR MCMXCVI

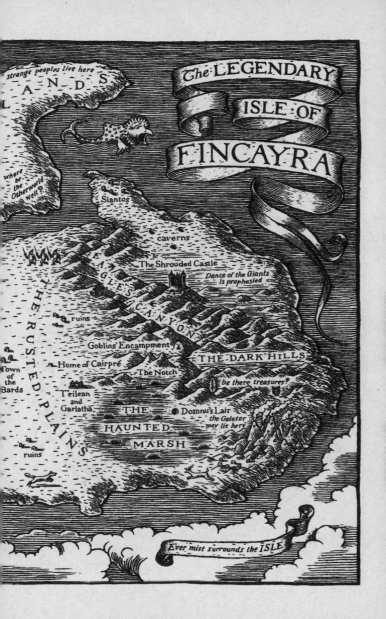

The LEGENDARY ISLE·OF FINCAYRA

strange peoples live here

LANDS

where be the Otherworld well?

Slantos

caverns

The Shrouded Castle

Dance of the Giants is prophesied

EAGLES' CANYON

ruins

Goblins' Encampment

Home of Cairpré

THE·DARK·HILLS

be there treasures?

The Notch

THE RUSTED PLAINS

Town of the Bards

T'eilean and Garlatha

Domnu's Lair
the Galator may lie here

THE HAUNTED MARSH

ruins

Ever mist surrounds the ISLE

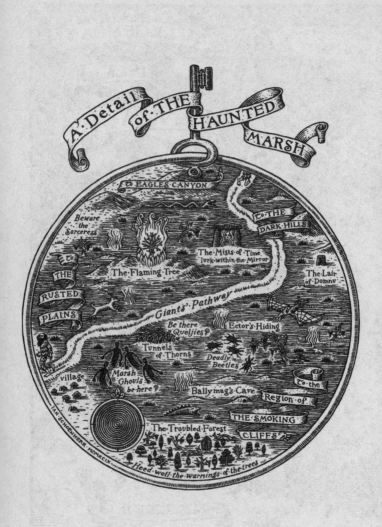

contents

PART THREE

AUTHOR'S NOTE

One thing never changes about Merlin: He continues to surprise.

That is true in the earliest tales, first sung by Welsh bards fifteen centuries ago; it is no less so today. It is true in Merlin's fabled elder years, when he has become the mentor to King Arthur, mage of the Round Table, and central figure in the wondrous tragedy we call Camelot. And it is no less true in Merlin's youth, as he struggles to find his own name, his own self, and his own destiny.

Perhaps his knack for surprise flows from the sheer depth—and complexity—of his character. (As merely one of the latest in a long line of Merlin's chroniclers, I am struck by how much of his character, after fifteen centuries, remains still unexplored.) Perhaps it stems from the powerful magic that starts to emerge within him during his youth. Or, perhaps, from the mysterious future that awaits him—as alluring as it is terrifying.

Or his ability to surprise may flow from something far more simple, far more basic: Merlin's own humanity. In this volume, the fourth in *The Lost Years of Merlin* epic, his surprises come less from his swelling gifts and dawning greatness than from his fundamental human frailties. For all his growing powers, and growing passions, he remains a mortal man.

To be sure, Merlin has come a long way from the fateful day that began the saga of his lost years. On that day a bedraggled, half-drowned boy washed ashore on a strange coastline. Almost instantly, death pursued him. Yet, for all the fears that filled his thoughts, he felt mainly aware of what he lacked: He had no memory of his childhood, his parents, nor even his own name. It was, in his own words, a day "harsh, cold, and lifeless . . . as empty of promise as my lungs were empty of air."

Although Merlin survived that day, his more challenging journey had only just begun. Since then, he has discovered some of the secrets of Fincayra, a land as elusive as the mist that swirls about its borders, an island resting in between the mortal Earth and the immortal Otherworld. He has learned much about his past, though less about his identity. He has found his parents, and the truth about his birth. He has gained a few friends—and lost a few, as well.

And Merlin has succeeded on other fronts: He has healed a wounded dragon, run like a deer, spawned the Dance of the Giants, discovered a new way of seeing, solved the riddle of the Seven Songs, heard the whispers of an ancient shell, survived being swallowed by a living stone, taken the spirit of his sister into himself and borne her to the Otherworld, triumphed over creatures who devour magic, and mastered the legendary Wheel of Wye. He has built a musical instrument of his own design—and realized that its music lay less in the strings than in the hands that plucked them.

Yet despite all his successes, Merlin's greatest challenges lie ahead. He must somehow come to understand the depth of his own humanness: its capacity for triumph, and also for tragedy.

How else can he ever become, in his later years, that mentor to King Arthur we know so well? To play his part in the Arthurian cycle—and in the even grander cycle of myth that stretches long before and after—Merlin must know humanity well. Immensely well. He must know our highest aspirations, as well as our deepest frailties. He must understand that even the best intentions may be riddled with flaws, that even promised salvation may hold serious dangers.

He must, in short, know himself. But how to see himself in the truest mirror? And where might such a mirror be found? Perhaps its reflections are seen in disparate places, if only in disguised form. Perhaps its images, whether highly luminous or deeply shadowed, hold some surprises of their own.

Only when Merlin can view himself with utter clarity can he hope to guide a young, idealistic monarch. To support him in creating a new social order, with the Round Table at its heart, even though it is doomed to fail in its time. To help the young leader, despite everything, to find hope. And, perhaps, to try again.

As Merlin reveals the secrets of his lost years, and continues to surprise me along the way, one thing never changes: I am deeply grateful to the friends who have encouraged and counseled me. As always, I owe a lasting debt of thanks to my wife, Currie, and my editor, Patricia Lee Gauch. In addition, I am most grateful to Kylene Beers, for her unwavering faith, as well as her wisdom. Kristi Dight deserves thanks for encouraging *The Tale of the Whispering Mist,* which Hallia tells her companions on a dark night in the marshland. Special thanks also go to Deborah Connell, Kathy Montgomery, Suzanne Ghiglia—and, as always, the elusive wizard himself.

T. A. B.

In misty dreams and shadowed memories
Of fabled cities I have dwelt apace . . .
In crystal splendor I have spanned the seas
And clothed myself in legendary grace.

—From a sixth-century poem,
SONG OF DYFYDDIAETH

The world from which the stories came
lies still within the astral mists . . .

—W. B. Yeats

PROLOGUE

Many are the mirrors I have examined; many are the faces I have seen. Yet for all these years—lo, all these centuries—there is but one mirror, with one visage, I cannot forget. It has haunted me from the start, from that very first instant. And it haunts me no less to this day.

Mirrors, I assure you, can cause more pain than broadswords, more terror than ghouls.

Under the stone archway, mist billowed and swirled, roving about like an all-seeing eye.

The mist did not rise from the ground, or from some steaming pool nearby. Rather, this mist formed out of the very air under the arch, behind the strange, quivering curtain that held it back as a dam might hold a swelling tide. Even so, the vapors often pushed past, licking the purple-leafed vines that wrapped around the pillars. But more often, as now, they churned deep within the archway, forming and dissolving shapes in endless procession: ever changing, ever the same.

Then, without warning, the curtain of mist shuddered, hardening into a flat sheet. Beams of light struck its surface, breaking apart like shards of glass; vague shapes from the surrounding marshes reflected there. Somewhere behind the reflections, clouds continued to churn, touched by dark, distorted shadows. And a mysterious light, glinting from the depths beyond.

For this curtain was truly a mirror, one filled with mist—and more. A mirror with its own movement, its own pulse. A mirror with something stirring far beneath its surface.

Suddenly, from the very center came a waft of vapors, followed by something else—something slender. And twisted. And alive. Something very much like a hand.

With long nails, sharper than claws, the fingers reached outward, groping. Three of them, then a fourth, then a thumb. Wisps of mist from the marsh curled around them, adorning them with delicate, lacelike rings. But the fingers shook free before closing into a fist.

For a long moment, the fist squeezed itself tightly, as if testing its own reality. The skin, nearly as pale as the surrounding vapors, went whiter still. The fingernails dug deeper into the flesh. All over, the fist quivered from strain.

Ever so slowly, the hand started to relax. The fingers uncurled, flexed, and worked the air. Hazy threads wove themselves around the thumb and stretched across the open palm. At the same time, the mirror itself darkened. From the edges of the crumbling stones, deep shadows seeped inward, covering the surface. In a few moments, the whole archway gleamed like a black crystal, its smooth surface unbroken but for the pale hand squirming in its center.

A sharp creaking split the air. It might have come from the mirror, or the ancient stones themselves, or somewhere else entirely. With it came a scent—compellingly sweet, akin to rose blossoms.

A wind stirred, carrying away both the sound and the perfume. Both vanished into the rancid terrain of the Haunted Marsh. No one, not even the marsh ghouls themselves, noticed what had happened. Nor did anyone witness what happened next.

The hand, fingers splayed wide, lunged forward. Behind it came the wrist, forearm, and elbow. The gleaming surface suddenly shattered, melting back into a shifting, quivering mirror, as restless as the mists within its depths.

Out of the archway strode a woman. As she planted her boots on the muddy ground, she smoothed the creases on her white robe and silver-threaded shawl. Tall and slender she stood, with eyes as lightless as the interior of a stone. Glancing back at the mirror, she smiled grimly.

She gave her black, flowing locks a shake, and turned her attention to the marsh. For a long moment she listened to its distant wailing and hissing. Then she grunted in satisfaction. Under her breath, she whispered: "This time, my dear Merlin, you shall not elude me."

With that, she gathered her shawl about her shoulders and strode off into the gloom.

PART ONE

1

SHADOWS

I strained, throwing all my strength into the task, but my shadow refused to move.

Again I tried. Still, the stubborn shadow would not budge. Closing my eyes—a meaningless gesture, since they couldn't see anyway, having been replaced by my second sight over three years ago—I tried my best to concentrate. To perceive nothing but my shadow. That was not easy, on a bright summer day like this, though it still seemed easier than my task.

All right, then. Clearing my mind, I pushed aside the sound of rustling grasses on this alpine meadow, and of splattering streamwater nearby. No smells of springmint, or lavender, or pepperwort—almost strong enough to make me sneeze. No boulder, roughened by yellow lichens, resting beneath me; no mountains of Varigal, streaked with snow even in summer, rising above me. No wondering about whether I might encounter my old friend, the giant Shim, in these hills so near his home. And, most difficult of all, no drifting into thoughts about Hallia.

Just my shadow.

Starting from the bottom, I traced the shadow's outline on the grass. There were my boots, leather straps dangling, planted firmly on top of the boulder. Then my legs, hips, and chest, looking less scrawny than usual because of my billowing tunic. Protruding from one side, my leather satchel—and from the other, my sword. Next, my arms, bent with hands resting on hips. And my head, turned sideways just enough to show the tip of my nose, which, much to my consternation, had started to hook downward in recent months. Already more beak than nose, it reminded me of the hawk who had inspired my name. Then, of course, came my hair: even blacker than my shadow. And, I grumbled to myself, just as unruly.

Move, I commanded silently, all the while keeping my own body motionless.

No response.

Lift yourself, I intoned, focusing all my thoughts on the shadow's right arm.

Still no response.

I released a growl. Already I had wasted the entire morning trying to coax it to move independently. So what if shadow-working was a skill reserved only for the eldest wizards—true mages? I never was much good at waiting.

I drew a long, slow breath. *Lift. Lift, I say.*

For a long moment, I stared, exasperated, at the dark form. Then . . . something started to change. Slowly, very slowly, the shadow's outline started to quiver. The edges of its shoulders grew blurry, while its arms quaked so violently they seemed to swell in size.

Better. Much better. I forced myself not to move, not even to brush away the bothersome drops of perspiration rolling down my temples. *Now, right arm. Lift yourself.*

With a sharp jerk, the shadow's arm straightened. And lifted—all the way above the head. Though I held my own body fixed, a thrill raced through me— a mixture of excitement, and discovery, and pride in my growing powers. At last, I had done it! Worked my own shadow! I could hardly wait to show Hallia.

Though I felt as if I could fly off the boulder, I kept myself still. Only my widening grin betrayed my feelings. Returning my attention to the shadow, its arm still raised, I savored my success. To think that I, barely fifteen years of age, could move my shadow's—

Left arm? My whole chest constricted. It should have moved the right, not the left! With a roar, I stomped my boots and waved my own arms angrily. The shadow, as if in spite, did the same back at me.

"You foolish shadow! I'll teach you some obedience!"

"And when will that be?" asked a resonant voice behind me.

I spun around to face Hallia. Stepping as lightly as a doe, she seemed more supple than the summer

grass. Yet I knew that, even in her young woman's
form, she was ever alert to any possible danger—
ready to run like the deer she could become in an instant. As the sunlight glinted on her auburn braid, her
immense brown eyes watched me with humor. "Obedience, if I recall, isn't one of your strong points."

"Not me, my shadow!"

Her eyes sparkled mischievously. "Where leaps
the stag, so leaps his shadow."

"But—but I . . ." My cheeks grew hotter as I stammered. "Why do you have to appear right now? Just
when I've botched everything?"

She stroked her long chin. "If I didn't know better,
I might think you had been hoping to impress me."

"Not at all." I clenched my fists, then shook them
at my shadow. Seeing it wave its own fists back at me
only made me angrier. "Fool shadow! I just want to
make it do what it should."

Hallia bent to study a sprig of lupine, as deep purple as her robe. "And I just want to keep you a little
humble." She sniffed the tower of petals. "That's usually Rhia's responsibility, but since she's off learning
the speech of the canyon eagles—"

"With my horse to carry her," I grumbled, trying to
stretch my stiff shoulders.

"True enough." She glanced up and smiled, more
with her eyes than with her lips. "She can't, after all,
run like a deer."

Something about her words, her tone, her smile,
made my anger vanish like mist in the morning sun.
Even my shoulders seemed to relax. How, I couldn't
begin to explain. Yet all at once, I recalled the secrets

she had shown me of transforming myself into a
deer, as well as the joys of running beside her—with
hooves instead of feet, four legs instead of two; with
keen sight, and keener smell; with the ability to hear
not just through my ears, but through my very bones.

"It's . . . well, it's—ahhh . . . ," I stammered. "Nice,
I suppose. To be here. With you, I mean. Just—well,
just you."

Her doelike eyes, suddenly shy, turned aside.

Emboldened, I climbed down from the rock.
"Even in these days, these weeks, we've been traveling together, we haven't had much time alone." Ten-
tatively, I reached for her hand. "If it hasn't been one
of your deer people, or some old friend, it's been—"

She jerked her hand away. "So you haven't liked
what I've shown you?"

"No. I mean yes. That's . . . oh, that's not what I'm
saying! You know how much I've loved being here—
seeing your people's Summer Lands: those high
meadows, the birthing hollow, all the hidden trails
through the trees. It's just that, well, the best part has
been . . ."

As my voice faltered, she cocked her head. "Yes?"

I glanced her way, meeting her gaze for barely an
instant. But it was enough to make me forget what I
had wanted to say.

"Yes?" she coaxed. "Tell me, young hawk."

"It's, well, been . . . Fumblefeathers, I don't
know!" My brow furrowed. "Sometimes I envy old
Cairpré, tossing off poems whenever he likes."

She half grinned. "These days, it's mostly love poems to your mother."

More flustered than ever, I exclaimed, "That's not what I meant!" Then, seeing her face fall, I realized my gaffe. "I mean . . . when I said that, what I meant was—not, well, not what I meant to say."

She merely shook her head.

Again, I stretched my hand toward her. "Please, Hallia. Don't judge me by my words."

"*Hmfff,*" she grunted. "Then how should I judge you?"

"By something else."

"Like what?"

A sudden inspiration seized me. I grasped her hand, pulling her across the grass. Together we ran, our feet pounding in unison. As we neared the edge of the stream, our backs lowered, our necks lengthened, our arms stretched down to the ground. The bright green reeds by the water's edge, glistening with dew, bent before us. In one motion, one body it seemed, we sprang into the air, flowing as smoothly as the stream below us.

We landed on the opposite bank, fully transformed into deer. Swinging about, I reared back on my haunches and drew a deep breath, filling my nostrils with the rich aromas of the meadow—and the full-hearted freedom of a stag. Hallia's foreleg brushed against my own; I replied with a stroke of an antler along her graceful neck. An instant later we were bounding together through the grass, prancing with hooves high, listening to the whispering reeds and the many secret murmurs of the meadow. For a time measured not in minutes but in magic, we cavorted.

When, at last, we stopped, our tan coats shone with

sweat. We trotted to the stream, browsed for a while on the shoots by the bank, then stepped lightly into the shallows. As we walked upstream, our backs lifted higher, our heads taller. Soon we were no longer wading with our hooves, but with our feet— mine booted, Hallia's bare.

In silence, we clambered up the muddy bank and stepped through the rushes. When we reached the boulder, scene of my unsuccessful shadow-working, Hallia faced me, her doe's eyes still alight. "I have something to tell you, young hawk. Something important."

I watched her, my heart pounding like a great hoof within my chest.

She started to speak, then caught herself. "It's— oh, it's so hard to put into words."

"I understand, believe me." Gently, I ran my finger down her arm. "Later perhaps."

Hesitantly, she tried again. "No, now. I've been wanting to say this for a while. And the feeling has grown stronger with every day we've spent in the Summer Lands."

"Yes?" I paused, trying to swallow. "What is it?"

She edged a bit closer. "I want you to, to . . . know something, young hawk."

"Know what?"

"That I . . . no, that you—"

Suddenly a heavy object rammed into me, knocking me over backward. I rolled across the grass, stopping only at the edge of the stream. After untangling myself from my tunic, which had somehow wrapped itself around my head and shoulders, I leaped to my feet with a spray of mud. Grimacing, I grasped the hilt of my sword and faced my attacker.

But instead of lunging forward, I groaned. "Not you. Not now."

A young dragon, her purple and scarlet scales aglow, sat beside us. She was tucking her leathery wings, still quivering from flight, against her back. Her immense, gangly form obscured the boulder, as well as a fair portion of the meadow, which is why she had sent me sprawling when she landed. Only Hallia's quick instincts had spared her the same fate.

The dragon drew a deep, ponderous breath. Her head, nearly as large as my entire body, hung remorsefully from her huge shoulders. Even her wings drooped sadly, as did one of her blue, bannerlike ears. The other ear, as always, stuck straight out from the side of her head—looking less like an ear than a misplaced horn.

Hallia, seeing my angry expression, moved protectively to the dragon's side. She placed her hand on the end of the protruding ear. "Gwynnia's sorry, can't you see? She didn't mean any harm."

The dragon scrunched her nose and gave a deep, throaty whimper.

Hallia peered into her orange, triangular eyes. "She's only just learned to fly. Her landings are still a little clumsy."

"Little clumsy!" I fumed. "She might have killed me!"

I paced over to my staff, lying on the grass, and brandished it before the dragon's face. "You're as bad as a drunken giant. No, worse! At least he'd pass out eventually. You just keep getting bigger and clumsier by the day."

Gwynnia's eyes, glowing like lava, narrowed slightly. From deep within her chest, a rumble gathered, swelling steadily. The dragon suddenly stiffened and cocked her head, as if puzzled by the sound. Then, as the rumble faded away, she opened her gargantuan, teeth-studded jaws in a prolonged yawn.

"Be glad she hasn't learned yet how to breathe fire," cautioned Hallia. Quickly, she added, "Though I'm sure she'd never use it on a friend." She scratched the edge of the rebellious ear. "Would you, Gwynnia?"

The dragon gave a loud snort. Then, from the other end of the meadow, the barbed end of her tail lifted, curled, and moved swiftly closer. With the grace of a butterfly, the remotest tip of the tail alighted on Hallia's shoulder. There it rested, purple scales upon purple cloth, squeezing her gently.

Brushing some of the mud from my tunic, I gave an exasperated sigh. "It's hard to stay angry at either of you for long." I gazed into one of the dragon's bright eyes. "Forgive me, will you? I forgot—just for a moment—that you're never far from Hallia's side."

The young woman turned toward me. "For just a moment," she said softly, "I, too, forgot."

I nodded sadly. "It's no fault of yours."

"Oh, but it is." She stroked the golden scales of the barbed tail. "When I started singing to her in the evenings, all those songs I learned as a child, I had no idea she would grow so attached."

"Or so large."

Hallia nearly smiled. "I suppose we should never have let Cairpré give her such a weighty name, out of ancient dragon-lore, unless we expected her to live up to it someday."

"That's right—the name of the first queen of the dragons, mother of all their race." I chewed my lip, recalling the old legend. "The one who risked her own life to swallow the fire from a great lava mountain, so that she, and all her descendants, might also breathe flames."

At that, Gwynnia opened wide her jaws and gave another yawn, this time so loud that we both had to cover our ears. When at last the yawn ended, I observed, "Seems like the queen may need a nap." In a hopeful whisper, I added, "We may get to finish our conversation yet."

Hallia nodded, even as she shifted uneasily. But before she could say anything, a new sound sliced through the air. It was a high, mournful keening—the kind of sound that could only come from someone in the throes of death. Or, more accurately, someone for whom death itself would be a reprieve.

2

†HE BALLYMAG

The anguished cries, from somewhere near the stream, continued. Grabbing my staff, I dashed across the grass, followed by Hallia. The young dragon merely watched us sleepily, nuzzling her wing with her enormous nose. Even before I reached the bank, I realized that the wailing—so loud that it drowned out the tumble and splatter of water on the stones—was coming from a bend upstream. Hallia and I rushed to the spot, pushing aside some yellow gorse that grew by the water's edge.

There, struggling to pull itself onto the muddy bank, was the oddest-looking creature I had ever seen. His body was dark, rounded, and sleek, much like the seals of Fincayra's western coast, though smaller in size. Too, he possessed a scal's long

whiskers and deep, sorrowful eyes. But instead of
fins, this creature had arms, three on each side. Thin
and bony, the arms each ended with a pair of oppos-
ing claws resembling a crab's. From his well-padded
belly hung a net of greenish webbing—a pouch, perhaps—while his back held a row of long, delicate
tails, each one coiled tightly into a spiral.

Then I noticed the jagged cut, caked with mud,
that ran down his right flank. As the creature flopped
against the bank, moaning piteously, I knelt beside
him. Quickly, splashing him with stream water, I
tried to clean the wound. At first the poor beast, thoroughly consumed by his own suffering, didn't seem
to notice me. After a moment, though, he gave a sudden, violent shudder.

"Oh, terribulous painodeath! Horribulous bloody-
hurt!" he bellowed. "My endafinish, so soon, so
soon . . . And I so littleyoung, almost a barebaby."

"Don't worry," I answered soothingly, hopeful that
my own dialect sounded less strange to him than his
did to me. "I'm sure that cut hurts, but it's really not
too deep." I reached into my satchel and pulled out a
handful of healing herbs. "These herbs—"

"Are for killocooking little mepoorme, of course!
Such a dreadfulous, woefulous endafinish." His
whole body trembled, especially the thick rolls of fat
under his chin. "How I soverymuch sufferfled—only
to be cookpotted by a cruelous manmonster."

I shook my head. "You don't understand. Try to relax." Dripping some water on the herbs, I patted them
into a poultice. "This will help you heal faster, that's
all."

The creature shrieked and tried to wriggle free. "Manmonster! You want to fattenchew me up lightningfast. Oh, agonywoe! My painodeath so nearupon, my—"

"No," I declared. "Calm down, will you?"

"You'll imprisoncage me, then. Touroshow me, as your odditious beast! So more manmonsters can hurlastones at my cage, or pinchasqueal me through bars. Terribulous fate, horribulous end . . ."

"No!" I tried my best to work the poultice into the wound, but the creature's constant thrashing made it nearly impossible. Several times he nearly slid off my lap into the water—or into the gorse bushes. "I'm here to help you, don't you understand?"

"You? Manmonster? Whenevernever did manmonster do thingany punybit helpfulous for ballymag?"

"Ballymag?" repeated Hallia, bending lower. "Why, indeed he could be." Catching my puzzled look, she explained, "One of the rarest beings on the island. I've only heard stories—but, yes, this surely looks like one. Though what he's doing here, I don't understand. I thought they lived only in the remotest marshes."

"In Haunted Marsh itselfcertain," wailed the ballymag. "Outstraighten your factsattacks! Before you imprisoncage me, crunchabeat me, and cookscald me with a hundreddozen stale potatoes. Oh, woefulous world, disheartenous distress!"

Shaking my head, I examined the gash again. "Trusting fellow, aren't you?"

"Yes, most certainously," bawled the creature, tears brimming in his round eyes. "My natureborn, that is. Too quicktrusting, too foolgullible. Always eagerready to find happyhope in any situation, I am! Which is why it's my sorrowfate to shriekadie with stale potatoes. An assnasty turn!"

The ballymag drew a slow, unsteady breath. "Well, go ahead and killascream me. I'll crumplego honorously." For a full two seconds, he kept silent. Then, all at once, he bellowed, "Oh, terrorwoe crampymess! To be cookpotted now! So littleyoung. So bravely-strong. So—"

"Quiet!" I commanded, working myself into a sitting position on the bank. Baring my teeth, I glared at him fiercely. "The louder you protest, the more terrible your death will be."

Hallia looked at me with surprise, but I ignored her. "Yes, oh yes." I cackled murderously. "The only question is just *how* to kill you. But this much is certain: The more you fuss, the more painful I shall make it for you."

"Trulyreally?" whimpered the ballymag.

"Yes! Now stop your wailing."

"Oh, horribulous . . ."

"This instant!"

The beast fell silent. But for the occasional shiver, which made him jiggle from the top of his throat down to the bottom of his belly, he lay utterly still on my lap.

Gently, I placed my hands over the wound. I began concentrating on the deepest layers of flesh, where the tissue was most badly torn. At the same time, I inhaled deeply. I imagined that my lungs were filling not with air, but with light—the warm, soothing light of summer sun. Here, in the cherished lands of the deer people, where Hallia and I had romped so freely—and would again, I felt certain. In time, the light overflowed into the rest of me, brimming in my shoulders, running down my arms, flowing through my fingertips.

As the healing light poured into the ballymag's wound, his body, even his whiskers, began to relax. All at once he moaned again. But this moan was different, sounding less pained and more surprised— even, perhaps, pleased. But knowing how much delicate work lay ahead, I shot him a wrathful glare. Instantly, he quieted.

I began directing the light into the severed flesh. Like a bard restringing a broken harp, I turned from one strand of tissue to the next, binding and tightening with care, testing the strength of each before moving on. At one spot, I found a tangle of ripped sinews, cut almost to the bone. These I bathed in light for some time just to separate them from each other. At length, I loosened them, then gently reconnected the tissues, coaxing them back to strength, back to wholeness. Layer by layer, I worked higher in the wound, slowly drawing nearer to the surface.

Several minutes later, I lifted my hands. The ballymag's black skin shone smooth and unbroken. Feeling drained, I leaned back against the stream bank, resting my head against a gorse root. Blue sky shone through the yellow blossoms above my head.

At last I sat up. Lightly, I tapped the ballymag's flank. "Well," I sighed, "you're in luck. I've decided not to boil you after all."

The creature's eyes, already wide, swelled some more. But he said nothing.

"It's true, poor fellow. I never was going to harm you, but that was the only way I could get you to stay still."

"You're just toyannoying with me," he groaned, squirming in my lap. "Laugholously playfooling me."

Hallia looked at me warmly. "He doesn't believe you now. But he will, in time."

"Nowoe chancehappen of that!" The ballymag suddenly uncoiled several of his tails, wrapped them around a rock protruding from the bank, and wrenched himself free from my grip. He landed with a splash in the shallows at my feet. Spinning his six arms, he swam downstream at terrific speed. In a flash, he had rounded the bend and disappeared.

Hallia stroked her slender chin. "It's safe to say you healed him, young hawk."

I glanced over at my shadow, crouching beside me on the mud, whose pose seemed hopelessly insolent. "Glad I can get something right."

She ducked under a branch and moved to my side, as gracefully as an unfurling flower. "Healing, I think, is different from other magic."

"How so?"

Pensively, she rolled a twig between her fingers, then tossed it into the flowing water. "I'm not sure, exactly. But more of healing magic seems to come from within—from your heart, perhaps, or some-place even deeper."

"And other kinds of magic?"

"From, well, outside of ourselves." She waved at the azure sky. "From out there somewhere. Those powers reach us, and sometimes flow through us, but don't really belong to us. Using them is more like using a tool—like a hammer or a saw."

I pulled a mud-encrusted stick out of my hair. "I understand, but what about the magic we use to change ourselves into deer? Doesn't that come from within?"

"No, not really." Pondering her hand, she squeezed it into the shape of a hoof. "At the beginning, when I will myself to change, I can feel my inner magic— but only as a spark, a sort of invitation, that connects me with the greater magic out there. That's the magic that brings change in all its forms: night into day, fawn into doe, seed into flower. The magic that promises . . ." She paused to stroke a curling shaft of fern sprouting beside her on the bank. "That every meadow, buried in snow all winter long, will spring into life once again."

I nodded, listening to the splatter and spray of the stream. A snake, thin and green, emerged from a tangle of reeds by my feet and slipped into the water. "Sometimes I feel those outer powers—cosmic powers—so strongly they seem to be using *me,* wielding me like their own little tool. Or writing me like a story—a story whose ending I can't do anything to change."

Hallia leaned closer, rubbing her shoulder against mine. "It's all this talk, isn't it? Oh yes, young hawk, I've heard it, even from some of my clan who ought to know better. All about your future, your destiny, to be a wizard."

"And not just any wizard," I added, "but the greatest one of all times! Even greater than my grandfather, Tuatha, they say—and he was the wisest and most powerful mage ever to live. It's . . . well, a lot of weight to carry around. So much that sometimes it's all I can feel. As if my own choices, my own decisions, aren't really mine after all."

"Oh, but they are! They surely are. That's what makes you . . . *you*. That's why I wanted to tell you . . ." Her voice fell to a bare whisper. "What I wanted to tell you."

"So will you tell me now?"

"No," she declared, determined to stay on the subject. "Listen, now. Do you honestly think you have no more say in your future than the acorn that's destined to become an oak tree? That couldn't possibly become an ash or a maple, no matter how hard it tries?"

Glumly, I scraped the muddy bank with the heel of my boot. "So it seems."

"But you have your own magic, too! What I said about the outer powers is true—but they couldn't be used by us at all if we didn't have our own powers, our own magic, within. And you, young hawk, have an amazing ability to tap into the greater magic. To receive it, concentrate it, and bend it to your will. I see it in you all the time, as clear as a face in a reflecting pool."

"Maybe the reflection you see is yours, not mine."

She shook her head, so vigorously that her auburn braid flew over her shoulder, brushing against my ear. "Without your inner magic, you couldn't have healed the ballymag the way you did."

"But was I really using my own magic, and my own choices, to heal him? Or was I merely following my destiny, plodding through a scene in a story written by someone else, long ago?" My fingers drummed against the silver hilt of the weapon at my side. "Even this sword is part of my destiny. That's what I was told, by the great spirit Dagda himself. He commanded me to keep it safe, for someday I will deliver it to a great, though tragic, king—a king so powerful that he will pull it free from a scabbard of stone." I paused, trying to remember how Dagda had described him. *A king whose reign shall thrive in the heart long after it has withered on the land.*

Hallia raised a skeptical eyebrow. "A destiny foretold be not a destiny lived."

"Is that one of your people's old proverbs?"

"*Mmm,* not so old. It was my father who first said it. He thought a lot about such things." She nudged me hard enough that my shoulder bumped a branch, knocking loose some leaves. "Like someone else."

I grinned, glancing at my staff leaning against a rounded stone at the stream's edge. Water slapped the shaft, moistening the seven symbols engraved along its length, making them gleam darkly. "The more I think about things—destiny or anything else—the less I really know."

Suddenly Hallia laughed. "My father said the same thing! More times than I could count."

I gave her a nudge of my own. "What else did he have to say?"

"About destiny?" She thought for a moment. "Not much, though he did say something puzzling."

"Which was?"

"He said, if I remember rightly, that seeking your destiny is like looking into a mirror. You see an image, however blurred, in whatever light exists at the time. But if the light ever changes, so will the image itself. And if the light ever vanishes, the mirror will be empty. That is why, he concluded, the truest mirror is . . . how did he put it? Oh yes. The truest mirror is the one that needs no light at all."

Bewildered, I furrowed my brow. "No light at all? What did he mean by that?"

"No one in my clan has ever made sense of it, though many have tried. Some of the elders, I'm told, have debated it endlessly, with no result. So it's best not to spend too much time pondering. It could have been merely a jest, or a play on words. My father knew much, but he also loved to play tricks on people."

I nodded, still wondering about the curious pronouncement. It could well have been a jest. But what if it really held some meaning after all? Evidently the elders believed it did, or they wouldn't have wasted so much time trying to understand it. Perhaps someone, someday, would succeed. Perhaps . . . even me. For a moment I savored that thought—a lovely one, indeed. I, Merlin, might be the one to shed light on the old mystery. And on many other mysteries as well.

A sudden movement on the muddy bank distracted me. My shadow! Although I was sitting perfectly still, it seemed to be moving—indeed, shaking. Could it be just the play of light from the stream? I concentrated my gaze. No, there could be no doubt.

My shadow was shaking its head at me.

3

SECRETS

I growled at my insolent shadow, still mocking me on the stream bank. "Why didn't you just stay back there at the boulder?"

Hallia stiffened, slapping her hand on the muddy slope. "Young hawk!"

"Not you—oh, I'm sorry." I reached out my hand, but she swatted it away. I glared down at my shadow, which seemed to be quivering with laughter. "Hallia, I wasn't talking to you at all! Just my shadow."

Slowly, her expression softened. "Seems you're having as much trouble with that shadow these days as you are with Gwynnia." She pushed aside some branches to glance at the meadow where we had left her. "She's gone again. I wonder where."

"Probably just foraging down the stream. She's not

far away, that much is certain." I tossed a river stone onto my shadow—half expecting it to toss something back. "So tell me. How did your father come to know so much? Was he a scholar? A bard?"

"Neither. He was the healer of our clan, for many years." Taking her braid, she toyed with it, separating the strands, as if she were untying a much-knotted memory. "Even after we were forced to leave our ancestral lands by the sea, which nearly broke his heart, he continued his work. And he knew much more than the art of healing. He understood things no one else did about certain places. And . . . certain people." She swallowed. "That was why, I suppose, he was entrusted with caring for one of the Seven Wise Tools."

I started. "Really?"

She nodded.

"Which one?"

"I shouldn't say more. It's a secret among the Mellwyn-bri-Meath."

As I watched the water moving past our feet, my own memories flowed like the stream. I remembered well those legendary tools, having rescued most of them from the collapsing Shrouded Castle. There was the plow that tilled its own field, the saw that cut only as much wood as one needed—and what else? Oh yes: the magical hoe, hammer, and shovel. Plus that bucket, feeling almost as heavy as the plow, since it always brimmed with water.

Only the seventh one had eluded me—though not my thoughts. For while I didn't know its description, let alone its powers, I had often dreamed of finding it, usually behind an impenetrable wall of flames. Whenever, in my dreams, I had tried to rescue it, the searing flames burned my hands, my face, my useless eyes. All I could hear were my screams; all I could smell was the stench of my own burning skin. When I couldn't stand the agony any longer, I always awoke, soaked in sweat.

Gently, Hallia touched my hand. "I can see from your face, young hawk, that you know some secrets of your own about the Seven Wise Tools."

"That I do," I replied, still gazing at the stream. "I have held them all, even used them all—except for the one that was lost forever."

She gazed at me, weighing her thoughts. At last, she whispered, "It wasn't."

"What do you mean? That's what everyone said. Even Cairpré."

"Because that's what everyone thought. Except for my father, and the few of us he had trusted with the secret. You see, that Wise Tool was the one in his charge. And when the wicked king Stangmar's soldiers came to seize it, my father gave them not the tool itself, but a copy he had made—a fake. The real one he hid away, somewhere safe."

"Where?"

"He never told anyone. Soon after he made the switch, the hunters . . . found him."

Reading the grief in her eyes, I wrapped my hand around hers. For some time we sat there, watching the swirling current. As much as I wanted to share her secret, I wanted still more to share her burden.

At length, she spoke again. "It was a key, young

hawk, a magical key. Carved of polished antler, with a single sapphire on its crown. Its powers . . . oh, I can't remember—like so much else my father told me. I was so young then! It mattered a great deal to him, that's mainly what I remember." Her fingers entwined with my own. "Though I do recall his saying once that, as great as its powers were, they still couldn't rival a healing hand."

At that instant, we heard a wailing cry from somewhere downstream. The cry grew swiftly louder—and more familiar. A few seconds later, the ballymag came swimming straight toward us, his six arms splashing furiously. He swam up the channel, flopped onto the bank, and leaped into my arms, shivering and panting.

Eyes ablaze with fear, he blurted, "Troubledous terror! Mangledous murder! It's getcoming closer-gulp."

Before I could ask what he was talking about, an enormous head lifted out of a grove of hawthorns downstream. Gwynnia! Her stiff ear snapped a few branches, sending up a cloud of leaves, as she straightened her long, scaly neck. She stepped from the trees, wings folded tight against her massive back, and leaned toward us. The orange light of her eyes flashed on the water.

"The frightdragon!" squealed the ballymag, burrowing his head under my arm. "We're doomed-killed, every deadlastous one of us."

"Nonsense," I replied. "That dragon is our friend."

"She won't harm you," added Hallia.

Hearing her friend's voice, Gwynnia thumped her

tail vigorously on the ground. One of her strokes, however, struck a hawthorn, uprooting it. The tree toppled with a crash into the stream, spraying mud and branches across the bank. At that, the ballymag shrieked—and fainted. He lay in my lap, as limp as a drenched tunic. Even his tails, once so tightly coiled, hung loose against his back. Gwynnia's head, now nearly above us, cocked to one side in puzzlement.

I stroked the ballymag's smooth skin. "This little fellow just isn't cut out for adventures. I think I ought to send him back to where he came from."

"The Haunted Marsh?" asked Hallia. "That's the last place you should send him."

"It's where he came from."

"Then he was wise to escape! That's an evil place, a dreadful place, with deathtraps at every turn. My people—like every other people, except for the marsh ghouls—avoid it however we can."

"Look, he clearly needs to be near water. And away from dragons. How he came to be here, I can't say. But surely the best thing to do is send him back to his home."

Hallia, shaking her head, touched the ballymag's wet back. "It's foolish, I tell you. And, besides, that wretched swamp is all the way on the other side of the island."

Hearing the doubt in her voice, I stiffened. "You don't think I can do it?"

"Well . . . no. I don't."

I frowned at her, my cheeks burning.

"Leaping is one of the most hazardous skills of wizardry. You've told me so yourself."

My fist slammed the bank, spraying mud on my tunic. "So you think I can't."

"What if you send him to the wrong place by mistake?"

"I won't make any mistakes!" Noticing my shadow, which seemed to be shaking its head again, I bit my lip. "And if by chance I do, then at least he'll wake up someplace where there's no dragon staring down at him."

Carefully, I lay the unconscious ballymag down in the reeds at the water's edge. Then, grasping my staff, I stood. I planted my feet firmly, turned my back to Hallia, and began to concentrate. Almost instantly, I felt the powers building within me, pushing to the surface like lava in an erupting volcano. Finally, I intoned the intricate chant, calling forth the high magic of Leaping.

> *Voyage near, venture far—*
> *Lo! The leaping place and time.*
> *Find the center of a star*
> *In the dreaming Muirthemnar;*
> *Or the echo of a rhyme*
> *Ringing rightly as a chime.*
> *Ever honor, never mar—*
> *Lo! The leaping place and time.*

A flash of white light erupted on the bank. Water coursing through the channel sizzled into steam. At the same time, the ballymag vanished—along with Hallia and myself.

4

PAÏNODEATH

Pine needles! I rolled over and spat them from my mouth. Above, thick branches arched upward, looking sturdy enough to support the sky itself. And burly enough to obscure it: Only a few specks of light shone through the tight weave of limbs.

"Good work, young hawk."

I cringed, spat out a chunk of sticky resin, then turned my head toward Hallia. Like me, she lay on her back among the needles and broken sticks. "All right," I admitted. "So my Leaping was a little . . . off."

She sat up, watching me solemnly. "A little, you say? Seems to me you were trying to send the ballymag, not us. Now we're here, in some forest, while he's nowhere in sight! And wasn't the Haunted

Marsh your goal? I should be grateful, I suppose, your aim was so poor!"

She shook a needle off her nose. "Compared to your aim in Leaping, well, Gwynnia's aim in landing is superb." Her expression darkened. "Where is she, anyway?" She bounced to her feet, spraying me with sticks. "Gwyyyniaaa," she called, her voice flying into the forest like a sparrow hawk. "My Gwyyyniaaa."

No answer came. Hallia turned to me, her brow knitted with concern. "Oh, I do hope she's all right. She'd answer me if she could hear. You don't think we—"

"Left her behind?" I finished, pushing myself to my feet. I brushed the bark and needles off my tunic. "It's possible, I'm afraid. Very possible. I wasn't, after all, supposed to send her anywhere."

"You weren't supposed to send us, either! Oh, she'll be horribly upset." She glanced around the grove. "Maybe she's here somewhere, just out of earshot."

"Wherever *here* is," I muttered.

Tilting my head back, I peered up into the vaulting branches and drew a deep breath of air, poignant with the sweetness of cedar and pine. And something else, I realized: a slight odor of something rancid, or rotting, that lurked just beneath the sweetness. Nonetheless, I drank in the aromas, for as much as I disliked being lost, I always savored being in a forest. The darker the better. For the darker the grove, the older the trees. And the older the trees, the more mysterious, and more wise, I knew them to be.

A breeze rustled the needled branches, sprinkling my face with dew. Suddenly I thought of another day, in another forest—in the land of Gwynedd, called Wales by some. Pursued by a foe, I had escaped by climbing a tree: a great pine, much like the ones towering above us now. Moments later, I'd found myself caught in a rising storm. The wind swelled, and I clung with all my strength to the tree. When the storm finally arrived in force, I rode out all the swaying and twirling, rocking and twisting, supported—nay, embraced—by those branches. And when, at last, the storm subsided, leaving me drenched in the boughs of that rain-washed tree, I had felt refreshed, revived, and newly born.

Hallia tapped my arm. Just as I turned to her, another, stronger breeze coursed through the limbs above us. She started to speak, but I raised my hand to stop her. For in the creaking branches of the trees, I heard voices, deep and resonant. Yet . . . these voices did not seem to belong to a forest whose boughs lifted so majestically. They sounded full of despair, and of pain slowly deepening.

With all my concentration, I listened. The trees cried out to me, their great arms flailing. I could not understand all they said, for they were all speaking at once, sometimes in languages I hadn't yet mastered. Yet there were several whose words I could not mistake. From a stately cedar: *We are dying, dying.* From a linden tree whose heart-shaped leaves twirled slowly to the ground: *It is eating me. Swallowing my roots, my very roots.* And from a powerful pine, in mournful tones: *My child! Do not take away my child!*

As the wind, and the voices, subsided, I turned to Hallia. "This forest is in trouble somehow—great trouble."

"I feel it, too."

"It doesn't seem natural."

"No, it doesn't. Yet if you look closely, the signs are everywhere. Like those death-grip vines on that stand of hemlocks."

"And here, look at this." Reaching for the trunk of a nearby pine, I scraped a bit of gray, scraggly moss off its bark. "Rotting beard. I've seen it on trees before, but only after a flood. Never in a thriving forest."

She nodded grimly. "I wish we could do something to help. But what? Besides, we have our own troubles. How can we find our way back to the Summer Lands? And to Gwynnia, poor thing! And what about the ballymag? Who can tell where he might be now?"

Grinding my teeth, I stooped to retrieve my staff. "Look, I'm sorry. I had no idea that my Leaping would go all awry like this." Squeezing the gnarled top of the staff, I lamented, "I forgot the very first lesson, what Dagda called *the soul of wizardry:* humility."

Angrily, I slid the staff under my belt. "I need another hundred years of practice before trying something like that again! Why, I might have sent us to another land, or even another world."

Hallia shook her head. "No, no. My feet, my nose, my bones all tell me we're still somewhere in Fincayra." She scanned the shadowed trunks surrounding us. "This forest reminds me a lot of an ancient grove that I visited years ago, when I was still a fawn-child. The mixture of trees, the way they stand—it all feels so familiar. But that place was so much more alive! What kind of sickness could have attacked a whole forest like this?"

"Ehhh," groaned an anguished voice from behind the knotted roots of a cedar. "Terribulous pain-odeath."

We rushed to the spot. The ballymag, his round eyes more woeful than ever, stirred within the roots. Shards of bark and clumps of needles dangled from his claws, his padded belly quaked with the slightest movement, and his whiskers drooped morosely. Yet my second sight, keener than an owl's vision in the darkened grove, found no new signs of injury.

Bending toward him, I tried to pull a twig, sticky with sap, out of one of his tails. He shrank away from me, cowering. "You've no reason to fear now," I coaxed. "The dragon isn't here."

"But manmonster is!" He lifted his nose and sniffed, as his eyes grew wider still. "And worsemuch, verilously worsemuch, this is terrorplace I leastcringe wantbe!" He fell into a fit of shudders and groans. "Terrorp-p-p-place."

Hallia caught her breath. "So you know where we are?"

"Certainously," wailed the ballymag. "C-c-can't you smelloscent flavorous puddlemuck?"

"No, I can't!" I declared. "Whatever mucklescent means."

"Puddlemuck!" The ballymag shut his eyes, muttering, "Manmonsters! So verilously dumbilythick."

I shook him until his eyes reopened. "Where do you think we are, then?"

Balefully, he looked up at us. "The darkendous wood, edgesouth of Haunted Marsh."

I started. "The marsh? Are you sure?"

"Certainously!" His whiskers bristled. "Thinkyou I not smellknow my own puddlemuck?"

Hallia shook her head. "That can't be right. The forest I remember was in the hills a long way south of the marshlands—practically a full day's run."

"Are you sure?" I asked.

"Positive. I never forget a forest, certainly not an ancient one like this. And it wasn't even close to the Haunted Marsh."

"Ohwoe, but it verilously is!" squealed the bally-mag, his whole body shaking. Waves of jiggly fat rolled down his belly. "Manmonster, please . . . hurt-pinch mepoorme if you choosemust. Tearpull out these whiskerhairs, oneshriek by oneshriek. But takeget me hereaway!"

Scowling, I studied the quivering creature. "You're not making sense. Even if we *were* near the swamp, why don't you want to go back? I thought it was your home."

"Was, absolutously. But not nowlonger. Not safe-home."

My eyebrows lifted. "Why not?"

He twisted, trying to push his head under one of the roots. "Can't talkexplain! Too horribulous."

Staring down at him, I wondered what could possibly be more horrible than the Haunted Marsh I well

remembered. The putrid air, the gripping muck—
and, worst of all, the marsh ghouls. I had seen their
eerie, flickering eyes, and much more than that. I
never wanted to feel their rage, their madness, again.
Hallia, I knew, had been right: That swamp was the
least known—and most feared—place on Fincayra.
And for good reason.

The ballymag, raising his head again, sighed
through his shivers. "Oh, how I achemiss that homeplace, with its glorifous underwonders! Such a
sweetlygush homeplace, for such timelong."

I traded disbelieving glances with Hallia.

"Ah, those putridous pools," he continued, his eyes
glistening. "Those bafflingous bogs! All so
mooshlovely and wetsecret." He cringed. "Until . . ."

"Until what?"

"Ickstick!" cried the ballymag suddenly, pointing
all his claws at my feet. "A dangerscream!"

I glanced down at the thick, crooked stick beside
my boot, then back at him. "No more hysterics, now.
I've had enough! I'm not running from sticks—nor
should you."

"Butayou don't . . ."

"Enough!" I commanded, drawing my sword. A
shaft of light, slicing through the branches overhead,
caught the blade. It flashed brightly. "This will save
us from deadly sticks. Or wailing ballymags."

Hallia frowned. "Come. Let's find our way back
to—*aaaghhh.*"

Both hands flew to her neck, tearing at the
writhing, sinuous snake that had wrapped itself

around her throat. Her face lost its color; her eyes
bulged with terror. Raising my sword, I leaped to her
aid.

"Painodeath!" shrieked the ballymag.

All of a sudden, something heavy struck my lower
back. It slid with incredible speed up my spine to my
shoulders. Before I could even cry out, powerful
muscles clamped around my neck.

Another snake! My breath cut short. I barely
caught sight of Hallia collapsing to her knees,
wrestling with her own strangling snake, when things
started spinning. I tripped on something, kept myself
from falling—but dropped my sword. Clumsily, I
stumbled toward Hallia. I had to reach her. Had to!

My fingers dug deep into the cold flesh closing
around my neck. It felt hard, like a collar of stone.
Even as I tugged, the snake squeezed relentlessly,
drawing itself tighter and tighter. My head seemed
about to explode, my arms and legs weaker by the
second. Bolts of pain shot through my neck, head,
and chest. I couldn't stand, couldn't breathe. Air—I
needed air!

Stumbling, I crashed to the ground, rolling on the
needles. I struggled to stand. But I fell again, face-
down, still pulling at the serpent. Meanwhile, a
strange darkness crept over me—and through me. I
felt no more spinning, no more motion.

Magic. I must use my magic! Yet I lacked the
strength.

Something sharp jabbed my shoulder. I felt the cut,
saw the blood. My sword—had I rolled on it?
Vaguely, an idea glimmered in my mind. Using all

my remaining strength, I tried to wriggle higher on the blade. Weakly I twisted, but the world grew darker. I felt the blade slicing my flesh . . . and possibly something else.

Too weak to fight any longer, I ceased moving. A final wish flashed through my thoughts: Forgive me, Hallia. Please.

Suddenly—the snake's hold loosened. I drew a ragged, halting breath. My arms started tingling; my vision began clearing. Wrathfully, I tore the severed body of the snake from my neck. Hallia, I could see, lay so near. And so still.

Grasping the hilt of the sword, I crawled to her side. The snake that had attacked her uncoiled slightly, raising its head from under her chin. It hissed angrily, yellow eyes sizzling. It shot toward me—

Just as I swung the sword. With a slap, the blade connected. The snake's head sailed into the air, thudding into the trunk of a tree. It fell to the forest floor.

I dropped the sword and pulled myself to her side. Please, Hallia! Breathe again. I held her bruised neck, almost as purple as her robe, and shook her head. But she didn't stir. I stroked her cheeks; I squeezed her chilled hand.

Nothing. Nothing at all.

"Hallia!" I cried, tears dampening my cheeks. "Come back now. Come back!"

She made no movement. She showed no life, not even the faintest breath.

Crumpling in despair, I fell upon her, my face pressed against her own. "Don't die," I whispered. "Not here, not now."

Something brushed against my cheek. Another tear? No . . . an eyelid!

I lifted my face, looking into her own, even as she drew a struggling breath. And another. And another.

In a moment, she sat up. She coughed, rubbing her sore neck. Her eyes, so wide and brown and deep, caressed me for several seconds. Then they moved to the bloodstained sword by my side, and the headless snake lying among the pine needles.

Her lips quivered in a fleeting smile. "Maybe," she said hoarsely, "your aim isn't so bad after all."

5

FLAMES NOW ARISE

It took a full hour for us to regain our strength, and for Hallia to clean the slice on my shoulder so that I could will the tissues to heal. And it took nearly another hour for the ballymag to speak again, having been frightened completely out of his voice. Finally, we sat among the needles and gnarled roots, grateful to be alive—and entirely alert for any more snakes.

"You bravelysave," rasped the ballymag, leaning against a bulging root. He clawed anxiously at his whiskers. "Muchously more bravelysave than me."

I tossed a pinecone into the boughs of a sapling. "At least you spotted that one before it attacked. How did you know it wasn't really a stick?"

"The angryeyes. Almostously closed, but peekingstill yellowbright. Many terrortimes I findenhide themsame before."

"In the marsh?" I leaned closer, peering at his round face. "Those snakes came from there?"

"Verilutously."

I scowled. "The place you called your wonderful homeplace."

Hallia rubbed her neck gingerly. "Your word, I think, was *mooshlovely.*"

"Well . . ." The ballymag made an effort to clear his throat, while his row of tails twitched nervously. "I mightcould exaggersillied a bitlittle."

"A bitlittle." Puzzled, I shook my head. "What's happening with the marsh? Even if it's not so far from here, as you believe, why did those snakes leave it?"

His round eyes closed tightly, then popped open. "Probabously for dreadfulsame reason as Iself."

"Which is?"

"Too terribulous to tell, even whispersay." The ballymag shook his head, along with his six arms and most of his tails. "Whatever my worstshriek dreamfears, this be worsefulous. Bigamuch worsefulous."

"Tell us."

He shrunk down into the roots. "Nowoewoe."

Lightly, Hallia touched my arm. "He still doesn't trust you."

I growled with exasperation. "How many times do I have to save his life before he does? Well, no matter. He won't be with us much longer anyway."

The ballymag gasped. His claws started to clatter

with his shaking. "Manmonster plangoing to . . . chopochew me?"

"Tempting, but no." I clambered to my feet and studied him ruefully. "We're going to find our way, somehow, back to the Summer Lands. But since I brought you here, it's my responsibility to get you safely to water somewhere. No, don't worry, not your mooshlovely marsh! But we're bound to pass some watery place before long. And that's where I'll be leaving you, whether you like it or not. I don't care if it's a stream, a tarn—or a puddle."

The ballymag's eyes narrowed and he snapped a claw at me.

With a sigh, I tore off a strip from the bottom of my tunic, tied the ends together, and draped it around my neck like a saggy sling. Then, despite his constant wriggling, I gathered him in my arms and placed him inside. Though one of his tails protruded, coiling and uncoiling in time to his nervous moans, the rest of him disappeared in the folds of cloth.

Lightly, Hallia touched the moaning bundle on my chest—causing the ballymag to shriek and curl himself into a huddled ball. She studied the bulging sling. "He may not appreciate that you saved our lives, young hawk, but I do."

I tapped the hilt of my sword. "This is what really saved us."

She stamped her foot on the ground like an angry doe. "Come now. You sound as if you had nothing to do with it."

I gazed at the shadowed trees. "That's not what I

mean. But we came close, too close, to dying right there. If I really have all the powers that Cairpré and the others think I have—expect me to have—then I shouldn't have been fooled by those snakes to begin with."

"*Hmfff.* Why can't you make mistakes sometimes, like anyone else?"

"Because I'm supposed to be a wizard!"

She placed her hands on her hips. "All right then, great wizard, why don't you tell me something? Such as how are we going to get back to Gwynnia before she frets herself to death, or tears up the countryside looking for me?"

"Well, unless you'd like me to try Leaping . . ."

"No!"

"Then we'll have to walk." I patted the sling—and jerked away my hand just as a claw nearly snapped it. "With our friendly companion here."

Turning to the aged cedar by my side, I laid my hand upon its deep-rutted trunk. A waft of sweet resins came to me; I could almost feel them flowing beneath the bark. "I wish I could find some way to help you, old one. And the rest of this place, as well. But there just isn't time."

The branches above me stirred slightly, sending down a shower of dead needles. I glanced at Hallia, who had already strode off into the forest, following the slanting beams of the afternoon sun. I pressed my palm into the tree's bark for another few seconds, and whispered, "Someday, perhaps, I'll return."

Catching up with Hallia wasn't easy, since she was trotting speedily through the woods. No doubt she would have suggested that we change ourselves into deer, but for her awareness that I needed to transport the ballymag. Yet even with two legs, she leaped with ease over roots and fallen trunks, while I seemed to snag my tunic on every passing branch. The ballymag's heavy sling didn't help—nor did the occasional claw that would reach out and snap at me.

Panting, I finally caught up with her. "Do you," I huffed, "know where you're leading us?"

She ducked beneath a fragrant bough of hemlock. "If this is the forest I remember, the Summer Lands lie to the west. I'm hoping to find a landmark I recognize before long."

"And I'm hoping to find some water. To rid myself of this—" I slapped away the roving claw. "This baggage."

For a long while we trekked through the trees, hearing only the crunching of our footsteps or the occasional scurrying of a squirrel on a branch. Then, from a ravine below us, we heard a sharp thud, repeated several times. A sword. Or an axe, hacking and chopping. Suddenly, a tormented wind swept through the branches, rising to a cacophonous moan.

Both of us froze. I took Hallia's arm. "We can't do anything to save this forest, but maybe we can save at least one tree."

She nodded.

Following the chopping sound, we flew down the ravine, crashing through the thicket of blackberry bushes that covered the hillside. Though I tried my best to keep up with Hallia, she soon left me behind. Once I tripped on a fallen limb, landing with a thud on my chest. And on the ballymag, whose shrieks nearly deafened me. I regained my feet and again plunged down the hill.

A few moments later, the ground leveled out. I burst into a narrow, grassy clearing. There stood Hallia, arms crossed against her chest, facing a man holding a rough-hewn axe. His ears, like those of most Fincayrans, were slightly pointed at the top. But it was his eyes that commanded attention: They glowered angrily at the young woman who dared to stand between him and the tall, gnarled pine whose trunk bore a ragged gash in its side.

"Away with ye, girl!" His tattered tunic swirling about him, he waved his axe at Hallia. Behind him stood a woman, her expression as frayed as her uncombed hair. In her arms she held a baby who cried piteously while her thin legs thrashed the air.

"Away!" shouted the exasperated man. "It's only a wee bit o' firewood we be wantin'." He lifted his axe threateningly. "And soon shall be gettin'."

"For that you don't need to cut down a whole tree," objected Hallia, not budging. "Certainly not an old one like this. Besides, there's plenty of wood on the ground. Here, I'll help you gather some."

"Not dry enough for kindlin'," retorted the man. "Now stand ye aside."

"I will not," declared Hallia.

Panting from my run, I stepped to her side. "Nor will I."

The man glared at us, eyes smoldering. He raised his axe higher.

"Our babe, she needs warmth," wailed the woman. "And a morsel o' cooked food. She hasn't eaten a scrap since yesterday morn."

Hallia, her face softening, tilted her head in puzzlement. "Why not? Where is your home?"

The woman hesitated, trading glances with her husband. "A village," she said cautiously. "Near the swamp."

"The Haunted Marsh?" I asked, with a quick look at Hallia. "Isn't that a long way from here?"

The woman eyed me strangely, but said nothing.

"Wherever your village is," Hallia pressed, "why aren't you there now?"

Ignoring the man's gesture to stay silent, the woman started to sob. "Because . . . it be invaded. By *them*."

"By who?"

The man swung his axe in the air. "By the marsh ghouls," he answered gruffly. "Now move yeselves aside."

At that moment, the ballymag lifted his whiskered head above the edge of the sling. Then, at the sight of the axe, he whimpered loudly and promptly buried himself again in the folds.

"Invaded?" I repeated. "I've never heard of marsh ghouls doing such a thing before."

The woman tried to give her little girl a finger to suck, but the child pushed it away. "Our village be borderin' the swamp for a hundred and fifty years, and we never heard of such a thing, neither. Their screeches and wails, of course, we hear every night.

Louder than battlin' cats! But if we be leavin' them alone, they do the same for us. Until . . . that all changed."

Her husband took a step toward us, brandishing his axe. "Enough talkin'," he barked.

"Wait," I commanded. "If it's fire you want, I know another way."

Before he could object, I raised my staff high. Beneath my fingertips, I could feel one of the engravings on the shaft, the carved shape of a butterfly. With my free hand, I pointed at a tangle of needles and sticks near the man's feet. Silently, I called upon the powers of Changing, wherever they might be found. Though I felt no wind, my tunic suddenly billowed, sleeves flapping. Seeing this, the man gasped, while his wife drew back several steps.

In a slow, rhythmic cadence, I spoke the ancient words of the fire-bringer:

> *Flames now arise*
> *From forest or fen;*
> *Brighter than eyes,*
> *Beyond mortal ken.*
>
> *Father of heat*
> *For anvil and pyre;*
> *Mother of light,*
> *O infinite fire.*

A sizzling sound erupted from the wood. Brown needles curled downward, while bark split open and began to snap and pop. A thin trail of smoke rose upward, steadily swelling, until—flash! The sticks, bark, and needles burst into flames.

The man shouted and leaped aside. Even so, the hem of his torn tunic caught a spark and started to burn. Hastily grabbing a tuft of long grass, he swatted at the flames. His wife, holding tight to their child, backed farther away.

At last, the fire on his tunic extinguished, the man turned to face me. For a long moment, he stared in silence. "Sorcery," he growled at last. "Cursed sorcery."

"No, no," I replied. "Just a little magic. To help you." I waved at the crackling flames. "Come, now. Warm your family, as well as your food, by this fire."

He looked at his wife, her eyes filled with a mixture of terror and longing. Then he took her by the arm. "Never," he spat. "No sorcerer's flames for us!"

"But . . . it's what you need."

Heedless of my protests, they crossed the meadow and retreated into the trees. Hallia and I stood there, dumbfounded, until the sounds of snapping sticks and the crying child no longer reached us.

Glancing down at my shadow, I caught sight of it slapping its sides. Jeering at me! I roared, jumping on top of it. Hallia spun around, but the instant before she saw the shadow, it returned to normal, moving only as I did. She looked at me in bewilderment.

Fuming, I stamped out the fire with my boot. My shadow, I was irked to see, did the same but with a touch more vigor. With a sigh, I said, "I hadn't intended to frighten them—only to help them."

She observed me sadly. "Intentions aren't everything, young hawk. Believe me, I know." For an instant, she looked as if she yearned to say something more—but caught herself. She gestured in the direction of the departed family. "After all, they hadn't intended to kill this poor tree. Only to build a fire for their child."

"But they're one and the same!"

"Wasn't your trying to send the ballymag home, and sending us all here instead, also one and the same?"

My cheeks grew hotter. "That's completely different." I ground my heel into the coals. "At least this time the magic worked. Just not in the way I'd hoped."

"Listen, you did what you could. I'm only lamenting . . . oh, I'm not even sure what." She watched the dying coals. "It's just hard, sometimes, to do the right thing."

"So I shouldn't even try?"

"No. Just try carefully."

Still perturbed, I gazed at her. Then, turning back to the scarred pine, I winced at the size of its wound. "Maybe, at least, I can do one right thing today."

Kneeling at the base of the elder pine, I reached out a finger and touched the sweet, sticky sap oozing out of the gouge. It felt thicker than blood, and lighter in hue, more amber than red. Even so, it seemed very much like the blood that had flowed from my own shoulder not long before. I listened to the barely audible whisper of its quivering needles. Then, very carefully, I placed both of my hands over the spot, willing the sap to hold itself back, to bind the wound.

In time I felt the sap congealing under my palms. Removing my hands, I crushed some fallen pine needles and spread them gently over the area. Bending closer, I blew several slow, steady breaths, all the while sending my thoughts into the fibers of the tree. *Draw deep, you roots, and hold firm. Soar high, you branches; join with air and sun. Bark—grow thick and strong. And heartwood: stand sturdy, bend well.*

Finally, when I felt I could do no more, I backed away from the trunk. I turned to speak to Hallia, but before I could, another voice spoke first. I had never heard it before—so breathy, vibrant, and strange, made more of air than of sound. Yet I knew it at once. It was the voice of the tree itself.

6

BOUND ROOTS

To my surprise, the tree spoke not in the language of pines, that whooshing and whispering tongue I had come to know, but in the main language of Fincayra. The same language that Hallia and I spoke to each other! Yet its airy voice, and its cadence that swayed like a sapling, were different. Strikingly different. I had never heard anyone speak—or, in truth, sing—in such a way.

> *In deepening soil my under-roots toil:*
> *Following, swallowing—*
> > *Arboresque moil.*
> *For year after year, for centuries dear,*
> *I build my roots to stand on.*
> > *Grow grand on!*

While branches reach skyward
To make a crown royal,
I build my roots to rise on.
Grow wise on.
Grow wise on.

Uncertain, I backed away. After a moment, my shoulder bumped into Hallia's. Her eyes, even wider than usual, were focused on the tree. From within the folds of my sling, another set of round eyes, along with some quivering whiskers, edged higher. Suddenly the entire tree shuddered, with such evident pain that I felt myself shudder in response. Flakes of bark, wet with sap, drifted down from its branches, falling like tears on the meadow.

Too soon comes the day: O spare me, I pray—
Hacking, attacking—
  A man comes to slay.
I stand in his path, incur his great wrath,
Though never would I harm him.
  Alarm him!
My living, my learning,
  Would all end today,
Though never would I claim him.
  Or maim him.
  Or maim him.

The breathy voice grew shrill, almost like a whistle. I felt a sharp pain in my ribs, as if a blade had plunged into my side. But the tree continued:

Before lifesap ends, arrival of friends!
Braving, yes saving—
    Ere axe my heart rends.

At this, Hallia's hand slipped into my own. Whether from her touch, or the tree's new tone, the pain in my side started to recede. Gradually, my back straightened, and I stood taller, even as the tree itself did the same.

You challenge his will, defy him to kill,
So I shall keep on living.
    And giving!
My limbs gladly lift,
    My trunk freely bends,
So I shall keep on growing.
    And knowing.
    And knowing.

Exultantly, the great pine tree waved its uppermost branches. Then, with a loud creaking, it twisted its trunk a full quarter turn—first to one side, then to the other. The tree, I realized, was stretching. Preparing for some sort of strenuous feat.

Midway up the trunk, a pair of grooves opened between strips of bark—revealing two slender, undulating eyes, as brown as the richest soil. The eyes gazed at us intently for several seconds before finally turning downward. All of a sudden, the whole mass of roots began to quake, shaking the tree enough to shower us with needles, twigs, and bark. Wood creaked and snapped. Clods of earth, tossed loose by the roots, flew into the air.

Hallia's hand squeezed mine more tightly. The ballymag let out a frightened cry, then thrust his head deep inside the sling.

At that moment, a very large root twisted, buckled—and broke free of the ground. With a spray of soil, the root slapped the turf like a knobby, hairy whip. Slowly, it splayed its hundreds of tendrils for balance. The trunk leaned to the side, placing much of its weight on the unburied root. On the opposite side, another root broke loose. Then another. And another. Clumps of dirt sailed in all directions.

Finally, the tree stood still again. Yet now it stood not beneath the ground, but on top of it. As Hallia and I watched, peering into the soil-brown eyes, the tree lifted a broad root and took a step toward us.

We did not flee. Rather, we stood like rooted saplings ourselves, drinking deeply of the moist, resinous air that swirled about us, wrapping us in a fragrant cloak. For we knew that we had encountered one of the best-disguised creatures in all of Fincayra. A creature who could hide so well that decades, sometimes centuries, would pass without one of its kind ever being noticed. A creature whose name, in the old tongue, was *nynniaw pennent*—always there, never found.

A walking tree.

With heavy, halting steps, the walking tree came closer. Behind it, a trail of moistened grasses sparkled in the sunlight. At last, when it was almost

upon us, it stopped. Then, unhurriedly, the remotest
tips of the tree's roots wrapped lightly around our ankles, pressing against our skin. Hallia and I smiled,
for we both felt the same surge of warmth, flowing
up our legs and into our bodies.

In deep, breathy tones, the tree sang again:

Our heartwoods are tied, we stand side by side—
Trusting wind gusting—
    Folly to hide.
I know not your name nor whither you came,
Yet now we are kin roots.
    Lo, twin roots!
For though I felt lost,
    And silently cried,
Yet now we are found roots.
    Lo, bound roots.
    Lo, bound roots.

The final phrase seemed to rise on a breeze, stirring the branches of a graceful cedar nearby. The
drooping limbs lifted and fell, as smoothly as a single
breath. Other trees caught the same lilt, rustling the
air. Still others followed, until all around us branches
swished and whispered, swaying in unison. In time,
the whole grove, the whole forest, it seemed, joined
in the song of celebration.

Then, abruptly, the music shifted. Harsher, deeper
tones emerged; the branches started clacking and
moaning. As the dissonance swelled, it reminded me
of the first cries of pain I had heard from the trees.

But this time the wailing reverberated across the whole forest, as if the land itself were drowning in a wave of suffering.

Against this background, the walking tree raised its voice. It sang to us, in words heavy with sorrow:

On land where we thrive, the blight does arrive:
Cleaving, bereaving—
    Till none left alive.
Advancing by stealth, it chops at our health;
It poisons all our breedlings.
    Our seedlings!
Their leaves cannot breathe;
    Their roots not survive.
It poisons all our taplings.
    Our saplings.
    Our saplings.

I felt drawn, as never before, to the spirit of this tree—and to those many saplings, yearning to live, whose anguish it bore. "What is this blight?" I cried out. "Can't it be stopped?"

All of a sudden, the tree went rigid. Throughout the forest, the moaning branches fell silent, even as a new sound, a relentless pounding, rose in the distance. Louder and louder it swelled, as rhythmic as a great drum, shaking the ground and the trees anchored within it. Whether the sound came from somewhere in the forest, or from somewhere beyond, it was clearly approaching. Rapidly.

The walking tree stirred again. Its roots uncoiled from our legs, curled sharply downward, and plunged into the ground. As they worked themselves into the soil, the roots vibrated, humming in mournful tones that echoed the final phrase of the tree's song. *Our saplings. Our saplings.* An instant later, the tree's slender eyes closed behind lids of bark. As they disappeared, so did any sign that this was anything but another pine, one more tree among many.

Meanwhile, the clamorous rumbling grew louder. Twigs and flakes of bark, knocked loose from the vibrations, rained down on us. I felt the ballymag curl into a tight ball inside the sling, his row of tails twitching anxiously against my chest. A high branch split off and crashed down through the layers of limbs, thudding into the roots by our feet.

Hallia pulled my arm frantically. "We must run, young hawk. Away from here!"

"Wait," I objected. "I know that sound. We should—"

But she had already dashed from my side. I saw her legs, blurring with motion; her back, pitching forward; her neck, thrusting higher. Her purple robe shifted to green, then glistening tan. Muscles rippled across her back and legs, while her feet and hands melted into hooves.

Hallia, now a deer, bounded into the trees. I watched her vanish. Then I, too, started to run—not away from the rumbling, but toward it.

7

A FÍERY EYE

I dashed through the dark woods, drawing ever nearer to the swelling rumble. Pounding, pounding, like thunder of the land, it shook the towering trees down to their roots, making them shudder and groan. Every few steps, I heard the crash of a falling limb or a toppled tree whose roots had wrenched loose at last. Cracks opened in the soil; roots popped and split; stalks of fern, as delicate as dragonfly wings, trembled in unison. With the help of my staff, I kept my balance. And, despite the ballymag's shouts at every jostle and bounce, I kept my ears to the rumbling.

For I wanted to find its source.

The trees began to thin, allowing more light to reach the forest floor. I pushed past a net of vines, studded with red flowers. All at once, I broke into full, unobstructed sunlight.

I stood at the top of a long slope, surveying the vista. Auburn grass, swaying with shifting winds, fell away from me, almost to the horizon, finally merging in the far distance with a dark line of shifting, steaming vapors. It was, I knew with a shudder, a vast swamp: the Haunted Marsh.

So near! The ballymag had been right after all. Yet Hallia's memory of this forest, and its distance from the marshlands, couldn't have been more clear. Could the swamp be advancing, pushing its way into the forest? And so rapidly? Something told me that the forest blight, in all its forms, stemmed from the encroaching marsh—as did those strangling snakes, the ghouls that had driven the family from its village, and whatever forces had robbed the ballymag of his home. But what lay behind it all? Was it possible that something else, even more sinister than the marsh itself, was at work here?

At the bottom of the slope, near the swamp's edge, towered a grove of immense, ragged trees. Though a great distance away, they stood out sharply against the roving mists beyond. Almost as wide as they were tall, they stirred strangely, as if caught in a ceaseless, circling wind. Then, all at once, I realized that they were not trees at all. And that they were the source of the incessant pounding.

For as overwhelming—no, as terrifying—as that sound was, I had heard it before, and never forgotten. I knew its thunderous impact, its relentless rhythm. Nothing could shake, in that way, the soil and the air

and everything in between. Nothing—but the footsteps of giants.

Bracing myself, I watched the hulking figures
march steadily up the slope. With remarkable speed
they climbed, though they seemed as immense, and
heavy, as the tallest trees. Yet with each passing second their outlines grew more clear. Powerful trunks
transformed into legs, bellies, and chests; hefty
branches became arms covered with wild tangles of
hair. Necks, jaws, and eyes also appeared—along
with noses, some as sharp as pinnacles, others as
round as boulders.

A few giants wore little clothing but a ragged
beard and shaggy pants woven of leafy branches and
strips of turf. Others, however, wore colorful vests
and bristling cloaks. Earrings made of millstones and
waterwheels poked through their long manes; wide
belts carried immense hatchets and daggers the size
of grown men. For all the variety of their garb, however, they shared one common quality: sheer, stupen-
dous size.

As they drew nearer, the crushing blows of their
footsteps grew louder. Leaning against my staff, I recalled standing by the feet of my friend Shim,
stretching just to touch the top of one of his hairy
tocs. I glanced down at my own feet, so puny by
comparison. And I remembered seeing my footprints, glistening in the wet sand, on the day my
makeshift raft had somehow brought me to Fincayra's shore. That day seemed so long ago . . . and
yet so close at hand.

My gaze moved to my shadow. Like me, it quiv-

ered with every new wave of rumbling that shook the
ground. Only more so. It swayed and flailed wildly,
like a distorted reflection in the waters of a wind-
blown pond.

As I tried my best to stay upright, the ballymag
poked half his head out of the sling. Seeing the approaching giants, he gasped in horror. One of his
claws clamped on the neck of my tunic. He looked up
at me, eyes ablaze with fear.

"Ve-ve-verilously," he stammered. "Thereshriek
be tr-tr-treetall, thunderstepping crashgiants!"

I nodded, watching them march up the hill.

"Why manmoster not ru-ru-ru-runhide?" He
tugged on my tunic. "Nowspeed!"

"Because," I answered, raising my voice over the
rumbling, "I want to talk to them."

The ballymag's whiskers splayed in every direction, as stiff as dried grass. "Manmonster! You
wouldcouldn't—shouldwouldn't . . ." He turned toward the advancing line of giants. With a sharp
squeal, he fainted away, sliding limply back into the
sling.

I scanned the giants' craggy faces, looming larger
by the second. Their ancient race, Fincayra's first
people, possessed deep understanding of the land and
its mysteries. Immense as they were, I knew that their
keen eyes often noticed details that many smaller
creatures ignored. Sometimes their great height
above the ground allowed them to sense patterns that
others couldn't perceive. Perhaps, just perhaps, they
could explain the sudden growth of the swamp—and
all the trouble it had caused.

To be sure, something strange was happening in the Haunted Marsh. And though I didn't yet understand it, I felt a growing fear that it threatened more than the swamp's immediate neighbors. Pondering the dark, shifting vapors at the edge of the bog, I touched the chafed skin of my neck. Something down in that morass, I suspected, could choke off part of Fincayra's future, much as that snake had nearly choked me. And a wizard—at least a great wizard like Tuatha—would do everything in his power to prevent it.

Whether or not the giants would tell me anything was another question. They were shy and generally unwilling to share their secrets. Even though, thanks to Shim, I had spent some time among them, I was still an outsider. And a man. And, worse yet, the son of the wicked king who had hunted them down mercilessly.

As the ground rocked beneath me, and my heart galloped inside my chest, I fought to stay calm. Would any of them stop to hear me? Or would they crush me before I could even ask my questions? Then, borne by some faraway wind of memory, I heard again the words of a friend, whispered to me on my first visit to Varigal, the giants' ancient city of stone: *One day, Merlin, you may find that the merest trembling of a butterfly's wings can be just as powerful as a quake that moves mountains.* But whether this was the day, I had no idea.

Their gargantuan shadows fell over me. Anxiously, I reminded myself that giants were fundamentally peaceful. Most of the time, at least. One Fincayran

giant could flatten a tree with a single blow, drink a
lake dry within minutes, or crush a boulder with ease.
Once I had seen a brawny female lifting a chunk of
rock that would have required at least fifty people my
size to move; she had tossed it about like a bale of
summer hay. Still, thankfully, they rarely used their
strength to harm others. Or so I hoped.

There were six of them, each taller than the tallest
trees in the forest. And Shim, I could see, was not
among them. Worse, their faces looked positively
grim and wrathful. As they came closer, rocking the
ground with every step, I realized that they were
dragging something behind them: a huge bundle,
caked in mud, peat, and brambles.

"You are either very brave, or very foolish," declared a familiar voice.

Hallia! She was just emerging from the trees, her
form metamorphosing back into a woman. Briskly,
she stepped to my side on the open grass, her doe
eyes darting from me to the immense forms striding
up the slope.

I waved her back. "Stay in the trees—where it's
safer."

"Not if you are here."

My jaw clenched. "You were right to run away in
the first place."

"Until I realized you weren't coming. And that the
swamplands had grown so much, more than I would
have ever dreamed." Defiantly, she thrust out her
chin. "I'm staying with you, young hawk."

"But I don't—"

A booming voice, from high above our heads, cut

me off. "Behold! A manling and a womanling." It was one of the lead giants, a female whose serpentine hair, the color of rust, reached down to her knees. "They bring trouble."

"Naw," countered another gruffly. He licked his wide lips. *"Mmmmm,* they bring food! Not mm-much, but mmmore than that mmmeager taste o' swamp berries."

He reached toward us, his great hand grasping the air. Even as we started to back away, a third giant— whose dark beard was caked with the same mud that covered the bundle—roughly shoved his arm aside.

"Lettez 'em liven," he barked. "Ussez seen enoughen dyining fer onen days."

His companion closed his hand into a fist. "Nobody else, mmmainly you, can tell mmmee what to do!"

"Thatsen acuz yer so thickster yer nevers understandining nobody elzen." He beamed as two others guffawed at his joke. "Itzen truer, harrur-harrur."

Growling with rage, the ridiculed giant swung his fist. While missing his target, he clipped off several high limbs from a tree. Needles and broken branches showered us. Hallia jumped and started to dash away, but caught herself.

"Seeyen there! Yer canten evenz hitsen whats yer wantzen, hoho-hurr."

The other giant lunged at him. But his massive foot caught on the edge of the bundle, and he lost his balance. Bellowing angrily, he crashed on the grassy slope—so hard that both Hallia and I tumbled over backward. We righted ourselves in time to see the two belligerents start wrestling. Their huge bodies rolled over each other, arms and legs thudding the ground. The other giants moved closer to watch, shouting jeers at the two wrestlers, leaving the mud-covered bundle unattended.

And then the bundle groaned.

An avalanche of mud fell from the lower end, revealing a pair of huge, hairy toes. Then came another groan, and a sudden twist—spraying more putrid-smelling debris on the grass. A few paces from us, a fiery pink eye opened, blinking from all the muck weighing down its lid. Above the eye loomed a gargantuan, pear-shaped nose, its cavernous nostrils stuffed with stones, sticks, and ooze.

At the base of the encrusted giant's head, the layers of slop started vibrating. The faster the chin—or neck, or whatever lay beneath—shook, the more clumps of swamp matter flew into the air. Hallia barely dodged a decaying branch, which struck the grass beside her, splintering into shards. Then a crack appeared in the mountain of muck. Slowly, it widened into a crevasse-like mouth.

"Aaaraaarr," moaned the buried giant. "I ith feeling sickly sick. Certainly, definitely, abtholutely."

"Shim!" I exclaimed, recognizing his favorite phrase—if not his voice, due to all the muck blocking his nose. Rushing to his side, I shouted into his clogged ear, "It's me. Merlin."

The bulbous nose scrunched, breaking off an avalanche of debris. A good deal landed in Shim's mouth, causing him to spit and cough violently. That in turn dislodged more swamp muck, which he in turn swallowed, making him cough all the more. The fit lasted several minutes. To avoid being struck by his pounding head and flailing arms, I retreated to the very edge of the trees.

Hallia, back at my side, shot me an anxious glance. "You know this giant?"

"My, yes! Since before he got—well, so big. He helped me save the Wise Tools when Stangmar's castle collapsed."

"He could still crush you like a worm underfoot if you're not careful."

I waved my staff at the other giants, a short way down the slope. They were still so busy shouting at the two wrestlers, and roughly shoving each other, that they hadn't noticed Shim's revival. "They worry me a lot more. Shim's a friend. And he might know what's really happening down there in the marsh."

Seeing Shim's violent spasm coming to an end, I started back toward him. But Hallia's gaze, as piercing as a spear, halted me. "Listen, young hawk. Giants are bad enough, but at least you might outrun them. The Haunted Marsh, though, is something else again. What more do you need to know, other than it's already too near? Right down there, at the base of this hill! Let's get away, as fast as we can."

"Believe me, I understand. When I was there before . . . well, I don't want to go back unless it's absolutely necessary."

Deep within the sling on my chest, I heard a muffled groan. Even while unconscious, the ballymag was voicing his views.

"How can you even speak about going back there?" Hallia pressed. "Once should have been enough."

"All I know is something feels very wrong." I motioned toward the dark vapors rising from the swampland. "There's a presence down there, something I haven't felt in a long time. I can't quite put my finger on it, but I know it's dangerous."

She eyed me doubtfully. "Careful, young hawk. This is one time to be sure of your intentions."

"I am sure. I want to help the land—our land."

"Not just to be someone's image of a great wizard?"

"No!" I jabbed my staff into the turf. "And whether or not you believe it, I also intend to be careful."

She drew a slow, unsteady breath, and shook her head.

8

ARROWS THAT
PIERCE THE DAY

As Shim's thunderous cough faded into a rasp, I stepped nearer. "Tell me, old friend. What happened to you?"

He made an effort to sit up, then fell back to the grass with a resounding thud. The noise was lost, however, in the ongoing tumult from the wrestling giants not far down the hill. Their bellows and roars, punctuated by bodies slamming the turf with enough force to shake the entire slope, joined with the shouts of their onlooking companions. "My poorly node," moaned Shim. "So stuffed full of muckly muck. Can baredly breade."

His massive head turned toward me, spilling more mud and the twisted, barkless remains of a tree. "Merlin. What ith you doings here?"

"A mistake—my own. But it's good to see you again."

"And you, even wid so muj disgustingly muck." He groaned, lifted his hand, and took a swipe at his nose. "I'd be gladly to takes you homely, bud I cad hardly move. I feel so weakly! Certainly, definitely, abtholutely."

"What happened?"

His pink eyes glowed like a smith's tongs. "Dey tries to block da giants' roadway, de anciently way across da marth. Why, it's been dere since Fincayra wath bornded. And it's our bestly pathway for summer fishing in da eastern seath."

Glancing at the grappling giants, I shook my head. "Who would be so foolish? So brazen?"

"Marth ghoulth."

"Marsh ghouls?"

"Yeth!" His enormous hand closed into a fist. "When we tried to opens da roadway anew, dey attack us. Wid arrowth, murderly arrowth, so strong dey can pierce da day."

Behind me, Hallia gasped. At the same time, I could feel the ballymag starting to stir again in the sling upon my chest.

"What do you mean, Shim? Arrows that pierce the day?"

"Angrily!" he bellowed, ignoring my question. "I gets angrily! I chases dem off da roadway. *Arrrarrr,* dose ghoulth, dey trick me. I fall headfirstly into a deeply pool of muck."

I reached my hand to touch his earlobe, though it

was so caked with mud that only a few patches of skin shone through. "That was brave of you."

"Brave bud stupidly."

"Maybe so." I grinned. "But I remember a day when you weren't so brave. When you'd run until sundown just to avoid a bee sting."

Shim half guffawed, half coughed. "I never did like getting stingded." Then the edges of his mouth turned down. "Dis time, dough, I almost drownded. Only my friends' brawnily arms pulls me freely. And even den, I thinks I'm surely going to die from muckly muck."

Solemnly, I pondered his words. My heart beat almost as loud, it seemed, as the shouting giants down the slope. "But why, Shim? Why have the marsh ghouls suddenly turned so vicious? They were always frightening, to be sure, but only to those who entered their territory. Now they're attacking giants, terrorizing villagers . . . as if they're chasing everyone else—even the snakes—out of the swamp."

The great eye studied me knowingly. "I've seen dat look before, Merlin. You ith full of madness again."

"And your nose is full of muck. Here, let me see if I can help you."

Using my staff for support, I began to scale the slippery mountain that was the head of my friend. It took me some time just to climb over his tangled hair to the rim of his ear. Then, just as I mounted it, a new wave of mud slid over me, knocking me back to the ground. At the same time, a potent smell—heavy with fetid, rotting odors—filled the air, making my lungs burn.

Without bothering to brush off my tunic, I started up his head again. By wedging my staff under a mud-crusted stone, I finally managed to reach the top of his ear. Pushing higher, I surmounted his temple and crawled over his cheek, trying hard not to slip in the layers of ooze, until at last I reached the base of his massive nose. There, I found myself facing a pair of cavernous nostrils, completely blocked with debris.

Planting my boots firmly, I tried pulling out some of the muck and branches. Only a small amount came free: The nostrils were jammed tight. I tried poking at the blockage with my staff, without much success.

"Give ub, Merlin," moaned Shim, speaking softly so the force of his voice wouldn't knock me off his upper lip. "It's all too stuckly."

"Not yet," I replied. "Maybe if I try something else, I can break through."

I slid the staff under my belt and took the hilt of my sword. As I pulled it from its scabbard, the blade rang in the air, echoing like a faraway chime. As many times as I had heard that sound, it always reminded me of the sword's heralded destiny—and its connection, however mysterious, to my own. I turned the blade in my hand, flashing it in the sun. At one point, I caught the reflection of my own face, looking back at me with pride, and yes, even confidence.

Carefully, I aimed the sword at one of Shim's clogged nostrils. "Hold still," I commanded. "Very still."

"You ith full of madness," he muttered. "Just don't sting me wid dat pokingly blade."

I drew back the sword and plunged it in. Though I twisted it vigorously, no muck came free. I jerked it loose, raised the gleaming blade over my head, and jabbed again. This time, I wrenched my whole arm as I thrust.

At that moment, one of the other giants—the rust-haired female—turned around. "Hold!" she shouted, waving her long arms. "The manling is trying to kill Shim!"

All but the two wrestling giants immediately froze. They let loose a unified bellow of rage. At the same time several giants charged up the slope, their faces contorted with wrath. Immense hands reached toward me, eager to crush every bone in my body.

Whirling to face them, I pulled my sword free. Almost. Something in the jammed nostril caught the blade, holding it tight. I tugged and twisted—to no avail. I heard Hallia scream. At the same time, the sky above me went completely dark. The smell of sweaty hands replaced the odor of the swamp. In just an instant powerful fingers would close over me, squeezing the air from my lungs, the life from my body.

Suddenly an eruption, as violent as any volcano, threw me high into the air. My ears almost burst from the simultaneous roar. Arms and legs flailing, I tumbled helplessly, aware only of my own flight—and of the slimy, gray-green ooze that covered my face and chest.

For Shim, I knew beyond any doubt, had sneezed.

I struck the ground. After much rolling and bouncing, I finally came to a halt. Though my head was spinning, I lifted myself into a sitting position and wiped my cheeks and brow. Far up the slope, I could see the giants gathered around Shim, slapping and shaking him. I smiled—and hoped that, in time, he would feel strong enough to walk again. And that, at long last, his nose was clear.

A beautiful doe bounded over the grass toward me. Approaching a boulder, she leaped skyward, her muscular legs tucked beneath her body. As she sailed gracefully over the obstacle, she held perfectly still for a single, magical heartbeat. When at last she landed, the ground seemed to move toward her, lifting itself to greet her hooves. And when she sprinted the last few lengths toward me, my own face felt the rushing of air, my own thighs the pounding of turf. For I remembered, with aching clarity, the freedom of running like a deer.

Stretching my stiff shoulders, I thought about the legend, first told to me by Cairpré, that long ago all Fincayran men and women could fly. Everyone possessed wings, he claimed, wings that had been treasured, before they were somehow lost forever. Many times I had wished that I, too, could fly. Yet, as I followed Hallia's movement down the slope, drawing nearer to me with every bound, I knew that I would rather fly over the ground in another way altogether. With her at my side.

I watched as the doe slowed her gait to a walk. At the same time, she straightened up, lifted her head, and transformed into a young woman. She strode quickly to join me. Seeing me uninjured (and covered with swamp muck), she broke into a grin.

"You do have a way with giants, young hawk."

"Only ones with clogged noses." I clambered to my feet. With difficulty, because of all the filth sticking to my boots, I managed to step clear of the debris. But apart from a few bruises and a scraped hip, I felt no injuries. My staff, still hanging from my belt, was also intact. As was the ballymag—whose muffled ranting and howling from inside the sling told me that he had revived. And that he remained quite unharmed.

Hallia's grin faded. "Please, now, let us return to the Summer Lands. To my people, and also my dear Gwynnia. She'll be frantic by now."

Instead of replying, I turned my gaze toward the steaming bog that stretched all the way to the horizon.

Reading my thoughts, she persisted. "Perhaps you'll find some way to help—but later, when you know more. The elders of my clan might be able to tell you some useful things about the marshlands. And there's Cairpré, too. Surely he can advise you."

Still facing the marsh, I gave a subtle nod. "He could, that's true."

"Besides, young hawk, you just can't go in there. No one goes in there."

Slowly, I turned back to her. "Then why do I feel so drawn to it? Even as I feel so repelled by it—and whatever dangers it holds?"

She sighed. "I don't know. But shouldn't you look for the answer to that before you go any further?"

"I've been looking, believe me, but it's all a blur." I chewed on my lip. "A real wizard, I think, would see things more clearly."

Moving closer, she fingered the muddy sleeve of my tunic. "A real wizard would know what he can do—and what he cannot."

"I suppose . . ." I hesitated, clenching my jaw. "I suppose it's folly to rush into this. That forest has survived for centuries. Surely it can last a little while longer—long enough, at least, for me to learn more about what's really happening."

"That's right," she said softly. "And now let's run. Before the sun falls any lower."

"You lead," I proposed. Then, noticing my empty scabbard, I caught my breath. "My sword! Where is it?"

Hallia spun around. "There," she announced, pointing down the slope. "See where it landed?"

Indeed, it could not be missed. For my shining sword stood perfectly upright, its tip planted in the soil, its hilt held high. Rather than a weapon, it looked more like a marker, dividing the forested lands above from the swampy morass below. In the distance, the swirling vapors almost seemed to reach toward it, curling themselves around the hilt, clutching at the blade.

At that instant, a large, gray-winged bird swooped out of the sky. Without slowing its plunge, it clasped the hilt in its claws and wrenched the sword free from the ground. The bird gave a raucous shriek, flapped its powerful wings with a slow, rowing motion, and rose again into the sky.

"Come back!" I shouted, so taken aback that I couldn't have wielded any magic, even if I had known what magic to use.

Flapping slowly, almost wearily, the great bird flew toward the lowering sun—and the vast reaches of the Haunted Marsh. In what seemed like only a few seconds, and at the same time, an eternity, it entered the twisting columns of vapors. Then, with another shriek, it released its prize. My sword flashed bright once again, then plummeted downward, vanishing in the mist.

9

LOS✝

Aghast, I watched the dark vapors swallow my blade—and the bird who had stolen it. "Gone," I said in disbelief. "Gone! I must get it back."

"Wait." Hallia's round eyes peered at the distant swamp, whose contorted clouds lined the horizon. The sun, riding low in the sky, painted the entire vista gold, with a growing hint of scarlet. "It's all so strange. Why would a bird do such a thing? Unless, perhaps, it was . . ." She shook her head, as if hoping to banish an unwanted thought.

"What?" I pressed.

"A way to lure you into the marsh."

I raised an eyebrow. "A trap?"

"For you, young hawk."

"Not likely. Anyway, it doesn't matter. I still need my sword."

"There are other swords. You can let the marsh ghouls have that one."

"No, I can't. That sword is part of me. Part of my . . ."

"Destiny?" She scowled at me. "It's time you chose your own path, don't you think?"

"Yes," I agreed, my voice firm. "And now I am sure. This *is* my path."

Wincing, she closed her eyes for a moment. "So you're going down there?"

"And wherever else I must. Hallia, what if the sword is somehow tied up with the rest of this evil business? I have to do something, whatever I can." I studied her auburn hair, aglow in the light. "You should go back to your people. And Gwynnia. I'll rejoin you after the marsh."

As I spoke the final phrase, I felt the ballymag shudder against my ribs. His claws started clacking anxiously within the sling. Taking Hallia's hand, I added quietly, "I'll still be with you, you know. In one way, at least."

Her hand trembling in my own, she declared, "No, that's not enough." Her voice dropped to a whisper. "I'm coming with you."

"No, you shouldn't—"

"But I will." Her eyes darted skyward. "I only wish Gwynnia were here to come, too."

"Notame!" shrieked the ballymag, thrusting his seal-like face out of the folds of cloth. "Thinkyou I sufferfled such terrorwoe, such crampymess, just backgo to certainous dangerscream?"

He thrust a pair of hefty claws at me, snapping them under my nose. "You horribulous manmonster! You'll squealbring my endafinish—and mepoorme, just a barebaby."

"Sorry," I said, pushing away the claws. "I didn't want to, didn't know . . ."

"Excusemanure!" Tears gathered in the ballymag's eyes. "I mustshall be bravelystrong. Mustshall. I foundcrawled my ownaway to watersweet before, and hopefulously againwill. Ifsad . . . ifsad I'm not swallowgulped by dragonbeasts or manmonsters firstous."

Hallia reached her hand toward him. Lightly, she brushed one of his trembling whiskers. "We didn't mean to bring you back here. Just to help you."

The ballymag tried to growl, though it sounded more like a whimper. "Helpsave some otherbody nextatime." He drew a shaky breath. "Now I mustshould sufferflee. Butafirst," he added with a glance at my empty scabbard, "heedknow my warnsay: Unless you lusciouslove painodeath, staykeep away from terribulous marshplace."

I gazed at the swirling vapors of the swamp. "Can you tell us something, anything, about what's happening down there?"

"Please?" coaxed Hallia. "Anything at all?"

The ballymag, who was starting to climb out of the sling, shuddered. "The marshaghouls . . . they've started killattacking. Bodyevery, verilously bodyevery!" He looked anxiously toward the bog lands. "I knowanot reasonwhy. But their dreadfulous—"

A clamorous roar from up the slope cut him off. We turned to see one of the giants, standing taller than the trees behind him, at the top of the slope. The same one who had tried to eat me at the forest edge! Angrier than ever, he waved his massive fists in the air.

"There you are!" he bellowed. *"Mmmmm,* I can taste your mmmoldy little bones already." One of the other giants, standing over Shim's prone form, shouted something to him, but he waved the words away. "No mmmiserable mmmanling escapes from mmme, I say! I'll mmmangle him and all his friends."

With that, he started stomping toward us. The bally-mag shrieked and plunged his head back into the sling. Hallia grabbed my arm, jerking me down the slope. Together we ran, with loping strides, as the ground rocked beneath us.

"Come back here, mmmanling!"

With all our speed we fled, leaping over rocks and gorse bushes. The rumbling grew steadily louder, as did the giant's rasping breaths, while the turf shook ever more violently. Meanwhile the slope started to flatten, as the long grasses gave way to bare soil. Soon our feet were squelching over patches of mud and slapping through puddles. As mist swirled around us, the scent of things rotting fouled the air. Even over the giant's thunderous steps, I could hear strange cries and howls—and a distant screech, almost a laugh, echoing over the marshes.

Abruptly, Hallia slowed her running. "His footsteps! They've stopped."

Realizing she was right, I, too, slowed. Together, we came to a halt on a sagging mass of peat surrounded by a stretch of brownish-yellow bog grasses. Although the air reeked of decay, we stood panting, trying to catch our breath. I watched as thick vapors, tinted the color of rust by the setting sun, closed behind us, drawing together like a curtain that cut us off from the world that we knew. Those vapors offered us protection at this moment—and, I feared, imprisonment at another.

I took Hallia's arm. "Come. We've got to find some sort of shelter before nightfall."

"Ohwoe, ohwoe," moaned the ballymag from his hiding place by my chest. "Terribulous fate, horribulous end."

We plodded across the bog grasses, alert for any signs of snakes, or other creatures still more dangerous. Before long a continuous array of sounds—a loud bubbling from one side, a sharp whistling from another—rose all around us. We slogged onward, through a flooded plain where thorny vines clutched at our legs. Hallia, who had refused my offer to cover her bare feet with my boots, twisted her braid nervously as we walked.

As the mist darkened, the gloom deepened. Crossing a murky pool, I stepped on something hard—which suddenly moved. I pitched forward, falling face-first into the reeking slop. With help from Hallia, I righted myself, only to slip and fall backward with a splash. As I struggled to stand again, something slithered into the sleeve of my tunic.

"*Yaaah!*" I shouted, furiously slapping my sleeve. I rolled over in the pool, even as the creature—whatever it was—slid up my arm.

Finally I grasped it on my shoulder. With all my strength, I squeezed it through my tunic. Something popped—and the creature shrunk down like a collapsing bellows. I felt a sticky ooze dribble down my arm. When I shook the arm, a dark shape splatted into the pool. I turned away, having no desire to look any closer.

"Manmonster," grumbled the voice in my mud-splattered sling, "you be a verilous clumsyfoot."

"Ballymag," I replied, "you be a verilous whiney-mouth."

Hallia shook her head. "Quiet, you two." She pulled a clump of reeds out of my hair. "It's growing darker. And the—oh, listen."

A thin, unsteady wailing rose in the distance. At the same time, a distinctly stronger smell, as putrid as rotting flesh, washed over us. The wailing voice went on, never pausing, pulsing with anguish. And with something else, something like despair. Even as Hallia and I cringed, it was joined by other voices—bleating, crying, groaning. The voices swelled, rising into a hideous chorus.

The ballymag's head edged out of the sling. "It's . . . it's . . . the ma-ma-marshaghouls," he sputtered. The rolls of fat around his neck quivered. "They're comekilling."

We stood, up to our knees in murky water, as the

anguished dirge grew louder. At the same time, the last traces of daylight began to fade. Then, not far away, a single spot of light appeared, hovering eerily over the marsh. Faintly it pulsed, wavering like a wounded eye. Then another light appeared, and another, and another. Slowly, slowly, they started approaching, advancing on us.

"Ohwoe, ohwoe . . ." moaned the ballymag. "Quicklynow! Follow fastously!"

He jumped out of the sling and splashed into the bog. Instantly, he swam off, with his broad tail flapping and all his arms whirling. Hallia and I dashed after him, even as the eerie lights pressed closer.

Through the slimy pools we raced. Dead, twisted branches tore at our clothing; thick mud sucked at our feet. As we ran, the rancid air stung our throats and eyes. Yet we fought to stay close to the ballymag. And ahead of the marsh ghouls.

Suddenly the ground grew drier, though also less stable. Like a carpet overlaying a tarn, it seemed as much water as land, billowing and shivering with our every step. I tripped, and nearly fell, but kept running. Our feet, like the ballymag's claws, slapped against the undulating turf. His heavy gasps kept time with our own.

All at once, the ballymag fell silent. He was nowhere to be found! We halted, panting, uncertain what had happened. Had he fainted? Been captured?

"Where are you?" I called.

No answer came.

I turned toward the floating lights, wavering unsteadily on all sides. Now they were almost upon us.

The mournful wailing shifted into echoing peals of harsh, grating laughter. The voices rose, higher and higher, ready to drown us like an evil wave.

Hallia and I bolted, stumbling on the uneven ground. The lights were now so close that I could see my shadow, fleeing before me on the quaking turf. Just as the marsh ghouls seemed to grasp us, we reached a darkened pool. We dashed across—and instantly sank into deep, syrupy muck. We had no chance to cry out, no chance to swim. The ooze closed over my head before I could even take a final breath. I gasped, choking, as mud filled my nose and mouth.

My last thoughts burned with rage and regret. That Hallia, too, would drown. That my sword would never fulfill its destiny. That I, having come so far and sought so much, would lose everything down a forgotten pool in a forsaken marsh.

10

THE WORD

Mud—all around, everywhere. The harder I struggled, the tighter it pressed, eager to swallow me whole. Soon it was all I could feel, sliding over my skin, filling my ears, pushing into my nostrils. Mud, thicker than any blanket, suffocated me.

In the deepening darkness of my mind, I cried out to Hallia, knowing she could not hear. *I wish you hadn't come! I am sorry—so very sorry.* And to the powers of the cosmos, to Dagda himself: *Please, forget me if you must. But save her. Save her.*

A jolt, a sucking sound—then silence. I dropped deeper, thudding into something. Though my head still whirled, my body, it seemed, had landed somewhere. At the bottom of a mountain of grime, no doubt. Too much to move. My arm lay twisted underneath me, crushing my hand, but I lacked the strength to straighten it. I lay still, as still as someone dead and buried. Buried by mud.

Breathe. I needed to breathe. I opened my mouth, more from habit than from hope. I knew that I would only taste mud again, for the very last time. And so I allowed myself to fill with . . . Air! I spat out some mud, forced myself to breathe, coughed, and breathed again. Slowly, slowly, my strength started to return.

In the darkness, I rolled over, freeing my arm. Cautiously, I felt around with my fingers. I was lying on my side, upon something soft. And flexible— bouncy to my touch. When I pressed against it with my hand, it pressed back. And when I pushed my nose into its contours, inhaling its rich aromas, it smelled wet, and lush, and alive.

Scanning with my second sight, I traced the flowing, curving slopes that surrounded me. This could be a cavern, a crystal cave of some kind. Yet the walls of this cavern were so moist, so supple, that its crystals, I sensed, would be different from any I had ever known. Looking closer, I noticed the thin, delicate hairs—each one with a plum-shaped fruit at the top—that covered every surface. Thousands upon thousands of them lined the walls, surrounding me, supporting me.

I realized, with a start, that the hairs were moving. Bending and swaying along numberless pathways, the hairs danced slowly to their own secret music. I felt as if I were inside a river, over whose surface flowed many smaller rivers—each one rippling, each one remarkable. And with their movement came warmth. A deep, soothing warmth that glowed without light, while welcoming the dark.

Feeling whole again, I propped myself up on my elbows. Suddenly, a powerful spasm shook the cavern. The floor supporting me arched, tilted, and sent me sliding downward.

I tumbled down a maze of dark passageways, gliding through countless turns, rolling over slippery flats, and sailing through twisting channels. The slick hairs lining every surface made it impossible to stop. And as my speed gathered, so did my fear. I bounced softly from these walls, as gently as a pebble rolling down a hillside of moss, but what lay at the end? I spread my arms and legs, trying to slow myself down. Yet my speed only increased.

All at once, I broke through an opening. And into light, subtle and shifting. I landed on a springy, resilient cushion, covered with more fruit-tipped hairs, and bounced almost to the ceiling of a high chamber. When I landed, I bounced up again, and again, only gradually slowing to a stop. At last, I managed to sit up.

Only an arm's length away, a round face peered at me. Half of it lay in shadow, and half in the quivering green light that rippled through the chamber. But I could not mistake those whiskers. The ballymag! And behind him, I saw another face—one I had not expected to view again.

"Hallia! You're safe."

"Yes," she said with relief. "As are you."

The ballymag snorted. "Typical manmonster. Noteven a singlebitty kindolous wordothanks."

I tore my gaze from Hallia. "Er, thank you, of course. If you hadn't known about this place . . ." I stroked the moist carpet beneath us. "Where are we, anyway?"

"Questionsask, questionsask," grumbled the ballymag, patting the cushioned floor with two of his unfurled tails. "Inawhile I answerspeak, maybesee. But nowalously, rightmoment for scrubamuck."

My brow furrowed. "Scrubamuck?"

Hallia's gentle laugh echoed among the glowing green walls. "I think I know what he means. And I'd love to."

I shot her a puzzled look, but she only grinned in response.

Bracing himself with all six arms, the ballymag closed his eyes in concentration. He took a deep breath, then started to hum a high, lilting melody. A melody that lifted, curled, and twined, even as his several tails did the same. As the song expanded, so did the light within the chamber. Stronger and brighter it grew—yet without any obvious source.

Where could such light come from? The very air? The song itself? In a flash I understood. The tiny hairs themselves! Each one of them grew more radiant by the second, its fruited cap swelling with light. Meanwhile, the countless hairs continued to stream with motion. So as the walls grew more luminous, they also grew more textured. On every side, they sparkled and flowed, pulsed and danced.

This was, indeed, a crystal cave. Though very different from the one I sometimes dreamed of finding—yes, even inhabiting—one day, it held a marvelous magic of its own. And it was so completely hidden, a surprising secret of the marsh. Might there, I wondered, be others?

The ballymag opened his eyes. His song faded slowly away, the echoes encircling us for some time. As he watched the light play across our mud-streaked faces, he released a grunt that showed no hint at all of satisfaction. Still, while it might have been just a trick of the light, I thought his whiskers turned upward ever so slightly—the hint, perhaps, of a smile.

Then he set to work. Sliding close to one wall, he unfurled all his tails and spread them out like long, slender fingers. Holding them rigid, he brought them very close to the wall, but not so close as to touch it. He held them there, motionless, for a long moment. He seemed to be waiting for something, like a hawk poised to feel the slightest gust of wind on its feathers.

Without warning, the remotest tip of one of the tails quivered. Slowly, ever so slowly, the motion spread down its entire length. Another tail suddenly bent, quaking along its middle. The other tails soon came alive as well. In a few seconds all of them were vibrating, shimmering in the dancing light of the chamber.

In a single snap, the ballymag whipped all the tails into the air. He started whirling them around and around, faster and faster, until they were only a blur of motion. In the middle, a glowing green bowl, larger than the ballymag himself, began to form. The more rapidly the tails spun, the more solid the bowl appeared.

An instant later, the ballymag pulled back his tails. He deftly rolled to the side, just as the gleaming bowl dropped to the soft floor. Hallia and I leaned over its rim, and gasped in unison. For the deep bowl contained a radiant, green fluid, every bit as dazzling as the walls themselves.

"Liquid light," I whispered in amazement. "A bowl of liquid light."

The ballymag scowled. "Whatsomething else forado scrubamuck?" He heaved a sigh. "Oh, painawoe . . . It's my cursafate alwaysever have intruderguests so stupidslow."

With that, he bent his back and threw himself into the air. He landed with a splash in the bowl. Completely oblivious to us, he splattered and scrubbed himself, humming as he did so. At last, he lifted his head, grunted, and pulled himself over the rim. He sprawled on the floor, glitteringly clean.

Next came Hallia. I turned away so that she could undress and bathe with privacy. And I twisted the ballymag's head around so that he did the same. For several delighted minutes, Hallia splashed around. When she finally emerged, she took a moment to wash her purple robe and the band of heather she wore around her wrist. And when she stood before us again, she fairly glowed.

Nevertheless, I hesitated before taking my turn. Unsure what to expect, I cautiously pulled off my boot and dipped my toes into the green liquid. My shadow, even more hesitant, dallied at the edge of the bowl. Suddenly I felt a delicate thrill, like warm rain falling inside my foot. As I pulled off my tunic and leggings and climbed fully inside, I couldn't help but sigh with pleasure. Only then did my shadow finally follow suit, sliding itself into the bowl. By now, my whole body tingled. Not just my skin, but every particle underneath. My bones felt more sturdy, my muscles more responsive, my veins more pure. And the longer I stayed, the deeper the cleansing. Before long, every element of my being felt somehow renewed. Scrubbed, like never before.

In time, I emerged and quickly rinsed my clothes. And also my staff, my leather satchel, and—though it gave me a pang to see it empty—my scabbard, studded with purple gemstones. I marveled at how, despite all the putrid muck we had washed off, the liquid of the bowl shone as clear as ever.

I dressed and gave the ballymag a slight bow. "Whatever magic you used to fill that bowl, and us, with liquid light, it was marvelous indeed. If I didn't thank you properly before, I do now."

His tails curled and uncurled in unison. "Don't flatterwoo me, manmonster."

"It's true," added Hallia, leaning her back against the soft, glistening wall. "You have great magic, as does this place. I've never seen or heard of a spot like this. To think it's right beneath that swamp! It's really the reverse of all that horror above, and yet somehow connected to it, too."

I ran my open hand along the flowing contours of the floor. "It's so lush, so verdant, so rich in here.

Like a garden. No, no, that's not it. More like . . . a womb."

Hallia's eyes danced in the light. "Yes. Like being inside of a womb."

I moved closer to her side. "Even that doesn't quite describe it. Maybe it's just one of those things that simply can't be reduced to a word."

"Wrongfoolish," grumbled the ballymag. "There be a verilous, perfectsay word."

Annoyed, I glared at him. "All right, then. If there is a word, what is it?"

The ballymag's whiskers lifted slightly. "Mooshlovely."

PART TWO

11
A TRAIL MARKED UPON THE HEART

We slept, nestled against the soft walls of the ballymag's underground home. When finally I awoke, however many hours later, I felt pinched with hunger. And painfully stiff in the tender spot between my shoulder blades. As I stretched my arms, Hallia, who was already awake and seated next to the ballymag, handed me a thick brown roll. It was a leaf, stuffed with a doughy substance that smelled like a mixture of honey, nuts—and mud.

Hungry as I was, I took several quick bites. The ballymag, his tails rhythmically coiling and uncoiling, watched me expectantly.

"It's very . . . filling," I said, trying not to offend our host.

"You thankously welcomesay," he replied, proudly

twirling his whiskers. "Thisotreat cametook from winterstores, callit gobblejoy."

"Gobblejoy." I tried, with difficulty, to swallow my mouthful.

"And heretaste for drinksome." Using three claws, the ballymag scooped up a wooden drinking bowl. He rested it on his prominent paunch, which protruded like a shelf. "Makeyou easytime for gulpchew."

"*Mmmff,*" I answered, still trying to swallow the first course.

Hallia took a sip from her own wooden bowl. "It's like spice soup, but cold. Try it."

Taking the bowl, I peered into it cautiously. On the surface of the clear broth, I saw my own wavering reflection. My face, even my hair, had taken on the green hues of the walls around me. Then, bringing the bowl to my lips, I drank. A burst of cloves, or possibly anise, struck my tongue. Then marigold, the low-lying sort that thrives in wet turf; a strong flavor of mushroom; and delicate hints of singing-rush and gingerroot. Lowering the bowl, I looked approvingly at the ballymag.

"Did you collect all the ingredients yourself? From up there, in the swamp?"

Quite suddenly, his customary look of fear returned. His eyes, glistening with green, narrowed slightly. "Somotime soonshort they findcome." The coiled tails lining his spine flexed tightly. "And killoscream horribulously."

I shook my head. "Really, I don't understand." I turned my face toward the ceiling of the chamber, watching the waves of light flow over it like a water-fall. "Why do they want to kill us?"

Hallia, still sipping her soup, grunted. "Because they are marsh ghouls."

"No, no, there's something more. You heard that woman in the forest. They have never acted so viciously before."

"Verilously," intoned the ballymag, giving his whiskers a stroke. "Butathey plentylots viciousmaim now."

Putting down her bowl, Hallia looked sullen. "The ghouls may be worse now, for some reason. But they've always been the bane of the marsh. Even in ancient times, when my people made the trek to the Flaming Tree—even then, marsh ghouls made sure that some never returned."

"Flaming Tree?" I asked. "What is that?"

"A wonder," she answered. "A tree, deep in the heart of the marsh, that was always aflame, since before the first fawn came to run upon this land." Her steady gaze swallowed me. "Long ago, when Fincayrans still wore their wings, the deer people were plentiful. So plentiful that we lived everywhere that grass could grow—even, it is said, on the shores of the Forgotten Island far to the west. Except for one place: this very swamp. But to prove their courage when they reached adulthood, every deer maiden and man came to this place all alone, and spent three full days by the Flaming Tree." She frowned. "Even though the marsh ghouls only stalk by night, they still waylaid many."

"Is that why," I asked gently, "the rite was abandoned?"

Shaking her flowing hair, she looked down at the floor. "That had to do, my father told me, with the same wickedness that cost us all our wings. And while your kind was doomed to remember your fall by the ache within your backs, in the spot where wings might have sprouted, my own kind received a different punishment. For us, the Flaming Tree—symbol of our lost courage and freedom—lurks always in our dreams. Though many generations have passed since deer people trekked there, it is said that any one of us could still find the way, for the trail is forever marked upon our hearts."

Pondering her words, I worked my stiff shoulders. To my dismay, my shadow leaped away from me and started dancing across the luminous walls, turning cartwheels and somersaults, spinning as lightly as a blowing seed. Although no one else seemed to notice its gyrations, I knew that my second sight hadn't deceived me. That shadow, once again, was mocking me! I wished I could tear it away from myself completely. Yes! And cast it into the remotest part of the swamp.

Hallia lifted her head—just as the shadow leaped back to my side. "Now you can see why I'm not surprised by the marsh ghouls' latest behavior. They are terrible creatures. Worthless creatures."

"Worthless?" I bristled at the word. "Are you certain?"

"You don't know them."

"I know enough." I pursed my lips. "Long ago, in

the most desolate land you can imagine, I was very nearly killed by a creature that everyone, including me, considered worthless. But later, when I had the chance to destroy it, I didn't—because I had discovered something about it that was valuable, truly valuable."

Her eyes narrowed in disbelief. "And what creature was that?"

"A dragon." I watched her expression slowly change. "The same dragon who became the father of Gwynnia."

She swallowed. Then, her face full of wonder, she gazed at me for a long moment. "Young hawk, you will make a fine wizard one day."

"So I've been told."

Still observing me, she began braiding her locks. "I didn't mean to upset you. But isn't being a wizard still your dream?"

"Yes, yes. It's just that, these days, everyone else seems to see my dreams more clearly than I do."

She paused in her braiding. "They're still your dreams, you know. Your visions of the future. You can change them if you want to."

"I don't want to! Can't you see? But the future itself, that can change. For years now, whenever I look into the future, what looks back at me is a wizard— and yes, a great wizard. That's what I see. Or, at least, what I *want* to see." I chewed on my lip for a moment. "Yet . . . what if that doesn't turn out to be true? Maybe it was only a false vision to begin with."

"Maybe it was," she replied. "And maybe not."

With a sigh, I said, "We should go now."

Tying off her braid, she nodded in assent.

Suddenly the ballymag leaped into Hallia's lap. His eyes at their widest, he moaned, "Nowoewoe, please! Makedon't mepoorme riskycome. Oh, nowoewoe."

"We won't," she answered, stroking his curved back. Gently, she entwined her fingers with one of his tails. "You've done enough for us already. And you have given us a gift we won't forget."

The ballymag wriggled closer to her and gave a high squeak that echoed in the luminous chamber. "Well . . . truthsay is, you diddo muchously wello-good to savehelp my lifetender." Then, with a glance at me, he clacked two of his claws. "Thoughnearly you maimkilled mepoorme thenafter."

"My apologies." I extended my hand. "If we must part company, then, let's do so as friends."

The ballymag watched me cautiously. Suddenly, in one swift motion, he slapped his tail across my cheek, so hard I fell into the wall. Before I regained my balance, he had jumped off Hallia's lap and van-ished down a thin crevasse in the floor. For a few sec-onds, the sound of his body sliding through moist tunnels came back to us. Then—nothing.

Hallia, her eyes laughing, stroked my cheek. "Something tells me that's not his usual good-bye."

I scowled. "He must save that for his dearest friends."

For a moment, we scanned the glowing surfaces, rippling with shades of green, all around us. When again would we see a place so lush, so alive—yet so near to another place reeking of death and decay?

Then, as one, we turned toward the end of the chamber where a large passageway opened. From the movement of light, I could see that it angled upward. "That's our route, I think. Are you ready?"

"No," came her hushed reply. "But I'm coming anyway."

Together, we entered the passageway. Soon the walls drew closer and the ceiling bent downward, forcing us to crouch. And before long, to crawl. In time, the green illumination of the walls began to fade, overpowered by the tentacles of darkness that probed ever nearer. The air grew rancid, heavy with the smells of things rotting.

At one point, Hallia hesitated, wiping her watering eyes with her sleeve. I started to speak, but her severe glance cut me off. An instant later we were crawling again, moving upward into the gloom. All at once, both of our heads bumped into something. Hard yet flexible, its slimy surface bent to our touch, like the peeling bark of a tree. It was, I realized, a slab of peat. Bracing myself against the wall of the passage, I prepared to push the slippery barrier aside.

Hallia, crouching by my side, squeezed my hand. "Wait. Just a moment longer. Before we go out there."

Under my breath, I cursed, "By the breath of Dagda, I'd rather not leave this place at all."

"I know. Down there, down deep, it's so safe and quiet and, well, complete. I haven't felt that way since . . . long ago, when we sat on that beach together, at the shore of my clan's ancestors. Do you remember?"

I drew a slow, thoughtful breath. "The shore where the threads of mist were woven together."

"By the greatest of the spirits himself," she whispered. "My father used to say that Dagda used as his needle the trail of a falling star. And his weaving became a living, limitless tapestry—containing all the words ever spoken, all the stories ever told. Each thread glowing, richly textured, holding something of words and something else, as well. Something beyond all weaving, beyond all knowing."

Listening to the echo of her words, I wondered about my own story, my own place in the tapestry. Was I a weaver? Or merely a thread? Or perhaps a kind of light within the thread, able somehow to make it glow?

"One day, Hallia, we'll go back to that shore. And to others, as well." I pulled my hand from hers. "Not now, though."

Pressing my shoulders against the soggy mass of peat, I heaved. A sucking, squelching sound erupted. At the same time, muddy water flowed over us. Plus a new wave of odors, more putrid than ever. Sputtering, Hallia crawled out into the swamp. I followed, dropping the slab behind us with a cold splash.

12

ᛏOO SILEᚾᛏ

Quiet lay the marshes—strangely quiet, like a heart at the very edge of beating. Gone were all the wails and moans, as well as the backdrop of pipings and creakings, that we had heard before. Hallia and I traded uncertain glances as we stepped into the swamp, our feet squelching loudly.

Steaming vapors rose all around, tying knots of mist, churning endlessly. Judging from the vague light filtering through the clouds, it seemed to be late afternoon, though it could easily have been some other time of day. While I felt a surge of gratitude that at least some daylight brightened the swamp, keeping the marsh ghouls at bay for the moment, I knew that it wouldn't last long. Soon darkness, thicker than the mud on my boots, would return. As would the ghouls.

We stood in a putrid pool, listening to the eerie quiet. The swamp seemed empty, a lifeless receptacle of molding plants and debris. So different from the vibrant underground world we had left behind! For an instant, I recalled the tingling touch of liquid light on my skin: my forearms, my lower back, the soles of my feet. Then the memory vanished, replaced by the reality of muck oozing inside of my boots.

Hallia stepped closer, sending ripples of slime across the pool. "It's so silent."

"Too silent."

Concentrating hard, I stretched my second sight as far as I could into the swirling vapors. Past the murky pool, banked with peat. Past the moss-splattered boulder where a lone crane perched, never blinking, ready to fly at the first sign of trouble. Past the gnarled tree in the distance, tilting almost to the point of toppling into the marsh grass. The tree shone as white as a skeleton, with only a few shreds of bark on its trunk and a mass of dead leaves clinging to one of its branches.

For the briefest instant I caught the scent of something new. Unlike the rest of the aromas assaulting us, this smell was actually pleasant—almost sweet. Although it vanished before I could be sure that I hadn't just imagined it, the smell reminded me of blossoming flowers. Yes, that was it. Rose blossoms.

Hallia leaned closer. "Where do we go now?"

Again, I tried to gauge the light. It seemed to be growing darker. I smiled sardonically, telling myself that at least for the time being I wouldn't be facing any more trouble from my shadow. What trouble we *would* be facing, though, I didn't want to think about.

"Best we find someplace to wait out the night." I pointed toward the leaning tree. "Over there, beyond that dead tree, is some sort of rise."

"Dry enough to have no snakes?"

"I think so. All I see growing there is some sort of shrubbery, dotted with berries, I think. Red ones."

Hallia followed the line of my gaze. "Your vision is so much better than mine in this mist," she lamented. "I can't even see the tree, let alone what lies beyond."

I sighed, stirring the murky water with my boot. "The most important things that lie beyond, I can't see either."

We started slogging through the muck, our footsteps echoing over the watery terrain. Rather than breaking the silence, our movement seemed to emphasize it, deepen it. After each step, the quiet took hold again, as if its own relentless steps were following just behind ours.

Through the steaming pools we trudged, doing our best to avoid the decaying branches floating there. At one point I saw, hanging from a branch, a single leaf that seemed to glow in the half-light. I paused to watch it swaying slowly, like a long-forgotten flag. Its fleshy interior had almost completely disintegrated, leaving only a delicate tracery of veins. Placing my hand behind it, I marveled at how much I could see through the open places—and yet how much of the shape of the original leaf still remained.

How could so much of it be invisible, and yet visible, at the same time?

Suddenly I heard Hallia groan. I whirled around to see her standing rigid, staring at something at the edge of a murky pool. Slogging to her side, my attention fell to a rotting, dismembered carcass that lay on the peat. What little of the hide remained shone tan and gray. A twisted leg, stripped of all its meat, stretched toward us, its hoof stained with blood.

Hallia groaned again and pressed her face against my shoulder. "A deer, poor thing. How could anyone have done that?"

I merely held her, the image of the glowing leaf now replaced by the gruesome scene before us. In time, without looking back, we started to plod again. Once more, we heard nothing but silence apart from our own movements. But now it seemed clearly the silence of death.

We crossed a mound of peat, which jiggled with our every step, then entered the field of marsh grass surrounding the tilting tree. Stiff stalks brushed against our legs as we approached the tree itself. As Hallia leaned against its trunk, I stood beneath its twisted boughs, trying to find a path we could follow to the rise—and, I hoped, to relative safety. In time, I picked out a suitable route. Pushing aside some brittle grass that reached to my chest, I turned to Hallia.

Suddenly the sharp cry of the crane echoed across the swamp. It lifted off from its perch on the nearby boulder, slapping the fog with its broad, silvery wings. Puzzled at what could have frightened it, I scanned the grasses, but saw nothing. Hallia's eyes told me that she, too, was puzzled, as well as frightened.

We stood rigid, listening. The beating of the crane's wings slowly faded away, swallowed by the silence. Then . . . I thought I heard something else. Merely an echo of the bird's flight? No, this sound seemed closer. Much closer. Rhythmic, like shallow, ragged breathing.

At that instant, something dropped out of the tree and thudded into my back. I fell face-first into the grasses, splattering mud in all directions. Before I could recover, I was tackled by a wiry form shrouded in a mass of torn robes. Over and over we rolled through the muck, each of us vying for control. The layers of tattered robes made my assailant hard to see—and even harder to grasp. At last, I felt my arm wrenched tightly behind my back. A strong hand clamped around my neck.

"Yield," barked a voice, "if you prize your life at all."

Sputtering from all the swamp water I had swallowed, I couldn't respond. The attacker twisted my arm still harder, almost splitting my shoulder in two. Finally, I answered hoarsely, "I . . . ah! Yield."

"Tell your companion to do the same," he commanded.

Quick as a deer, Hallia leaped at us from the trunk of the tree. She plowed straight into our foe, sending him careening into the marsh grass. I jumped to my feet and ran to him. Instinctively, I reached for my sword, expecting to hear the ring of its magical blade. Finding it gone, I cringed, remembering—and drew my staff instead.

Brandishing the staff's knobby handle over the huddled figure, I growled a command of my own. "Now," I declared, "tell us your name."

Hallia planted a bare foot on one of his legs to keep him from wriggling away. "And why you attacked us."

From out of the mass of torn robes, a face slowly lifted. It was not, as I had expected, the face of a warrior goblin. Or that of a grizzled outlaw, bent on harm. No, this face was altogether different, and altogether surprising.

It was the face of a boy.

13

ECTOR

The boy stared at us, his face full of anguish. His cheeks, though smeared with mud, still showed a naturally ruddy complexion. Above his flinty blue eyes, yellow curls dangled—barely visible for all the twigs, bracken, and clumps of mud in his hair. His shredded robes hung from him like wilted petals, making him look like an elderly beggar. Yet he couldn't have been older than twelve.

Still feeling the ache in my shoulder, I waved the staff angrily. "Your name."

"It's, well . . ." He paused, licking his lips. "Ector, sir." Wriggling his leg under Hallia's weight, he said, "And I didn't mean to attack you."

I bristled. "That's a lie."

"I, well . . . meant to attack. But not you." He

scratched his head, shaking loose a cluster of twigs, then gazed at me plaintively. "I didn't know you were a man, you see. I thought you must be a goblin, or something worse." His brow wrinkled as he stared at my staff, and the strange emblems carved upon it. "You're not going to hurt me with that, are you?"

I straightened myself, rubbing my shoulder. "No, though by rights I should show you the same kindness you showed me."

"I'm sorry," declared the boy. "Truly sorry. That was, er, rather rude of me."

Hallia removed her foot from his thigh. "Rather."

I studied him pensively. There was something about this boy—despite my aching frame—that made me feel forgiving. That made me want to give him a second chance, even if he didn't deserve one. I shoved the staff into the belt of my tunic. "I suppose I can understand your confusion, if not your brashness. This swamp is a bit frightening."

Ector lowered his eyes. "That it is."

Extending my hand, I helped him to his feet. "No need to fret, young man. Everyone deserves a chance to make a good healthy mistake now and then. Giants' bones, I've certainly had my share."

His lips quivered in a grin. "You sound like . . ." His words trailed off. "Like someone I know."

"Well, I hope you don't greet him by pouncing out of a tree."

The grin widened. "Only on Tuesdays."

"Good. Let's call this Tuesday, so I'll have at least a week for my poor body to mend."

He eyed me gratefully. "Tuesday it is, then."

"The ways of men are strange indeed," said Hallia. She stepped forward, her bare feet crunching on the stalks of marsh grass. "Yet I will entrust you with my name, as you have told us yours. I am Eo-Lahallia, though my friends know me as Hallia." Tilting her head my way, she added, "And this is young hawk." I started to protest, when she smiled at me and continued. "He goes by other names, as well. But that, I think, is his favorite."

Softly, I replied, "It is indeed."

Ector nodded. "I am glad to meet you, Hallia. And you, young hawk."

I studied the boy's face, hopeful despite the gathering gloom. Why did I feel this strange urge to help him, even protect him? After all, he had tried his best to pummel me only moments ago. Glancing up at the tree where he had been hiding, I wondered whether the feeling stemmed from my own memory of escaping, as a youngster, to the boughs of a tree. Or whether, in fact, it stemmed from something else, something I couldn't quite fathom.

Facing him squarely, I asked, "Whatever brought you to this place? Are you lost?"

He pulled a soggy shaft of fern from his neck. "No—and yes. I came here looking for . . ." He turned aside. "For something I cannot name. I'd tell you if I could, really. But he made me promise."

"Who did?"

"My master."

I lowered my voice a notch. "Then who is your master?"

A sudden wind arose, stirring his tattered robes

and whistling through the grasses. The dead tree, tilting precariously, gave a single, sharp creak.

"Who is it?" I asked again.

"I, well—" Ector bit his lip. "I can't tell you that, either."

Hallia cocked her head suspiciously. "You won't say any more than that?"

Ector shifted nervously, splashing the murky water at his feet. "Well . . . I can tell you I'm lost."

"How forthcoming," I said sarcastically.

Meekly, he added, "I wish I could say more." His blue eyes began to glisten. "Believe me, I don't want to spend another night—another minute—in this wretched swamp. But now it seems I'm going to fail my mission, as well as my master. I just . . . well, I just don't want to fail my word as well."

Taken aback by his sturdy sense of honor, I felt a renewed touch of sympathy. "Keep your secrets, then. But if you won't tell us where you're going, or what you're seeking, we can't be any help to you."

The boy worked his tongue as if he were about to say something. Then, catching himself, he swallowed. "Then I must do without your help." He tried to square his shoulders. "Would you, though, tell me just one thing?"

"It depends."

He glanced worriedly at the rising vapors. The darkening mist churned, clutching at our legs, entwining about our arms. His voice a whisper, he said, "A few minutes before you appeared, the whole swamp went suddenly quiet. Hear it now? Not even a peeping frog, let alone some of those other, er, noises. That's when I climbed the tree." His youthful brow furrowed. "Do you know why it happened? What it means?"

"No. But I'd wager it means trouble."

Hallia cocked her head, listening to the silence. "Feels like an enchantment to me. An evil enchantment."

Ector drew an anxious breath. "Perhaps," he asked hopefully, "we could travel together for a little while?"

I shook my head. "Our work is too dangerous. If you stay with us, it could be your ruin."

"And besides," added Hallia with an edge, "we'd need to know more about you. Much more."

Sensing her distrust, I felt a pang in my chest. Yet as much as I was drawn to the boy, I knew she was right. What really did I know about him? Except that he had jumped me from a branch? Resignedly, I extended my hand toward him. "Good luck to you, Ector."

He nodded morosely. Slowly, he lifted his hand and clasped my own. Despite his smaller size, he squeezed firmly, trying not to let his fear show through. In a determined tone, he said, "All right then. I've lasted a few days alone in this place already, and I can last a few more."

Though I could tell he felt less brave than he sounded, I said nothing. He turned and strode off, his torn robes swishing against the grasses, heading in the opposite direction from the rise that had caught my interest.

"Careful," I called after him. "Night will be falling soon."

Without turning around, he waved a hand.

"He's one courageous lad," I muttered, watching him trudge away.

"One devious lad, if you ask me." Hallia's eyes followed the shadowy figure as he disappeared into the mist. "I think we're well rid of him."

"Secretive, yes," I replied. "But devious? I'm not so sure. It's true, he could be someone who can't be trusted. Or he could be . . ."

"What?"

"Someone who just loves his master deeply. So deeply he'd do anything for him—even if it means wandering in this bog all alone."

"*Hmmff,*" she sniffed. "Deer who can't share their true motives can't run together."

By now no sign of the boy remained. I peered after him, but saw only veils of mist, ever swirling. Then, gradually, I noticed a change. Not in the marshlands, which remained as still and silent as before, but in the mist itself. While I watched, its once-fluid movements grew steadily more brittle. The clouds seemed to tense, their stillness of motion joining with the stillness of sound in the marsh.

The next instant, a harsh, buzzing noise erupted. As the silence broke, the vapors started to swirl again. Hallia and I shrank back toward the tilting tree. The noise seemed to come from everywhere at once, from the vapors as much as the land itself. Slowly, it grew more intense, more jarring—and more loud. And with it, though I could have been

mistaken, came the vaguest scent of something
sweet. As sweet as rose blossoms.

Suddenly, out of the darkening clouds burst a
swarm of enormous beetles, each of them as big as
my own head. I had barely enough time to whip out
my staff before they descended. Jagged, transparent
wings sliced at the air, while sharp claws raked at our
exposed skin. The beetles attacked from every angle,
buzzing so loud that I could hardly hear my own
thoughts.

Swatting wildly with my staff, I managed to smash
one as it dived at my face. Its purple armor, glinting
darkly, flew apart as the beetle plunged into the
muck. Hardly had I raised the staff again, though,
when three more of them were buzzing me, clawing
at my hands and eyes.

Hallia shrieked, falling backward against the tree.
A pair of beetles darted around her flailing arms,
seeking an opening to her face. I turned away from
my own attackers and swung with the staff. I felt a
thud—and one of the beetles spun into the marsh.
But there was no chance for elation. In just a fraction
of a second, the other beetle would break through.
And I had no time for another swing!

The beetle dived at Hallia. Its wings struck her
forearm, cutting her skin. Blood spurted. She jerked
her arm back, leaving half of her face exposed. Veer-
ing sharply, the beetle flew straight at her eyes.

Suddenly I heard a high, whizzing sound. Then a
splat—and the beetle exploded in the air only a hair's
breadth from Hallia's face. Purple fragments of shell
drifted down into the marsh grass. I whirled about to

see Ector, his eyes alight, holding a rough-hewn slingshot.

"Watch out!" he cried.

A beetle's sharp claws scraped my ear. I shouted and swung my hand. The blow connected, knocking the creature away—right onto my chest. Buzzing wrathfully, the beetle arched its back, revealing a mammoth, barbed stinger. The size of my fist, it lifted, ready to strike.

At the same moment, several other beetles swarmed at me. Pushing close, jabbing at my face. In desperation, I called to the deepest part of myself: the place most calm, even under such an assault; the place most primal, and mysterious, and close to the elements. *Air around us!* I cried, summoning all my will. *Throw them. Hurl them away. Far away from here!*

A sudden gust whipped the air. Buzzing frantically, the beetles fought against the whirling wind. Their wings screamed, their claws sliced, but to no avail. The wind was far too strong, tearing them away from our huddled bodies.

The beetle on my chest, clutching at my tunic, resisted a sliver of a second longer than the rest. And in that instant, it plunged its stinger down toward my ribs. I winced, expecting to feel it pierce my skin, but to my shock—and relief—the stinger halted, just above my tunic. From its barbed tip flowed a thin, gold line, as wispy as the thread of a spider. The thread expanded, flashing in the air as it coiled itself into a loop. Then, as quickly as it had appeared, the loop melted into the folds of my tunic. I felt nothing.

It happened so quickly, I was not really certain what I had seen.

Howling angrily, the wind tore the beetle from my flapping tunic. Swirling air bore the attacker, together with the rest of the swarm, in a frenzied mass over the marsh. Flying upside down, wings splayed, or jumbled on top of each other, the beetles vanished into the fog. Their buzzing soon faded away completely.

I felt suddenly weak. My legs buckled, and I dropped into a shallow pool of water. Marsh grass jabbed at my face, but I lacked the strength to brush it away. It was all I could do to remain sitting up.

Hallia rushed to my side. She lay her hand over my brow. "Are you hurt?"

"Not . . . seriously. I—I just feel . . . weak."

"You must have thrown all your strength into making that wind." Her voice, while gentle, seemed anxious as well. "You should rest awhile."

"That was quite a trick." Ector plodded over, kicking a half-submerged branch out of his way. "I'm not sure even my master, who makes his own magic sometimes, could have done that."

Hallia kept her gaze on me, but spoke to the boy. "And your slingshot—that, too, was quite a trick." She looked his way just long enough for her eyes to say thanks. "You didn't have to come back."

Replacing the weapon inside his torn robes, he shrugged modestly. "I always enjoy a little practice with this thing."

Weakly, I smiled at him.

Hallia stroked my brow. "I am worried, young hawk. You feel . . . wrong somehow."

"I'm fine. Just drained." Feeling a slight prick in my ribs, I remembered the beetle's strange behavior. "Nothing worse happened than one of those beetles . . ."

"Stung you?"

"N-no. Not exactly." I pulled open my tunic. There, on my ribs, lay the loop of golden thread. Stretched flat, it was about as large as my hand. It quivered slightly on my skin, as if it were alive. Something struck me as odd: I hadn't noticed any hole where it had passed through my tunic.

Hallia gasped. The color drained from her cheeks. Tensely, she reached her hand toward the loop. Her long fingers knitted the air as they approached. Just as she was about to grasp it, the golden filament stirred, twisted, and wriggled downward. It buried itself in my skin, leaving no mark.

A jolt of pain shot through me. I cried out and clutched my rib cage. Hallia's fingers scraped at my skin. All too late. The loop had vanished, working its way deeper into my chest.

14

†HE BLOODΠOOSE

The loop sank further into me. I could feel it melting into my skin, slipping between my ribs. And I felt certain—though I had no notion how—that it was heading for my heart.

With all my concentration, I tried to muster the power to stop it. Yet, as drained as I was, I couldn't find the strength. Whatever magic I sensed instantly slipped away from me, faster than the very winds I had conjured. I couldn't stop the loop's progress. Nor even, I feared, slow it down. All the while, I could feel it working its way deeper and deeper into me.

I gazed at Hallia, her frightened eyes the mirror of my own. "What is it?"

"I think . . . it's what my father called a bloodnoose."

Ector, bending over my chest, caught his breath. He ran a hand through his mud-clotted curls, frowning deeply.

Bloodnoose. The very sound of the word made me shudder. I reached over to the leather pouch on my hip and tapped it. "Will any of my . . . healing herbs . . . help?"

Hallia's head lowered. "No. The bloodnoose, once inside you, moves rapidly. There's no way to stop it." She took an uneven breath and looked at me. "When it finally reaches your inner chest, it wraps itself around your heart. Then it squeezes tightly, until—"

"My heart . . . splits in two?"

She nodded, her eyes brimming. "I don't want to tell you what my father said about the victim's agony. Just that . . . oh, young hawk! That dying is the better part of it."

The curling vapors of the swamp thickened. The dead tree, leaning so close to our heads, seemed to withdraw farther and farther into the mist. Night, I knew, would come soon.

Gently, Ector touched my ribs. "You are very brave. It must feel terrible." He started to say something else, but cut himself off. "I just wish I could do something."

"Your slingshot," I said feebly, "can't do much for me now."

Again he started to speak, struggled with his words, then abandoned them. All the while, his hand remained on my ribs, anxiously stroking the skin. At length, his agonized expression faded, giving way to one of resolve. "Wait," he said, fumbling in his robe. "This might help."

He produced a small vial, burgundy in color. Pulling out the cork, he carried it closer. A pungent, slightly burned aroma filled the air. Hallia, looking alarmed, reached out her arm to block him. For a breathless moment, she held him in her gaze.

"It's an elixir," he explained. "Something my master gave me, in case I got hurt on this, ah, errand. He told me to use it only in gravest peril—and warned that it can't outright heal a bad wound. But it could win some time. Enough time, perhaps, to find a proper cure."

Hallia ground her teeth. "And if it doesn't work?"

"Then he'll be no worse off."

Another spasm of pain struck me. Groaning, I clawed at my chest.

"Please," Ector urged me. "Drink some. It might help."

I peered at his earnest face. Even in the deepening darkness, his eyes glowed with youthful passion. "No, no. I can't let you do that. What if you should need it later . . . for yourself?"

He answered firmly, "I think it should be used when it's most needed."

At last, Hallia lowered her arm. The boy knelt in the shallow pool, bringing the vial to my lips. This time, I didn't protest. Very slowly, he poured the burgundy liquid into me. It tasted like charcoal from an old fire. But I kept swallowing, even as I grimaced. In a few seconds the vial was completely empty.

Even as Ector withdrew, a subtle thrill, like taking a first breath of crisp morning air, coursed through my chest. Upward and outward it spread, filling my middle with new, pulsing warmth. The feeling spread rapidly through my whole body. I felt lighter—and sturdier. Fresh rivers of blood raced through my limbs. My fists clenched, feeling their former strength return.

Hallia smiled, wiping her eyes. She threw her arms around my head and held me, squeezing tight. In time, she released her embrace and turned to Ector. "We are grateful," was all she could manage to say.

"Very grateful," I added.

The boy grinned shyly. "Just say it's an apology for what I did to you before."

I reached for my staff, half buried in muck. With a sharp tug, I pulled it free, though its top now bore a thick earthworm. Shaking the passenger loose, I grasped the gnarled top and clambered to my feet. I faced Ector. "Apology accepted."

"How long," asked Hallia, "will your elixir last?"

His expression clouded. "I don't know, but I have a feeling it's not very long."

Taking my hand, Hallia probed me with her gaze. "This is your chance, young hawk, to save yourself. Come. Leave your sword for later. With any luck, we can find our way out of this marsh before the chance has flown."

I looked down at my empty scabbard. Even in the dim light, the purple gemstones glittered. It was the scabbard of a magical sword, the sword of a wizard—and a king. *A king whose reign shall thrive in the heart long after it has withered on the land.*

"No," I said, my hand tightening around hers. "I can't do that. Especially not now. Hallia, there's something wicked, utterly wicked, happening in this marsh. Unlike anything that's been going on before. And my sword is only part of it. I know that now, as surely as I know your face. What it really is, I can't quite name, but I have the strange feeling that it's something I've met somewhere before."

She pulled her hand away. "You can't do much good if you're not alive! If we can just get to Cairpré—or your mother, the healer—they might still be able to save you. Then you can come back here if you choose."

"It may be too late by then."

Her eyes narrowed. "Whose expectations are you trying to meet, young hawk?"

I sucked in my breath. "My own."

She frowned at me, her eyes full of doubt.

Leaning on my staff, I scanned the steaming decay surrounding us. And I noticed, for the first time, that the sounds of the swamp had started to return. Over there, a strange bleating. And there, a deep-throated burbling. A series of low, moaning howls echoed across the marshlands. Soon, I knew, they would be joined by other sounds. And by other things.

"Come," I declared. "We need to find shelter before nightfall." I nodded at Ector. "And by *we,* I mean to include you. Will you travel with us?"

Thoughtfully, he rubbed his chin. "For a time."

Hallia brushed my chest lightly with the back of her hand. "And does *we* still include me?"

"Of course—that is, if it's what you choose."

She blinked her round eyes. "It's what I choose."

"Then let's go." I pointed toward the bush-covered rise, now just a dark hump against a background nearly as dark. "Let's hope those shrubs are thick enough to hide us."

I started off, followed closely by the others. Stretching my second sight as far as I could, I led them through the marsh grass to a narrow mound of peat that wound its way through the thickening fog. At one point we passed a pile of loose, jagged stones, whose cracks revealed a pair of thin yellow eyes that watched us closely. Cautiously, we moved past. Though the peat, unlike the softer mud around us, didn't suck at our every step, it remained wet enough to form tiny pools of water in our footprints. Once, as I paused to wait for the others, I watched the string of watery prints behind us gradually fade away. In a moment's time, they melted into the land as completely as one spiral of mist melts into another.

At the edge of the peat mound, I spotted a twisted vine with curling leaves. Nearly buried in the mud at its base lay a squarish vegetable, reddish-purple in color, that seemed quite familiar. Suddenly I remembered the time I had seen, and eaten, one just like it. My mouth watered. How marvelous it had tasted! Even so, I hesitated. What if it wasn't really the same vegetable? In the end, my churning stomach prevailed and I reached over, plucked it, and placed it into my satchel.

As we pressed ahead, the rise grew more prominent. Drawing nearer, I realized that what I had taken for shrubs covering it were actually low, densely branching trees. Their trunks, where they showed at all through the mass of branches, looked as stout as giants' toes; their bark, as deeply wrinkled as my own leather boots. What had, from a distance, looked like red berries, I saw now were the red undersides of their leaves.

At the end of the winding mound of peat, we came to the edge of a wide, slimy pool. Even in the gathering shadows, I could tell that it bubbled and stirred ominously. Crossing its dark green expanse was surely the shortest route to the rise, but I didn't particularly like its look—or smell. Still, with night fast approaching, going straight across could save precious time.

Cautiously, I tested its depth with my staff. It seemed shallow enough. I stepped forward. Although fluid seeped into my boots, the bottom held firm, seeming slippery but passable. I traded glances with my companions, then took another step.

Whatever I stepped on moved, slithering into the reeds at the pool's edge. I jumped back, but lost my footing. With a splash, I landed on my side in the slimy water. Then, to my horror, I felt something wrap around my leg. It hardened, like a flexing arm, then pulled me deeper into the pool, dragging me downward.

"Something has me!"

Hallia and Ector leaped to my aid. They grabbed me by the arms and tugged hard. Whatever held me, though, tugged back. Ector's boots slipped on the peat, causing him to fall to his knees. Still he kept pulling. Hallia's braid lashed her shoulders and back as she twisted this way and that.

At last I broke free. We toppled backward, falling in a heap on the soggy ground. For some time we just lay there, panting, while thick vapors curled above our bodies. Finally I shook the mud from my hair and sat up. Noticing the slick black ooze that covered my lower leg, I scraped away as much as I could with the base of my staff.

Wordlessly, we helped each other to our feet and set off again, working our way around the pool. The last light faded swiftly, as the swamp noises swelled around us. Fog swirled, opening into dark mouths with shifting teeth and vaporous tongues. Dead branches caught on our clothing and scraped our shins. Yet such obstacles did not concern me. For I had noticed an eerie glimmering at the edges of my vision. A glimmering that grew stronger by the minute.

At last we reached the rise. Although not very high, it was, as I had hoped, drier than the surrounding marshes. But my heart sank. There was no clear pathway to higher ground! The thick stand of trees formed a tight mesh of branches, so closely woven that even my second sight could not see past the outer rim. Only a few gaps in the growth gave glimpses of the woody tunnels among the trees. Tunnels . . . The idea made me start. Perhaps we could still find shelter here after all.

Hallia grabbed my shoulder. "Those lights!

They're coming this way. It's the marsh ghouls, I'm sure!"

An eerie, anguished shriek arose from the marsh. It was followed by another, and another.

"Come quickly." I darted to the trees. Stepping over the burly roots, I led the others to a narrow gap in the branches. "Careful, now. These thorns look murderous."

More of the chilling cries rose behind us as we ducked into the narrow tunnel. Instantly, darkness overwhelmed us, along with the scent of fir cones, sharp and sweet. The tunnel bent to the left, toward the center of the stand, then right, then left again. Whenever it forked, I chose the most difficult passage, hoping it might afford more protection. As I crawled deeper, thorns ripped at my tunic, stabbed at my knees, neck, and shoulders. Behind me, Ector gave a shout of pain. More than once, Hallia's fist pounded the ground like a doe stamping angrily with her hoof.

We reached, at length, a wide place in the tunnel. Four or five of the gnarled, grooved trunks surrounded us. The ceiling of thorns was too low for us to stand, but left plenty of space for sitting or kneeling. I guessed that we had arrived near the center of the cluster of trees.

I leaned back against one of the trunks, licking a cut on the back of my wrist. "Well, here is our accommodation for the night."

"I've had worse," offered Ector, pulling his robes around his battered shins.

Hallia curled herself, like a fawn, in a hollow

among the roots. "Yes, this will do fine." She touched my thigh. "How are you feeling?"

"Well enough."

"All we need," said Ector in the darkness, "is a bit of supper."

Remembering the vegetable, I pulled it out of my leather satchel. A bit crushed though it was, its skin remained intact. I broke off a section, brought it to my nose, and smelled. At once, I recognized the robust aroma, as rich as meat roasting over a fire.

"What's that smell?" asked the boy.

"Our supper," I replied. "It's a vegetable used by the bakers in Slantos, far to the north, to make one of their special breads. I found it in the marsh."

Hallia slid closer. "Do you trust it?"

I broke open the juicy vegetable, then licked my fingers. "I'm too hungry to doubt. And besides, I could never forget this smell."

Handing each of them a section, I then proceeded to extract the wide, flat seed from the center. Even in the dark, my second sight glimpsed its deep red sheen. Placing it on the ground, I struck it with the base of my staff, cracking it into pieces. These I distributed around, but not before popping a few into my own mouth. As I chewed, the bits of seed burst apart, exploding with flavor. As well as something more, something that made me feel that I would, in fact, regain my sword—and live to wield it once again.

"*Mmm,* good flavor," commented Ector, a river of juice dribbling down his chin. "The bread must be wonderful."

"It is," I replied. "The people of Slantos say it can fill your heart with courage."

"I like it more and more," said Hallia, chewing avidly. "That's what we really need."

"Right," agreed Ector, breathing a heavy sigh. "Courage to face the future."

I handed him another section. "The future can be frightening, can't it?"

"In a place like this most of all, young hawk. Where every step you take means . . . choices. Hard choices." He took another bite and chewed thoughtfully. "So whichever path you choose, it's bound to be partly right and partly wrong."

I nodded. "Life itself often feels that way to me: unfamiliar trails, shrouded in mist so thick you can hardly see what choices you really have." I swallowed my own mouthful. "I suppose all you can do, all any of us can do, is try to do the best we can."

"Despite the mist?" he asked plaintively.

"Despite the mist."

"But what if . . ." His words trailed off. "What if the choice before you is clear, but it's simply impossible? Say you're trying to help someone, maybe someone you love a lot—and yet if you succeed in helping him it means that you can't, well, help someone else. Someone who also deserves to be helped. What do you do then?"

Stretching out my hand, I clasped one of his ankles. "I don't know what it is you're searching for, Ector, or who it is you're trying to help."

He stirred, at the very edge of speaking, but held himself back.

"And yet," I went on, "I can tell you one thing with certainty. Whatever difficult times the future holds in store for you, this thing will never change." My voice deepened. "You have helped someone, beyond any doubt, on this day. And Ector . . . I will never forget it."

Silently, he nodded, even tried to smile. Yet underneath his face remained grim. While I could tell that my words had touched him, they hadn't lightened his burden as I had hoped. Could it be, I wondered, that he knew something more about the future than he could reveal?

At length he placed his smaller hand on top of mine. "I'm glad you found these trees, young hawk. And I'm also glad you found me."

For a long moment, we said nothing. In time I lifted my arms toward the ceiling of thorns, trying to stretch my back. "I suppose we should try to sleep a little. Trouble is, I don't feel sleepy."

"Nor do I," he agreed.

"Nor I," whispered Hallia, shifting her weight among the roots. "Especially with all that wailing and howling, muffled as it is, going on out there."

"For me," I confessed, "those sounds aren't as troubling as . . ."

"The bloodnoose?" she asked sympathetically.

"Yes, cursed thing! I can't help but wonder when the elixir is going to run out. And what that will feel like."

"What we really need," suggested Ector, "is a good story. The kind that can take your mind off, well, everything else."

"I know a gifted storyteller," I volunteered. "Someone who grew up in a clan whose life is rich with all manner of tales." I nudged Hallia's thigh. "Would you?"

"Yes, please," echoed the boy. "Would you?"

She drew a long, slow breath. "Well, I suppose." For a moment, she looked at the ground, thinking, before raising her head again. "All right then," she said at last. "I shall tell you a story, famous among my people. It is the story of a girl named Shallia. And it is a tale about mist, about friendship, and about choices. Impossible choices."

She sat, legs crossed and hands resting in her lap, gazing at the wall of branches. It seemed, by her expression, that she could see right through the sheltering trees into the swirling clouds beyond. Then she began, her voice as smooth as an evening breeze by the sea: "Hear me now, for I shall tell you *The Tale of the Whispering Mist.*"

15
THE TALE OF THE WHISPERING MIST

By a faraway shore on a faraway sea, the mist rises nightly from star-shining waves. Over the darkening sea it spreads, stretching thin, wispy fingers out to the land. And on this night, as on so many nights before, the mist reaches first to touch a single place, a single rock—the rock still remembered as Shallia's Stone.

For there Shallia came often.

Legs dangling from the rock's edge, she would sit hour after hour. To watch the sun plunge into the sea, or the stars swim like luminous minnows through the eel-black sky. To feel the first curls of mist touch her toes. And, above all, to listen: to the slap of waves and the cry of gulls; to the spray of whales, heaving breaths as deep as the waters themselves; and, on some nights, to another sound—unlike waves, unlike whales—a mysterious whispering that seemed almost alive.

The whispering, somehow, made her recall her youngest years, her gladdest years. Although she had never known her mother, who had been taken by the gods of Sea and Shore while giving birth, her father had stayed always near. How they had laughed when they leaped into the waves, uncovered clams together, and chased each other through the pools of flashing fish at low tide! How they had lived, utterly one with the waves and themselves.

Until that day it had all ended—the memories drowned, like her father, after he stepped on the spines of a poisonous spike-fish hidden in the shallows.

Taken in by her grandmother, Shallia moved to a mud hut at the outskirts of the village. She had no brothers or sisters, no friends her own age. Yet as much as she longed for companionship, she kept to herself. She felt no room in her heart for anything but loneliness—and the unending longing to sit by the sea.

"Don't stay all alone by the water," her grandmother warned. "Especially at night. For that, my child, is when the sea ghouls come closest to shore."

Sea ghouls, the old woman explained, lived in the shadowy realm between water and air. More dangerous than a circle of spike-fish, they could take any shape they chose, much like the mist itself. They could drive people mad, and often did. Many were the tales of villagers who, lingering too long after dark, had been lured into the waves by sea ghouls.

Carried off by the currents, they were never found alive—or never found at all. Only their footprints in the sand remained, fading with the moonlight.

Shallia had heard all the stories. But she had also heard, much more clearly, the faraway call of the waves. How could that whispering, soothing enough to wash away her grief for a while, be dangerous? Just to think of closing her ears to that sound made her feel sad, more lonely than ever. And so every night, when her grandmother slept, Shallia stole silently down to the shore.

Every night she sat there, watching, as liquid darkness poured into the great bowl of the sea. Sometimes she closed her eyes and imagined her mother and father returning to her, stepping out of the shallows. Or a true friend, someone who knew her so well that they would need no words at all to know each other's thoughts. Yet she knew these were only dreams, no more real than her grandmother's tales.

One night, Shallia followed the full moon's path down to the sea, stepping over broken shells and shards of driftwood. As the turf gave way to sand, a huge wave slammed against the shore, pounding like thunder. Slowly the wave withdrew, sloshing over the reef. Shallia saw that her rock, wet with spray, glowed eerily.

She climbed onto her barnacle-covered seat. Moonlight sparkled on the waves; manes of mist streamed from every crest. The briny breeze tousled Shallia's curls, and she shivered. Not so much from the evening chill as from something else, a feeling she couldn't quite name. Part uncertainty, part hope, part dread.

She gazed at the open ocean. Tonight the mist churned even more than the water, forming into wild, phantomlike shapes before shredding again into nothing. She saw a moonbeam strike a spiral of mist, revealing—for half an instant—shapes within the shapes, shadows within the shadows. And always, from somewhere out there, the continuous whispering swelled and faded.

Then a dark, lumbering mass of mist gathered in the distance. Shallia watched, her heart racing, as it started to rush toward shore. Toward her. The whispering grew louder and louder, drowning out the surging sea. She tensed. Should she leap off her perch and run back to the hut? But her fingers only clutched the stone more tightly.

The dark mass approached, leaning into the land. Great, writhing arms protruded from its face, reaching out, stretching toward Shallia. The whispering became a rumble, the rumble a roar.

Suddenly, the whole mass stopped. Mist hovered over the lone girl, embracing her, quivering slightly where its edges melted into the air. Yet the mist came no closer, never touching her, just as it never quite touched the beach.

At the same moment, the full moon's light cut through the vapors. There, deep within the curled arms of mist, Shallia saw other arms: more delicate, more wispy, more . . . like her own. With elbows. And hands. And long, slender fingers. Fingers that moved! One misty hand, shimmering with moonlight, reached up to comb strands of flowing, silvery hair. Then a shoulder appeared, a neck, and a face—the face of a tall, glistening girl standing inside the mist.

Shallia started, almost tumbling off the stone. In response, the mist maiden turned sharply, placed her hands upon her hips, and gazed through the vaporous window that separated them. Her eyes, gleaming like starlight on the waves, fixed on Shallia's. For an instant, the whispering ceased, as if the sea itself were holding its breath.

All at once, the mist maiden threw back her head—and laughed. Although Shallia couldn't hear her voice, she clearly felt her mirth. In her own bones, in her own veins, in her own mortal flesh. And then Shallia, without thinking, did something she had not done for a very, very long time.

She laughed out loud.

The mist maiden nodded her head, raining moonlight on her shoulders. As she placed a silvery hand upon her chest, the whispering resumed, swelling into a sound like *Maaalaaashhhaaa.*

Slowly, her skin tingling, Shallia rose and stood upon her stone. "Malasha," she repeated. Then, touching her own chest, she uttered her own name.

Shhhaaaliaaa, echoed the mist.

With a sweep of her hand, as graceful as a wave rolling over a reef, Malasha beckoned toward the beach. Shallia hesitated briefly, then clambered down from her perch. As she stepped on the coarse, wet sand, she left deep footprints in her wake. Meanwhile, Malasha moved in the same direction, always staying within the wall of mist, leaving no footprints at all.

Walking parallel to each other, the two girls followed the shoreline. Shallia sensed somehow that her companion could not leave the shroud of rippling vapors, just as she herself could not move beyond her own, more solid world. Yet even though mist and sand could never merge, they still could touch—almost.

Speaking no words, the pair wandered down the beach together. When Shallia picked up a spiraling conch shell, turning it over in her hand, Malasha bent to gather something of her own. It looked like a sinuous, glowing ribbon: a mist-serpent, perhaps, or some sort of plant made of air and light and half-remembered dream. Intrigued, Shallia traced the shape of a circle in the wet sand at her feet, whereupon her companion drew a luminous circle in the mist itself.

And, once again, both of them laughed.

Malasha turned and padded silently through the folds of mist, lifting her hands as if to feel some invisible spray. And Shallia followed, her feet slapping the shallow pools on her side of the boundary.

Suddenly Shallia spied a sea turtle laboring to dig a nest in the sand. As she halted, bending nearer, Malasha halted, too, leaning as close as possible to the turtle's bright eyes and mottled shell. For some time, the mist maiden watched in fascination—as well as frustration. Shallia knew that her companion wanted to break through the wall of mist, to walk between their worlds. For Shallia wanted the very same.

All evening long, the two girls explored the edges of their shared shore. They leaped like dolphins in the moonlight, chased spinning stars of mist, strutted sideways with crabs, tried to grasp at moonbeams. And whenever one of them had a new idea, the other readily understood. With no words at all.

As the yellowing moon dropped nearer to the horizon, the evening light shifted. The undulating wall of mist turned from silver to gold, gilding the hair of both girls, and the wings of a passing gull. Shallia sat on a tangle of driftwood, watching the glowing mist and her newfound friend within it. The whispering swelled a bit, caressing her with soothing sound. She felt so different than she had only a few hours before. Glad—no, more than glad. Revived, in truth. Like a parched voyager, finally given water.

And yet . . . while she and Malasha had found each other, they couldn't truly share each other's lives. They couldn't speak. They couldn't touch. Over her shoulder, Shallia glanced at the setting moon. The trees lining the beach shimmered with golden light, no less than the mist. If rays of moonlight could pass between the worlds, why couldn't she do the same?

Shallia sighed, filling her lungs with cool, salty air. Even as she exhaled, she saw Malasha tilt back her head and lift her chest, as if she, too, were sighing. Just then, a great whale spouted somewhere in the distance, drawing a deep, full breath of his own.

A smile slowly spread over the two girls' faces. Though they could not share the same world, their worlds shared the same air. And so did they. For the breath of the whale, and the gull, and all the creatures of the sea—was their own breath, as well.

For a long moment they gazed at each other, breathing in unison. Their bond pulled stronger than ever, yet so did their longing for more. Then Malasha, wrapped in mist, took a step nearer. She leaned into the vaporous wall, pushing it aside, tearing it apart with her hands.

Hope and fear raced through Shallia, faster than a pod of dolphins leaping through the waves. "To me! She's coming to me."

The whispering of the waves grew louder and shriller. Malasha hesitated for an instant, then continued tearing at the barrier between the worlds. Anxiously, Shallia stood. Walking to the very edge of the beach, she reached into the mist, hoping to clasp the hand of her friend in her own.

All of a sudden Malasha's eyes widened, her face contorted in pain. She clasped her foot and tumbled backward into the swirling vapors.

"Malasha!" cried Shallia.

No answer came but the rising whispers, even more shrill than before. The wall of mist shuddered, darkened, and started to shred. As Shallia watched, dumbfounded, the misty curtain melted away—vanished completely, along with her friend.

The whispering ceased. All that remained upon the waves were the last golden rays of the vanishing moon. Seconds later that, too, disappeared. In deepest darkness, Shallia stood alone on the beach. She called. She stomped on the sand. And then she fell to her knees, sobbing.

Every evening thereafter, Shallia returned to her stone, watching the waves until dawn. She saw no more mist, heard no more whispers. Yet night after night she continued her vigil. She no longer cared if her grandmother discovered her hideaway. Or if some angry wave rose out of the sea and swept her away. She cared only about finding again what she had known for an instant—then lost.

"Malasha, where are you?" she called over and over again to the sea.

But her friend never answered.

One night, as a crescent moon lifted, hooking the edge of the horizon, Shallia sat alone. She had already lost so much in her life. And now Malasha, too. Her fists clenched. She wouldn't allow that to happen. She wouldn't! But what could she do? She had no idea, except that she would pass through a sea of spike-fish—through the very mist itself—if that were the only way.

She bit her lip. Through the mist itself . . .

Slowly, she stood upon her stone, raising her arms to the sea. "Come for me, please! Take me to my friend."

The sea, as always, gave no response. Shallia's arms fell to her sides. Dejectedly, she turned to leave. Then, one last time, she glanced at the ocean.

In the distance, a long arm of mist, as pale and slender as the moon itself, lifted out of the waves. Soon it was joined by another, then another. The wispy arms began thrashing about, raking the sky, as if whipped by a violent storm. Yet there was no storm, at least none that could be seen.

Suddenly a wave of mist lifted above the water, growing taller by the second as it rushed toward the shore, toward the stone—and Shallia. Just as it reached her, the great, shimmering wall arched forward, curling over her upturned face. Then it plunged downward, submerging her completely.

All at once the churning mist shredded into nothing. The air grew calm, as did the sea. But Shallia was not there to see the change. For her stone had been swept clean.

Shallia found herself sitting on a strange, soft hillside. A gentle wind, smelling of salt, tousled her hair. The ground, if it could be called ground, felt as moist as moss after a rain, and so supple that her hand could almost pass through it. Before her stretched a swirling, shifting landscape. Ridges rose and fell like foaming waves, canyons yawned and closed and opened again, and colorful clouds glowed like melting rainbows.

Then she noticed an eerie sound, rising from all around her. Its slow, sweeping rhythm reminded her of waves washing ashore. Yet this sound was deeper, richer—full of feeling, like a thousand voices chanting in unison. Like something she had heard in another land, another world.

Where, she wondered, had she heard that chanting before?

The air around her shimmered, as silvery shapes began to form on every side. Shallia leaped to her feet, unsure whether to stand or run, or where indeed she might go if she ran. Swiftly the shapes thickened into people, tall and somber. They stood in a circle, gathered around something she could not see. Softly they sang, adding their voices to the rhythmic song— a song that grew more sad, more longing, with every note.

One of them, a man whose cloak fluttered as gracefully as fronds of kelp, turned to face her. For a long moment, he observed Shallia. At last he spoke, his deep voice trembling like an underwater bell. "Child of the hardened world, I did not wish to bring you here. But my daughter, who calls you friend, did. And though I doubted the wisdom of doing so, I could not bear to refuse her."

"Malasha?" Her bare feet sinking into the moist ground, Shallia stepped nearer. "You are her father?"

The man's mouth pinched, even as the despairing chant swelled a little louder. "Yes. And her father I shall remain, even after she dies."

His words struck Shallia like an icy wave. "Not again," she whispered. "Please not again."

The man lifted his silvery hand. Two of the chanting figures stepped aside, revealing a slender form lying on a bed of mist. It was, indeed, Malasha. Shallia moved closer. Her friend lay still, as lifeless as a shard of driftwood.

Gently, she lifted Malasha's frosted hand—the very hand she had yearned to touch on the night they met. At that moment, Malasha's eyelids opened a sliver. Yet the once-bright gleam behind them had nearly vanished. Blinking back her tears, Shallia squeezed the hand. She knew, as before, that she did not need to speak for her friend to know her heart. And, in any case, she did not know what to say. She could only stand, and ache, and hope.

But soon she could hardly even hope. Malasha's eyes closed again, with the finality of the sun falling behind the horizon. The heads of the people in the circle fell lower. The steady chanting dropped slowly away, fading with the life of the young girl.

Shallia pressed her friend's palm against her own chest. "Don't die," she pleaded. "I want you to live again. To breathe again."

Breathe again.

Somewhere in Shallia's memory, a whale spouted, breathing the same misty air as two newfound friends.

Breathe again.

Holding the limp hand, Shallia thought of how breath was not just air, and not just body, but something more besides. Something that could move between her own world and Malasha's as easily as mist moves between water and air.

Please, Malasha. Breathe again.

The mist maiden's silvery hair quivered, touched by the breath of her friend. The breath of the whale and the gull and the turtle. The breath that filled every sighing shell, that powered every rolling wave. The breath of the sea. The breath of life.

All of a sudden, Malasha stirred. Her chest shifted, then rose ever so slightly. Her fingers curled around Shallia's own. Her eyes opened, glowing with the light of stars upon waves.

The chanting returned, surrounding them, embracing them. No longer despairing, it resounded with joy. At last, Shallia understood. The chanting, in this world, was the whispering she had so often heard in her own! She was embraced as never before by the music of this world, the music of the mist.

Shallia gazed at her friend. She knew that they would never part again. And she knew that, in the morning, the people of her village would find only a trail of fading footprints in the sand.

By a faraway shore on a faraway sea, the mist rises nightly from star-shining waves. Over the darkening sea it spreads, stretching thin, wispy fingers out to the land. And on this night, as on so many nights before, the mist reaches first to touch a single place, a single rock—the rock still remembered as Shallia's Stone.

16

QUELJIES

I leaned my head against the tree trunk, still hearing the rhythmic swell of waves upon a faraway shore. In time, I turned to Hallia. "That was wonderful."

"I'm glad you liked it." She slid deeper into her hollow among the roots. "It was one of my father's favorites. He felt a special closeness to mist, so very hard to control or contain."

"Or even," I added, "to define. My own mother used to say that mist was neither quite water nor quite air, but something in between."

As Hallia nodded, the phrase echoed in my mind. *Something in between.* My mother had used those same words, as well, to describe Fincayra itself—on that day long ago in our meager thatched-roof hut. And what else had she called it? *A place of many wonders; neither wholly of Earth nor wholly of Heaven, but a bridge connecting both.*

Glancing down at my empty scabbard, and at the spot where the bloodnoose had plunged into my chest, I sighed. She should also have called this island a place of many perils. And choices—many of them clear one moment, then gone the next, like a reflection in a pond that is suddenly disturbed.

In the darkness, I leaned toward Ector. "Did you enjoy the story, young friend?"

His only answer was a series of slow, rhythmic breaths.

"No doubt he did," said Hallia dryly, "as long as he was awake." She yawned. "In fact, a little sleep isn't a bad idea. Maybe you and I should do the same."

"Yes," I agreed, listening for a moment to the distant screeching sounds of the marsh beyond the sheltering trees. "But one of us should stay awake. I'll take the first watch."

"Are you sure?" She yawned again. "I could do it if you'd rather rest."

"No, you sleep first." I drew my knees up to my chest. "I'll wake you when it's your turn."

She shifted herself, laying her head against a burly root. Minutes later, her own breathing was as slow and regular as Ector's. I straightened my back against the trunk. To keep myself alert, I trained my second sight on a succession of objects—a jagged thorn here, a cluster of leaves there. When my attention fell to one of the small knotholes that lined the thickest branches, I started.

For the knothole, I was certain, had blinked.

I stiffened, staring at the spot. Again the knothole blinked—but no, not quite. It was more like a movement inside the dark spot, a shadow within a shadow. As I watched, hardly daring to move, a vague, shimmering light kindled inside the hole. It glowed subtly—the same dull orange as a fire coal on the verge of dying out. The light pulsed and wavered. I shivered with the feeling that this luminous eye was studying me.

"Sssso," hissed a thin, airy voice. "He thought he'd be ssssssafe in here."

Just as I seized the handle of my staff, another light winked from a different branch. "Say-hay-hafe?" it asked. "Who-oo-oo could be say-hay-hafe in su-hu-huch a swa-haw-hawmp?"

"No one, eh-heh, but us," chortled a third voice. "Eh-heh, eh-heh." It came from a branch almost directly over Hallia's head. Although she didn't waken, her fingers twitched anxiously as the quivering light touched her.

"Who are you?" I demanded.

"Not fre-heh-hends."

"Not enemies. Eh-heh-heh-heh."

"Jusssssst . . . queljiesssss."

I sucked in my breath. "Queljies? What's that?"

"We ar-har-har the wa-ha-hatchers of the swa-haw-hawmp. Oh, ye-he-hes! No-ho-hothing misses u-huh-hus. We see-he-he it a-ha-hall. And we tra-ha-havel in three-hee-hees."

"Like trouble," piped one of the others. "Eh-heh, eh-heh, eh-heh."

All three of the flickering creatures burst into sustained laughter. Their guffaws filled the canopy of branches, drowning out the voices of the swamp. My cheeks burned; now I felt more angry than afraid. I raised my staff, planting its base on a root beside me. The handle nearly brushed the thorns of the ceiling. "Do you intend to bring us harm?"

"Har-ar-arm?" sniggered one. "How-ow-ow could anywuh-hu-huhn har-ar-arm you mo-ho-hore?"

"More?" I asked. "More than what?"

"He's already lost his way, eh-heh. And don't forget, eh-heh, his sword."

I froze. "What do you know about my sword?"

"Just that it's lost, eh-heh-heh-heh. Like you! Eh-heh, eh-heh."

"Sssssomething elsssse will be losssssst very sssssoon. Yesssss, quite sssssoon."

"What?" I asked, turning to the wavering glow.

"Your life, that'sssss what." The creature broke into a raucous giggle. "Sssssee what we told you? Trouble doesssss come in threesssss."

A chorus of harsh, grating laughter washed over me, along with splashes of light from the queljies. At first, my anger rose again. I nearly lashed out—then thought better of it. Perhaps another tack might yield a better result. Mustering my patience, I waited until their laughter had faded.

"My dear queljies," I began, "you are good-humored, to be sure."

"He-ee-ee's trying to fla-ah-ahter u-huh-hus."

"Think sssssso?"

"You may be good-humored," I continued, "but

you clearly don't know as much as you let on. In fact, it's obvious you're much too delicate to do any exploring out there in the swamplands. So you can't have learned anything really important."

"Sssssuch an inssssssult."

"It's all right," I said soothingly. "Better to stay safe than expose yourself to dangerous knowledge."

"You-hoo-hoo have no ide-ee-eea what we-ee-ee know-oh-oh!"

I waited a moment before responding. "Really? Then if you know so much, tell me something I don't already know."

"Like wha-ha-hat?"

"Oh, I don't know." I paused, chewing my lip thoughtfully. "Like . . . where something lies hidden."

A knothole flickered. "Hisssss sssssword! We know where that liesssss."

Though I started perspiring, I waved my hand nonchalantly. "I guess that would do. But of course, you don't really know."

"Yesssss we do! It'sssss—"

"Si-hi-hilence!" came the stern command from another branch. "Ha-ah-ave you forgot-ot-otten?"

The other lights glimmered, but didn't speak.

"There," I pronounced. "My proof. You really don't know."

More flickers. More silence.

"Ah, well." I yawned, stretching my arms. "I suppose all I've heard about queljies is true: lots of bluster, but no knowledge."

"Not true!" squealed all of them in unison.

At this, both Hallia and Ector awoke. Both of them, seeing the wavering lights in the branches, gasped in astonishment. I waved them silent.

"Show me, then," I coaxed. "Tell me what you know."

"Not about your sword, eh-heh, eh-heh. She would surely hurt us, eh-heh-heh, for telling you that."

"She?" I asked, puzzled.

"She, eh-heh, is—"

"Si-hi-hilence! Spe-he-heak no mo-oh-ore of her."

"Yes, well, there it is." I spoke lazily, trying hard to conceal my eagerness. "More proof."

A tense moment of quiet ensued, broken only by the muffled noises from the marsh. Hallia and Ector fidgeted nervously, their faces half lit by the strange glow. Both concerned and confused, they kept watching me, turning aside only now and then to scrutinize the gleaming knotholes. I could almost hear their heartbeats, along with my own, under the ceiling of branches.

At length, a thin voice broke the silence. "We cannot sssssay anything about your ssssssword. But we know many other sssssecrets. Many other treasuressssss."

I shook my head. "I don't believe you."

"Yesssss! It'sssss true." The glow within the knothole intensified. "Why, we even know the sssssecret hideaway of the sssssseventh Wisssssse Tool."

Hallia stiffened. She reached for my arm and squeezed hard. Ector, meanwhile, peered at the branches, mouth agape. Doing my best to remain calm, I merely shrugged. "That can't be true. The last of the Wise Tools was lost long ago."

"Oh yesssss?" Now the voice hissed with utter indignation. "You think sssssso?"

"You've shown me no proof. None at all."

No response other than orange flashes, brighter by the second.

"You poor beasts," I said, shaking my head sadly. "So small, so frail. At least, I suppose, by never venturing out of your safe little nests you never get into trouble. It's much better for you, really, that you know nothing of any value."

"Li-ie-ies!"

"Ssssstupid man."

"You are the one, eh-heh, who knows nothing."

Relaxedly, I spoke to Hallia and Ector. "Go back to sleep now, friends. These little creatures are just senseless babblers."

"Isssss that sssssso? Then how could we know thisssss?"

The lights flared in unison as the voices recited:

"Ce-heh-henter of the swa-haw-hawmp—"

"By a flaming, eh-heh, tree—"

"Liesssss the missssssing treasure: Ever preciousssss key."

I leaned back against the tree trunk. "Well now, queljies, I am truly impressed. Just imagine knowing such a thing." As their lights faded away, submerging us in darkness once again, I turned to Hallia. Though I felt frustrated at my inability to learn anything useful about my sword, I couldn't help but grin that I had, at least, pulled something interesting out of them.

Hallia released her grip on my arm, although she continued to stare at me, her eyes swollen with amazement. And with something else—something urgent. "Young hawk," she whispered anxiously, "I remember now."

"Remember what?"

"What my father told me, some of it anyway, about the powers of the key, the seventh Wise Tool. It can—" She caught herself suddenly, glancing over at Ector.

"It's all right," I said, motioning toward the boy. "You can trust him."

"What about those . . . creatures?"

I shook my head. "Them, I have no idea. They might well know already what you're about to say. On the other hand, they might not. If you're worried about them, you could just wait until tomorrow to tell me."

Hallia grunted. "Tomorrow someone else, much less friendly, could be listening. And besides—I want to tell you now. It's too important."

At the edge of my vision, I saw Ector crane his neck toward us. No doubt he felt glad, at last, to be trusted. Yet he seemed to be frowning, concerned about something, though it could have been just a trick of my second sight.

In hushed tones, Hallia spoke again. "My father said this about the magical key that was, for so long, in his care: It can unlock any door—to any palace, any chamber, any chest of treasures. Or it can do something else, if held by someone with deep enough magic."

She paused, making sure her words hit home. "A person of deep magic could use it to unlock not a door—but a spell. Any spell. And forever, young hawk. That spell can never be inflicted again."

It was my turn, now, to be amazed. "Did he say anything else?"

"Y-yes," she answered hesitantly. "There was more. I'm sure of it. A warning, I think, about its powers. But . . . I just can't remember."

Ector fidgeted on the ground, shifting his weight uneasily.

"But nothing," she continued excitedly, "matters as much as what I've just told you. Why, don't you see? The key—if we can truly find it—could save your life. It could! You can use it to unlock the spell of the bloodnoose!"

I sat up sharply, my hand upon my heart. "Why, yes, of course! Then, fully healed, I can regain my sword at last—and do whatever I can to halt the rest of this wickedness. But first I must find the key."

"*We* must," she corrected.

"Yes, we! And the Flaming Tree the queljies spoke about . . ."

"Must be where my father hid it!" She slid across the ground to my side. "Of course, I'm sure that's right. The Flaming Tree of old, deep in the marsh, would have been the safest possible place." Rubbing her hand along a root, she said dreamily, "I can see the spot now, at the highest part of a treeless ridge . . .

oh, young hawk! And we are close—very close. I can feel it in my bones! A half day's walk, no more."

"*A trail marked upon the heart.* That's what you said before."

"And that's what it is! Let's go there right away, shall we?" She halted, listening to the distant shrieks beyond the rise. "At dawn, when the marsh ghouls are gone."

Gently, I stroked her slender chin. "I'm grateful to your father—and even more, to you."

Her head tilted toward me, resting on my hand. After a moment, I suggested, "Now why not get a little sleep? It's still my watch, so rest well. And tomorrow morning, you can follow that trail on the land, as well as your heart."

17

A WALL OF FLAMES

When I awoke, a hazy light drifted through the web of branches. Hallia lay across from me, encircled by thick roots. Hearing me stir, she looked up, her long auburn hair a tangle of mud, burrs, and bark.

I lifted an eyebrow. "And how are you this morning?"

Her doe's eyes smiled. "You didn't wake me for my turn at watch."

"That's because," I confessed, "I fell asleep myself. But no harm came of it."

"I could use another one of the ballymag's baths right now."

"We both could." I scratched my cheek, peeling off a hard clump of mud. "That bath was the last thing I expected to find in this swamp." My gaze moved to the three knotholes, now dark, where the strange creatures had appeared. "Almost."

She, too, scanned the knotholes. "Did they say anything more?"

"No," I replied, emptying some pebbles out of my boot. "They never reappeared. But while they were here, they said enough, didn't they?"

She sat up. "That they did. I've been hearing it even as I slept:

> Center of the swamp,
> By a flaming tree,
> Lies the missing treasure:
> Ever precious key."

Gingerly, I touched the center of my chest. "Let's hope your father was right about its powers."

"He was right, I'm sure of that." She squinted at the thorny ceiling. "I wish I could remember what else he said. It was about how to use the key, I think."

I tapped her shoulder. "No matter. I'm glad you remembered as much as you did." Turning to the spot, still shadowed, where Ector had slept, I said, "I'd better wake up—"

My whole body went rigid. "Hallia! He's gone."

"No!" she cried, slapping the sides of her face. "He wouldn't . . ." She turned to me and scowled. "I knew we should never have let him join us."

Still stunned, I slowly shook my head. "I can't believe he'd betray our trust like that. Maybe he just left early to continue his own search."

She continued to scowl. "Without bothering to say

farewell? No, young hawk, I'll tell you where he went—and what he's searching for. The key."

Grimly, I nodded. "I'm afraid you're right. But I really thought he gave more value to friendship—the way Shallia did, in your story."

"Apparently not."

I rolled over and started crawling into the thorn-rimmed tunnel. "Come. He could have a sizeable lead."

As we emerged from the jumble of branches, a cacophony of howling and chattering greeted us. Much as I disliked the notion of going back into the swamp, I felt a wash of relief that, at least, we would not have to face the marsh ghouls. And that their new aggressiveness hadn't prompted them to terrorize by daylight. Even so, something that Shim had said still troubled me. Or perhaps I just hadn't heard him correctly. But he had, I thought, said something or other about the marsh ghouls in the day. Whatever—they were nowhere to be found right now.

Standing at the edge of the rise, I discerned a slight yellowing of the vapors in one direction. It gave a golden hue to everything, even the large, burbling pool where I had nearly drowned last night. Of course! The rising sun.

Hallia, following my gaze—and, as usual, my thoughts—swiveled and pointed toward a stretch of twisted shrubbery and steaming pools. "There," she pronounced. "The treeless ridge lies over there."

Just then I spotted a glint of moisture on the ground near the base of the trees. Gleaming gold, it snaked down the slope before disappearing into the muck. Hallia and I ran over to the spring and knelt by a small, clear pool formed by a curved root. We thrust our faces into the water, drinking eagerly, slurping and gasping in turn. At last, we looked at each other, hair dripping onto our shoulders.

Hallia glanced anxiously toward the marsh. "If only Gwynnia were with us now! She could carry us straight to the Flaming Tree."

"We could turn ourselves into deer," I suggested.

She shook her head, spraying me with droplets. "No, in this kind of muck, any legs are a problem. Four would, in many cases, be even worse than two."

"Then let's go."

Together we rose, and plunged again into the swamp. Thick mud oozed into my boots; moss-coated branches tore at my legs; clouds of vapor, smelling of sulphur, swirled so close at times that it seemed more like dusk than early morning. I felt a strange sense of foreboding—something in the air, or the sopping terrain, or perhaps the depths of my own chest. Even my shadow, stepping alongside me, seemed shrunken and subdued.

A circle of questions ran over and over through my mind: Would we arrive at the hiding place of the key, only to find that Ector had already taken it? How could that boy who had affected me so surprisingly, who had felt such loyalty to me that he gave me his precious elixir, do such a thing? And how much longer would the elixir be able to hold off the bloodnoose?

For two or three hours we trekked, through murky shallows and desolate flats. The marsh seemed endless, the misty light unvaried. Yet Hallia's sense of direction never wavered, just as her pace never slowed. Whenever I wondered how she could possibly judge distance and direction on such a landscape, I remembered the continual ache between my shoulder blades. Perhaps her own people's curse, and her vision of our destination, remained equally constant.

As we struggled across a wide pool, trying to keep to stones and mounds of grass—anything more solid than bogwater—I noticed a single, wide-leafed lily growing on the surface. Its pointed white petals thrust upward, ringing the bright yellow bud in its center. In the hazy light, it looked almost like a crown, resting upon the water.

Instinctively, I fingered my empty scabbard. Would I ever know the heft of that bright blade again? And, more important, would I ever be able to fulfill my promise to Dagda, to deliver the sword safely to the virtuous king who would call it his own? At this point, that promise seemed more a dream than a destiny.

Finally, we reached higher ground. We started ascending a steep hill, covered with stubby brown grass and jagged stones that rose sometimes to our shoulders. As we pushed through an immense cobweb strung between two of the stones, Hallia stopped abruptly. She stood, poised, for a frozen moment. I said nothing, listening to the chattering and wailing of the marsh.

She turned to me at last. "Do you smell it?"

I sniffed the pungent air, but found nothing new. "Smell what?"

"Smoke."

Without waiting for me to answer, she started off again, leading us higher on the slope. A few moments later I, too, caught the scent of something burning. And, though I couldn't be sure, the fleeting aroma of rose blossoms once again. The mist, heavier and darker than before, swallowed us, obscuring any view.

As the terrain began to level, the smoky smell grew stronger. Then . . . a glimmer of light appeared. We drew closer, hearing an unfamiliar sound: a wavering, unsteady roar, loud enough at times to overwhelm the other noises of the swamp. Pressing ahead, we found ourselves gazing at a whirling circle of flames.

Pouring out of a ring of vents in the ground, the fire blazed forth, licking the clouds. Every so often it would sputter, choking back, only to rise again with still more fury. Even from a distance, the intense heat burned my cheeks. I fell back a step, remembering the flames in Gwynedd that had scarred my face forever. Those flames had cost me my own eyes—and another boy his life.

The fire dropped down again, releasing a burst of black smoke. The smoke billowed forth, then suddenly parted. There, in the center of the blazing circle, stood a single, contorted tree. Its wood long since replaced by glowing coals, it remained standing somehow, whether by the force of gases from the vents, or by some peculiar magic of its own.

With awe, I watched the blackened form disappear behind a rising wall of fire. "The Flaming Tree."

Hallia bit her lip. "It looks impossible to reach."

"You're right about that."

We whirled around to face Ector. His robe, even more shredded than before, showed many charred threads. One side bore three or four holes eaten by fire. His face, somehow, had lost its youthful air; his blue eyes seemed blank.

Averting his gaze, he shifted from one foot to another. "I'm sorry I left without you," he said remorsefully. "But I couldn't wait."

My brow knitted. "You mean you didn't want to wait. You wanted to find the key before we did."

He glanced at the circle of flames, making half his face glow like a fire coal. "Yes, that's true. And I wanted something else."

"What else," demanded Hallia, striking the ground with her foot, "would justify betraying us?"

"I wanted . . ." he began, then swallowed with difficulty. "I wanted to save my master."

"Save him?" I asked skeptically. "Just how?"

His head drooped forward. "He is locked up—imprisoned. If he isn't set free, and soon, terrible things will happen! And, though my master hasn't said so directly, I'm sure that he will also die." His expression hardened. "When I left him, his command was clear: Find the key, and let no one else use it for any purpose."

Hallia slammed her fist into her hand. "If young hawk doesn't get to use the key, then *he* will die."

The boy turned to me, his face twisted with anguish. "It's what . . . what I feared would happen. This is the choice I've been wrestling with ever since

last night." He drew a ragged breath. "But I think—
no, I'm sure—my first loyalty must be to my master.
If I could do something for you, believe me, I
would."

Feeling so much pain in him, as well as in myself,
I said nothing.

"The vial," he went on, "was mine to give. The
key, though, is my master's."

"No!" cried Hallia. "The key belongs to no one!
Where was this master of yours when my father stole
deep into this marsh, risking his life to keep the key
away from Stangmar's soldiers?" Her eyes narrowed.
"Who *is* your master, anyway?"

Ector hesitated, working his tongue. "I can't say. I
promised."

"Well your promises—and your master's commands, for that matter—aren't worth someone's
life."

"Wait now," I announced. "I have the solution."
Squarely, I faced Ector. "You will not violate his
command. But *I* will."

"But—"

"This will work, I tell you!" I grabbed him by the
arm. "You can still bring the key to your master. He
can do whatever he likes with it! But first, I shall use
it to save myself."

"My master said . . ."

"Forget what he said." I glared at him. "He'll just
have to share it."

"But he must have had a reason," protested the boy.

"Silence!" I jabbed my staff into the stony ground.

"I'll hear no more about your master. As far as I can tell, he has the courage of a newborn hare and the wisdom of a jackass! Sending a lad your age into the middle of this swamp! If the stakes were so high, he should have sent an army."

Ector started to respond, but my severe look silenced him.

Turning to Hallia, I declared, "The real problem is how to get it out of there." I winced as the wall of flames swelled higher, towering over our heads. "No mortal could pass through such a blaze and survive."

She cocked her head in puzzlement. "Yet my father was mortal. How did he get in there?"

My face brightened—from more than reflected flames. "He didn't."

"How then did he hide the key?"

I slid my hand down my staff. "Through his own power of Leaping."

She started. "He did know some magic. But enough to do that? It's possible, yes." Her expression darkened. "Do you think, though . . ."

"That I can do it?" Pensively, I watched the blaze. "I really don't know. Leaping is hard to control. I might send it—well, somewhere else by mistake, as I've done before. All I can do is try."

She touched my cheek and turned my face toward hers. "Then try, young hawk."

My attention turned back to the circle of flames, and the twisted tree within it. Using my second sight, I probed the charred soil at the tree's base. Finding nothing there, I moved to the vents, lined with rocks that had been burst apart by the unending heat. Again, nothing. I scanned the tree itself—roots first, then trunk, then limbs. Still nothing.

Where in this inferno was the key? Carved from an antler, Hallia had said. With a sapphire embedded in its crown. I kept searching, following every contour of the tree—until at last I spotted an unusual shape. It was a small, contoured object, resting on a burl on the trunk. Peering closer, I spied a flash of bright blue, as bright as a sapphire.

Concentrating, I focused on the key. Somehow, I sensed that my powers were not as strong as I remembered. But this was no time for self-doubts. I trained all my senses upon the object, grasping it with hands of magic.

Leap to me.

The flames surged, forcing all of us to step backward. Hands of heat slapped my cheeks. The very air crackled, while the roar swelled, assaulting our ears. Still, I kept my focus.

Leap to me. Through the flames.

As if sensing my intrusion, the inferno grew even greater. The blast of heat singed my eyebrows; the raging flames of heat groped at my tunic. And at my memory of other flames—so relentless, so deadly.

I felt my strength fading rapidly. My legs wobbled. It was all I could do just to keep standing. Whatever I held in my grasp would surely fall, surely burn as I had done. With a final effort, I tried to heave my powers through the conflagration.

Out of the writhing flames, the key appeared. The polished white form glowed from the fires that surrounded it, and from an inner light of its own. Borne by invisible wings, it sailed through the blazing wall. Sizzling fingers tugged at it, trying to hold it back, but it pulled free. Even as I sank to my knees on the ground, struggling to catch my breath, it fell into my open hand.

Hallia, trembling, reached to touch it. She moved her fingers from the finely wrought base, up the shaft, over the looping crown adorned with a sapphire. "You did it," she whispered. I could tell that she was speaking both to me—and to her father.

At that instant, something whizzed just over my head. Some sort of weapon! I glimpsed it slicing into the circle of flames. Then, to my horror, I saw that it had left behind a dark trail—not of smoke, but of emptiness. Nothing, not even light, remained along the path of its flight.

It was, I knew with a shudder, an arrow. Not a traditional arrow, but one with special properties. One that could, as Shim had warned, pierce through the day.

18

ROSE BLOSSOMS

Leaning heavily on my staff, I struggled to stand. Carefully, I avoided touching the dark ribbon that the arrow had cut into the air—a void where nothing, not even light, remained.

Hallia, looking ashen, backed up until her shoulder touched my own. Ector stood next to us, his eyes wide with terror. Together, we watched as a vast phalanx of warriors strode out of the vapors. But for the dark shimmerings in the air that were their bodies, and the vague glimmers of light from their eyes, they remained almost invisible. Yet they could not be missed, for each of them wore a stout, curved sword, hung from the waist with a belt of woven vines. And each of them bore a heavy wooden bow, nocked with a charcoal-black arrow that was aimed directly at us.

"Marsh ghouls," muttered Ector, edging closer to my side. "Where can we go?"

Nowhere, it seemed. Behind us roared a deadly inferno—the Flaming Tree and the blaze that surrounded it. Before us stood forty or fifty marsh ghouls, armed with menacing weaponry. I could feel, almost touch, their scorn for anything alive that stood in their way. Even the swirling vapors of the marsh seemed reluctant to touch their wavering forms. My own shadow withered, shrinking down to a mere wisp of gray at my feet.

Propped against my staff, I tried to think of something—anything—we could do. As waves of dark mist rolled over us, my mind raced, but with no result. And my quivering legs didn't help matters. I felt weak, hardly able to stand. So how could I possibly fight? Was I simply drained by my act of Leaping or, as I feared, by the fading power of the elixir?

"They hate us," said Hallia, her voice hush. "I can feel it."

"So can I." Then, with a slight shudder, I realized that I also felt something more. It was an uncertain, elusive feeling; a sensation I could almost grasp, but not quite. "They hate us, yes. And yet . . . I have the feeling, somehow, that they hate something else. Even more."

She gave me a bewildered glance.

Turning my flagging powers toward the phalanx of marsh ghouls, I probed their shadowy selves. I pushed to see behind their shimmering forms, beyond their visible shapes. Wrath—more potent than poison hemlock—flowed from them. Probing deeper,

I sensed betrayal. And could it be? A deep, unflagging sorrow.

Gradually, ever so gradually, their shapes came more clear for me. They had heads, long and narrow, topped by hoods; dark brown tunics that fell to the ground; and enormous, clawed hands. I saw more of their faces—twisted, harsh, hateful. And then I saw something else, something so surprising that I couldn't believe it at first. They were wrapped, held tight, by a kind of rope. No, not rope. Something far more heavy, far more cruel.

Chains.

Yes, there could be no doubt. Someone, or some force, had bound the marsh ghouls. Stolen their freedom—and, perhaps, their will. As much as they raged at the three intruders who dared to venture on their land, they raged much more at some hidden oppressor.

Hallia jerked, craning her neck. "Do you smell that?"

Indeed, I did. Rose blossoms! Again I smelled that striking aroma, so very different from the sulphurous smoke of the blazing vents or the rancid air of the swamp. Faint though it was, it brought a sudden memory of spring roses, fresh and alluring. And . . . something else, a dream perhaps, too distant to recall.

Just then, the line of shadowy warriors parted. Through the opening strode a woman. Tall and proud, she wore a glistening white robe, untouched by mud, and a silver-threaded shawl about her shoulders. Her hair, black like my own, fell midway down her arms. Seeing us, she smiled grimly. Her eyes seemed as devoid of light as the arrow's dark trail.

For an instant, I thought somehow I knew this woman. Her stride, her curling lips, her hair—all reminded me of a girl I had met in another part of Fincayra. A girl who had betrayed me. Whose name was Vivian . . . or, as she preferred, Nimue. I pushed those thoughts aside. How could a girl my own age, who had tried to steal my staff only two years ago, suddenly have grown into a woman? Yet the resemblance was strong. Very strong. I almost recognized her, just as I almost recognized that scent of rose blossoms.

I started. For the woman pulled from behind her back something that I most definitely did recognize. My own sword! Its blade, catching the light from the circle of flames, flashed brightly. It almost seemed to be calling to me, imploring me to take it back.

Ector's body tensed. Then he spoke a single word—a name—that froze the blood in my veins. "Nimue."

"Indeed, little servant," she answered in a voice that sounded only a shade huskier than the voice of the girl I had once known. She waved the sword at Hallia and myself. "Wouldn't you like to introduce me to your friends? *Hmmm?* Or can you not recognize them under all those layers of mud?"

Hallia, her indignation overcoming her fear, stepped forward. "I am Hallia, of the Mellwyn-bri-Meath—a people who learned long ago that finely wrought clothing can't mask a poisoned heart."

The woman's eyes narrowed. "A people who

learned long ago to run away from trouble instead of confronting it." Without waiting for Hallia's response, she turned to me. "And you, young wizard. Who might you be?"

Though my weakened body trembled, I stood as tall as I could. "We have met before."

"Ah, yes. So we have." She examined my staff. "A long time ago, *hmmm?*"

I said nothing.

"Too bad." Glumly, she clacked her tongue. "You know, I think I liked you better before. In your younger form." She sent Hallia a knowing glance. "Is he any better at romancing now? He was, believe me, dreadfully clumsy back then."

Hallia's eyes flared angrily.

"My sword," I declared. "You have my sword."

Carelessly, Nimue twirled the silver hilt in her hand, watching it sparkle. "Ah yes, so I do."

"I want it back."

"Really?" She scanned the rows of marsh ghouls, arrows at the ready. "You wouldn't be thinking of fighting me, would you? That would be rash, very rash. These marksmen are not seasoned fighters, like warrior goblins. But I have trained them to shoot my own dark arrows—and shoot well."

I glared at her. "You're not only older. You're crueler."

She stabbed at the air with my blade. "The blessings of age! The same thing will happen to you, young wizard. Ah, yes." She released a long, low cackle. "If you should survive this day, that is, which is most unlikely."

She leaned closer, the glow from the inferno dancing on her pale skin. When she spoke, her grating whisper made me shudder. "And if you should, by some miracle, survive, this sword will not be the last thing I shall steal from you. That, little wizard, I can promise."

She straightened herself, patting down her robe, then scanned her ring of warriors. "Yet even as I speak, I am tempted to show you some mercy."

"I don't need mercy from you," I spat back.

"Oh no?" She scrutinized me with mock concern. "You don't look at all well, *hmmm*." Her lips creased, almost smiled. "Is it possible you could be having some sort of problem . . . with your heart?"

I cringed.

"Huntress," snarled Hallia. "It was you who sent the beetles!"

"Perhaps, you slab of venison! And perhaps I've brought some other blessings to this marsh, as well."

Several of the marsh ghouls stirred suddenly, releasing wrathful growls. Nimue turned to them, raising her eyebrows. They instantly quieted, though their shadowy forms continued to quiver.

She turned her gaze back to me. "As I was saying, right now I am feeling merciful." She strode forward, raised my sword, and plunged it deep into the ground. Charred dirt flew up, soiling her dress, but the marks instantly disappeared. All the while, she observed me. "The terms of my bargain are quite simple. If you give me that key in your hand, I will give you back your sword."

I caught my breath. The blade seemed aflame itself, flashing in the firelight. "You would do that?"

"I would."

My sword . . . I could almost reach it, almost feel it. But one look at Nimue, watching me smugly, struck me like a falling stone. My fingers tightened around the sapphire-studded loop. "I'll make no bargains with you," I proclaimed. "Even for the sword."

Her hands, creamy white, clasped together. "Ah, well, such a shame. I shall just have to tell my soldiers to kill you. And your friends, as well. Then I'll take the key anyway."

"You are a witch, Nimue," blurted Ector. "If my master knew—"

"Leave your foolish master out of this. Or I shall turn my marksmen on you right now, servant boy."

Bristling, he swung to face me. "Don't do it, please! If she gets hold of that key, then all will be lost."

Nimue cackled softly. "I suppose I might give you one more gesture of mercy, *hmmm?* Just to prove my intentions are honorable."

I sneered, "You don't know the meaning of the word."

"Skeptical? Ah then, just listen. Before you hand the key over to me, I'll allow you to use it. That's right. To heal yourself."

"No, young hawk!" cried Ector. "That would—"

Nimue swatted the air, as if brushing away a fly. Ector flew backward, rolling down the slope. He stopped just short of the conflagration, though his sleeve burst into flames. While he labored to put it out with handfuls of dirt, she watched him with amusement. "Someone," she said, "should teach that boy some manners."

Turning back to me, she coaxed, "Go ahead, now. Use the key to mend that little trouble with your heart." Her perfume wafted over me. "Before I change my mind."

"Wa—wait," I stammered. "Why would you let me do that?"

"Mercy, as I said. And also gratitude."

"For what?"

The ring of flames roared, surging higher. From every side it spouted sparks that landed, still aglow, on the ground. A few tufts of grass caught fire, sending thin trails of smoke into the mist.

"For leading me to my precious key, of course. Why, I've been searching for it for quite some time now."

Seeing my look of astonishment, she smirked. "I don't mean you, little wizard, but your large-eyed friend there."

Hallia gasped. "Me? I wouldn't lead you—"

"Not knowingly, of course." She stroked her hair with evident satisfaction. "That was the beauty of it, you see. Once I learned that a deer man had carried the key into the marsh, I figured you would lead me to it eventually." She pointed a long finger at my chest. "Especially if you had the proper incentive."

With a frown, she waved at her shadowy soldiers. "The timing was fortunate, too. I was beginning to grow a little, shall we say, *impatient* with my good friends here."

A few of the marsh ghouls grumbled, tensing their bows, before she cut them off with a glance. "They had done well enough, I'll grant, at keeping unwanted intruders out of the marsh. And at widening the borders where I required more room to search. Yet they had done miserably at helping me find what I really wanted."

"So you're responsible for destroying that forest," I fumed. "And also that village."

"Oh, more than just one village, I daresay. And more than just a few trees here and there! You have no idea." Looking very pleased with herself, she flicked a spark off her dress. "Ah, but all this was not so easy as it sounds. It wouldn't have worked to have *me* clearing intruders out of the marsh, oh no. That would have roused too much suspicion—not to mention the few enemies I still have on this antiquated island."

She paused, straightening her silver-threaded shawl. "The solution, of course, was to give a good deal of my power—not all of it, mind you, but enough to raise serious havoc—to some other people." She pondered the marsh ghouls for a moment. "Preferably people who were almost as wicked, if not as clever, as myself. That way no one would suspect that I was involved." In a silken voice, she added, "And the marsh ghouls, I can assure you, were delighted to cooperate. More than eager! How else could I have entrusted them with my own magic? And my own weaponry?"

She flicked her finger at the blade of my sword, causing it to ring softly. "Hence my gratitude, and this little moment of mercy. So now, tell me. Do you accept my offer to use the key, or not?"

Hallia, her hair aglow from the flames, leaned toward me. "I don't trust her any more than you do. But you can't refuse this chance to spare your life."

"Wise words, deer woman." Nimue placed her hands on her hips. "All right, then. Make your choice."

Slowly, I nodded. My hand quivering, I brought the key to my chest. As it came nearer, I could almost feel the bloodnoose tightening around my heart. My life.

"All you need to do," offered Nimue, "is fix a clear image in your mind of the spell you would like to break. Then turn the key." She eyed the sparkling sapphire. *"Hmmm,* hurry now. I'm growing rather bored with being merciful."

I drew a deep breath. My chest throbbed; now even breathing seemed an effort. I looked into Hallia's eyes, then at the key. At last, I concentrated my thoughts on the spell that, beyond all others, I knew must be destroyed.

Suddenly, I turned the key around—pointing it at the marsh ghouls. Nimue cried out in surprise. Before she could do anything more, I turned the key.

Instantly, a new sound rent the air: the sound of heavy chains splitting apart and clattering to the ground. The shimmering forms of the marsh ghouls released a cheer that drowned out the roaring from the inferno. At the same time, some of them hurled their bows, arrows, and swords into the fire. The flames rose higher, spitting and hissing while consuming their weapons. Meanwhile, the marsh ghouls themselves melted into the vapors—freed forever from Nimue's spell.

She clenched her fists tightly. "How dare you?" she shouted. "I needed them still! I had more plans for them. And now they are roaming freely, with powers that belong to me!"

All at once, her rage dissipated. An inscrutable grin spread over her face. "So be it. But mark my words, young wizard. In trying to harm me, you have only doomed yourself. Ah, yes! More completely than you know."

Gathering her shawl, she chortled softly. Then she turned and strode off into the swirling clouds. In a moment, no sign of her remained, but for the lingering aroma of rose blossoms.

19

GREAT POWER

Weakly, I sagged on my staff, driving it deeper into the dirt. My head spun from the intensity of the confrontation with Nimue. The place between my shoulders ached like never before.

Hallia peered at me, confused. Firelight glowed in the strands of her hair. "What happened to the marsh ghouls? And why, young hawk, didn't you heal yourself?"

"I felt their rage, as you did. But I also felt their pain. She had chained them, forced them to serve her. So I made a choice: to set them free. And if that spoiled Nimue's plans, so much the better." An unsteady breath seeped into my lungs. "Also, I couldn't help feeling that if she wanted me to use the key on myself, then it must be wrong somehow."

"You were right about that." Ector, his face smeared with soot, trudged over to us. The cloth of one sleeve sent thin trails of smoke into the air. His whole body drooped, nearly as much as my own.

"Are you all right?" I asked.

"My body? Fine." He shook his mass of curls. "My quest, though—it's ruined."

"Why? We still have the key. I've already told you that after I use it, you can take it to your master."

He sighed. "You can't use it. Nor can he."

"Why not?" I lifted the enchanted object, last of the Seven Wise Tools. "She didn't take it."

"For good reason," he answered glumly. His blackened hand snatched it from me. "Just look at it."

Both Hallia and I stiffened. For the sapphire no longer gleamed from atop the polished crown. Now, in the gem's place, sat something else: a lump of charcoal. The entire key had lost its luster—and, I could tell, something far more precious.

Ector's voice sounded hollow. "That must have been why he warned me to let no one else use it! For its powers, as great as they were, could only work once. Now he is doomed."

I groaned, sinking lower, until my knees crunched against the charred soil. "So am I."

The boy, biting his lip, placed his hand on my shoulder. "You didn't know."

"Through my own arrogance! You tried to tell me. Now the only ones who will ever gain any benefit from the last Wise Tool are a troop of marsh ghouls."

Hallia, her lips pinched, turned toward the roaring

blaze encircling the tree. "All my father's efforts . . . for what? He would be sickened." She stamped on the ground. "The marsh ghouls won't even be grateful. It's not in their nature."

I shook my head morosely. "What a fool I am!" Sullenly, I turned to Ector. "Forgive me, if you can."

His crystalline eyes studied me. "I can. I only hope my master can do the same for me."

I dropped the useless object on the ground. Though it still reflected the glow of the flames, its inner fire had vanished. "Now both of us must die."

"Wait." He ran a hand through his curly hair. "Not both of you. Not necessarily."

I drew a ragged breath. "How so?"

"My master—he might still be able to save you. If we can get you there in time."

Hallia and I exchanged doubtful glances. I shook my head. "Why would he do that? After what I've done to him?"

Ector smiled wistfully. "Because, well, he's a very good man. And the healing arts are his specialty. If he can help you, he will. Of that I'm certain." He rubbed his blackened chin. "And besides, there's something about you, young hawk, something . . . different. My master, I think, will see it, too."

Hallia stared at the knotting vapors. "I do hope you're right. It could be our only chance."

She helped me to my feet. Then, leaning on my staff for support, I hobbled over to my sword. The blade, brightly shining, seemed ready to greet me as an old friend. I took the hilt and tugged, hoping to pull it free. The blade twisted a bit, creaking in the turf, but didn't lift at all. Frustrated at my lack of strength, I tried again—with no success.

"Here," offered Ector, "let me try." He wrapped his own hand around the hilt. All of a sudden he froze, a look of wonder in his eyes. "This sword . . . feels strange somehow."

I nodded. "It has a power, and a destiny, of its own."

Bracing himself, he tugged. To my surprise—and annoyance—the sword slid upward, as easily as a fish leaping out of water. Ector, his eyes still alight, handed me the weapon. I took it, pondering his expression. Then I plunged the blade into my scabbard, glad to have it with me once again.

Stroking my chin, I examined the slender hole in the ground left by the blade. "Why, I wonder, did Nimue leave it behind?"

"Simple," answered Ector. "She had no further use for it. She needed it only to tempt you—to lure you into her wicked little trap. Once she saw that wouldn't happen, she cast it aside. Just as she does to anything, or anyone, she no longer needs."

"She's horrible," growled Hallia. Her round eyes darted to me. "What she said there was a lie, wasn't it? There never was anything, well, *between* you, was there?"

"Of course not! She tried one time to trick me out of my staff, that's all." I frowned in puzzlement. "I can't fathom how she's grown so much older."

"I can explain that," declared Ector. "She comes from the same place I do."

"And where is that?"

The boy's voice dropped to a whisper. "From a country called Wales, part of the isle my master calls Gramarye. And from a time . . . in the future."

My legs, already wobbly, nearly buckled. "Help me understand. You're saying that both you and the older Nimue traveled here to this marsh from another time?"

He nodded gravely.

"That must have required great power."

"Yes." Even beneath the soot, I could see his cheeks flush. "But it's not a power that belongs to any person. It belongs to the Mirror. That's how I came here. And that's how I'm going to take you back to Gramarye."

PART THREE

20

THE MISTS OF TIME

We trudged through the swamp for the rest of the day, the light dwindling along with our strength. Hallia and I hadn't swallowed anything but a little water since last night's supper of vegetable slices; Ector, I was certain, felt no less hungry. And lack of food was the least of my own worries: Deep inside my chest, I felt a slow, relentless tightening.

My whole body ached, as my strength withered. Walking, even breathing, grew more difficult, while my eyes and throat throbbed painfully. I remembered one time, as a fevered child, thrashing about on my pallet of straw; I could still hear my mother singing softly as she pressed cold cloths against my forehead and poured soothing potions down my throat. The memory made me miss her, though I knew that none of her healing herbs could help me now. Why then did I think Ector's master, whatever his skills, could do any better?

To my surprise, Ector seemed to know his route across the marshy terrain. He led us down the ridge and across a flooded field where mossy tree trunks stood like forgotten graves. Plodding willfully, he paused only to help one of us, usually me, through the most treacherous patches. From the moment we departed the Flaming Tree, he hardly slowed his pace, rarely changed direction, and never backtracked.

At one point, the muck sucked at my boot—so hard that it slid off completely. I fell forward, splashing into the bog. Thanks to my staff, I managed to stand again, though my head swam from the exertion. As I hopped, dripping wet, back to my boot, Ector slogged over to help. He grabbed the leather top, which was nearly submerged. With a loud slurp, it pulled free. "Here," he declared, scooping out some of the mud. "Not much farther to go."

"How do you know?" I asked, panting heavily as I forced my foot back into the boot. "Have you been this way before?"

He nodded. "It's the way I came before. But I'm not really guiding us. The Mirror is."

Still breathing hard, I shot him a puzzled look.

"Somehow it knows," he explained, "who has already passed through. It helps you find your way back—just as, when we pass through again, my master will bring us the rest of the way."

My confusion deepened. "Pass through?"

He stepped away, saying no more. In fact, during

the trekking that followed, none of us spoke at all, except now and then to curse the branches that clutched at our clothes, or the sulfurous clouds that seared our lungs. Amidst our silence, the howlings of the marsh seemed even louder than before. Yet I had little strength to worry about it. My frame continued to weaken, my legs to drag. Everything I carried—my staff, my boots, even my sword—felt heavier with each step.

What a terrible mistake I had made by using the key! Not only had I spoiled Ector's quest; I had probably condemned myself to die. And for what? Nimue still roamed the marsh. She was less powerful, perhaps, without the marsh ghouls and whatever powers she had granted them, but she remained as scheming and vengeful as before. I could still feel her malevolent presence, as tangible as my own staff. I couldn't rid myself of the feeling that she had not yet finished with her plans for the marsh—or, indeed, for me.

Finally, we approached what seemed to be a rough-hewn arch. Purple-leafed vines curled around the edges of the two stone pillars that supported the crosspiece. A tangle of thick moss, dripping wet, hung down from the top.

I trudged up to the others. Standing beside Hallia, I found my vision drawn to the arch—and the shifting mirror it contained. The surface, glinting strangely, reflected our own faces, though they looked shadowy and distorted, almost unrecognizable. All the while, the mirror bent and bubbled, as if it were not a mirror at all but a curtain of mist. Indeed, dark vapors churned within its depths—quite different, however, from the vapors of the marsh.

For the mist within the mirror moved with a pattern—almost, it seemed, a mind—of its own. Clouds would knot, then unravel, only to twist themselves into knots again; these, in turn, would open into misty vistas, showing glimpses of valleys, homes, or half-formed hills; then all the vistas would combine, flowing into one another, forming a single knot that would begin to unravel again. Again and again the process repeated, but with new variations each time.

"That mirror . . ." I began, peering at my twisted reflection. "It's almost alive."

Ector's head bobbed up and down. "My master would agree with you. He says the Mirror is really a passage, a doorway. It leads to what he calls the Mists of Time, though he says they've also had other names across the ages."

Leaning against my staff, I peered into the archway with a mixture of fear and fascination. *The Mists of Time*. I savored the name, as well as the idea. How often Cairpré, in teaching me the lore of Fincayra and other lands, had stopped just to ponder the notion of time. For he, like myself, sensed its mysterious powers. He also knew that I had always longed to move through time—even dreaming, as a young boy, about traveling through it backward. To grow younger, as the world around me grew older! It was a bizarre thought, I knew, yet one I still secretly cherished.

The Mirror bulged, contorting our faces. One of Hallia's eyes swelled until it seemed ready to burst, then suddenly fractured into a dozen tiny eyes, all staring back at us. Doubtfully, I asked Ector, "Are you sure that's where we go?"

He swallowed. "I'm sure." Looking down at his mud-crusted boots, he added, "It's coming out the other side I'm not so certain about."

Hallia and I traded worried glances.

"What did your master say to do," I probed, "when you wanted to return?"

Ector drew a long breath. "Just call to him. He vowed to bring me home."

My head throbbed. "He thinks you'll be bringing him the key. Is he depending on that, somehow, to help him find you in there?"

"I, well . . . don't know."

A bolt of pain shot through my middle. I shouted, collapsing to my knees on the muddy ground. Though the pain subsided quickly, it left me quaking, feeling even weaker.

Hallia knelt beside me, placing her hand on my brow. "You feel so hot! Oh, young hawk, this is foolhardy. To walk into—into *that*. It's less like a mirror than a terrible, angry storm! And what chance do you have of coming out alive? There must be a better way."

Feeling the pinch in my chest again, I coughed. "No, there isn't."

She winced. "So be it. But I'm coming with you."

"I wouldn't do that if I were you."

Hearing the voice, thin and whistling, we froze. It came from somewhere nearby. We stared, but saw nothing other than the stone archway and the shifting mirror within.

"Who are you?" Ector called.

I struggled to stand, holding on to Hallia's arm as well as my staff. "Yes. Show yourself."

"I only show myself when I like," whistled the voice.

Abruptly, a catlike paw lifted out of the moss on top of the arch. It twisted, stretching to its fullest length. As it flexed its claws, combing the air, a second paw shot upward. Then a third. A fourth. For a long moment, the paws stretched lazily. *"Ahemmm,"* said the voice. "You are fortunate this is one of those times."

Listening to the half-snarling, half-purring quality of the words, I wasn't so sure.

"And I really don't care what you think," said the creature, as if it had heard my very thoughts. It continued: "And you, deer woman, ought to be ashamed."

The color drained from Hallia's face.

"Thinking I might be a witch in disguise! One who smells of rose blossoms, no less. *Ecchhh.* A thoroughly disgusting idea."

Suddenly, the paws retracted. A pair of silver-tipped ears poked out of the forest of moss. The rest of the face followed, rising slowly upward. It would have looked exactly like a cat's face, brown speckled with silver, except for one thing: It lacked any eyes. Smoothly, the creature stood. It rolled its shoulders, stretching the muscles, then sat down near the edge of the crosspiece. As if we didn't exist, it started licking its forepaws.

In time, the eyeless cat spoke again. "It doesn't

matter, you see. All you need to know is I am . . . well, a friend of the Mirror."

Ector started to open his mouth, when the cat continued talking.

"You don't believe me?" Its voice whistled more sharply than before. "I really don't care whether you do or not." The cat's paw dragged over the stone, claws scraping. "Yet you might as well ask yourselves, if I am not a familiar of the Mirror, and the mists it holds, then how do I know so much about them?"

Though my head swam, I moved a few steps nearer. "What do you know?"

The cat arched its back, stretching. Eyes or no eyes, it seemed to be gazing right at me. Right *into* me. After a while its back relaxed.

"More than I care to say," it answered at last. "Though I will tell you this much. Those mists are full of, *ahemmm,* pathways—where you will encounter many voices, many shadows. And not puny little shadows like that meager one clinging to your boots, oh no. I speak of shadows far more immense, far more terrifying."

At that, my shadow started spinning its arms, flailing at the turf under my feet. Although nothing happened—not a single speck of mud flew at the creature on the arch—the shadow's intention couldn't have been more clear. For an instant, I almost pitied it.

The cat, however, ignored the attempted assault, calmly licking the backs of its forepaws. "All those pathways," it continued in a relaxed tone, "will be

difficult enough for one person to survive. Two, perhaps, could also make it, though the chances are
small." It exhaled, making a sound that was half
growl, half sigh. "Three, though, will never work.
All of you would die, as surely as if you were swallowed by a bottomless pit."

"But my master will help us," protested Ector.

"He will try," whistled the cat, giving the boy an
eyeless stare. "He will wrap you in a protective cocoon of his own, as he did when you traveled here.
That is why two of you just might survive. Two—but
never three." Again, he stretched his legs. "Of course,
I really don't care. It's your fate, not mine."

Hallia stiffened. Slowly, she turned to me. "He
speaks truly. I can feel it."

As much as my legs trembled, my voice did more
so. "So can I. Yet who . . . should stay behind?"

"Not you," she replied, her eyes uncertain. "And
not Ector, whose master we hope will find some way
to heal you." Her grip tightened on my arm. "I shall
wait for you, right here, whatever happens."

The cat purred faintly as it clawed at the moss.

Though my arms felt as heavy as tree trunks, I embraced Hallia. "I'll come back. I promise."

"Remember when, when I . . . ," she said awkwardly, "wanted to say something to you? Back at
the meadow?" She moved closer, her hands tousling
my hair. "Well, I want to tell you now, more than
ever. But it won't sound—can't sound . . . not here,
not this way."

It was all I could do to shake my head glumly. At
length, she pulled away. Without her support, I nearly

fell, but Ector moved swiftly to my side, standing where I could lean against him. With a deep breath, he threw back his shoulders and faced the mists churning within the Mirror.

"I am coming, Master! Coming with a friend. I beseech you, bring us both back home."

The glinting surface suddenly shuddered, splitting along a crack. Out flowed a long, writhing tentacle of mist that reached toward the boy. The vapors brushed his chin, curled around his ear, then drew back. All at once, the Mirror snapped completely flat. Our reflections, clearer than before but more deeply shadowed, confronted us. At the same time, the sound of a distant chime rolled out of the depths, rising from somewhere far beneath the surface. My own sword caught the sound, ringing faintly in response.

"Of course it means nothing to me," said the cat, grooming a paw, "but it might be wise to hold hands." It paused, flashing an invisible eye at me. "And never, *ever* let go. Unless you don't mind being lost forever."

As the cat went back to licking itself, I linked hands with Ector. I turned, glancing back at Hallia, feeling another, deeper pain in my chest. Then, on a silent command, the two of us strode into the Mirror.

21

VOİCES

Our bodies merged into our own reflections as we stepped into the Mirror. Something shattered—and a powerful force dragged us forward, plunging us into darkness. The air thickened, hardening, even as it turned suddenly cold, as if we had been buried under a mountain of snow.

I felt Ector squeeze my hand. But I couldn't turn to see him, for my body had gone rigid, compressed by the heavy darkness encasing us both. I struggled to break free, to lift my arms—without success. Breathing, even thinking, grew more and more difficult.

Then, miraculously, the Mirror's grip loosened. My shoulder twisted; my head moved; my lungs filled again. The air warmed and swiftly softened into mist, wispy yet somehow sturdy enough to support our weight. At the same time, everything grew lighter. I glanced over at Ector, who returned my gaze, his face full of apprehension.

We were standing, our feet planted on vaporous ground that stretched without limits in all directions. Billowing clouds of mist rushed toward us, then abruptly withdrew. Columns and spirals sprung up from the clouds, like trees appearing fully grown in a forest, before they vanished into nothingness. Forms—almost recognizable but never quite—arose continuously, hovering briefly at our shoulders. Hollows of mist swelled into canyons; canyons shifted into mountains; mountains vanished in an instant.

All around us, hazy traces of shapes emerged, transformed, and disappeared. While I couldn't recognize any images, I felt a rush of familiar feelings. Some shapes tugged on me, alluring, like a dream that I wanted to recall. Others, more disturbing, clawed at me, like a secret fear that had stalked me always.

Though we stood still, we were constantly moving deeper into the mist. We seemed to be riding some kind of current—a current that drew us toward a mysterious destination. Would it be our destination, I wondered, or the current's own? Whatever, even if I hadn't felt so weak, I could not have resisted the relentless pull.

As the vapors drew us deeper, I recalled the many ways that mist had moved through my life. Even as a child in Gwynedd, I had savored the sight of morning mist rising off the meadow grass, the trees, or the snow-draped summit of Y Wyddfa. How I had longed to touch it, to hold it, this ephemeral river that flowed upon the air! Yet I could never come quite close enough. Whenever my hands nearly grasped it, the mist fled from me.

When I first sailed to Fincayra, a wondrous wall of mist had met me, arrested me—then finally parted to allow me through. And later, when I had followed the secret pathway to the Otherworld, bearing Rhia's limp body as well as her spirit, a different kind of mist had swirled about me. It had grown brighter, more luminous, with every step I took, until everything around me glowed with the luster of polished shells. Even the Tree of Soul, whose massive roots lifted from the Otherworld to support the lands above, had sprung from the mist; its dewy branches were one with the clouds. And when Hallia had first told me the legends of her people, the stories themselves were woven from those same elusive threads.

Now Ector and I were entering another world of mist. Suddenly an immense wave of vapors rolled toward us, gathering speed as it approached. Once again Ector's hand squeezed my own. Even as I squeezed back, the wave washed over us. For an instant, I lost my bearings. I saw nothing but mist all around me; I felt nothing but its chill upon my skin. Just as suddenly, the wave dissolved. I stood, as before, one hand grasping my staff, the other holding—

No one. Ector had disappeared. I was standing alone.

The warning of the eyeless cat thundered in my mind: *Never, ever let go. Unless you don't mind being lost forever.* I staggered, almost falling. It took all my fading strength to stand upright. I could feel the wave of mist coursing about me, even as it carried me along. But to where? Dark vapors flowed into my mind, clouding my thoughts, though I felt increasingly sure that this place had become my tomb.

At last, the sweeping motion slowed. The wave seemed gradually to withdraw, both from my mind and from the world around me. Shakily, I watched as the mist before me wavered and darkened, coalescing into images both detailed and colorful. There were rocky hillsides, and trees bent by incessant winds—hawthorns, ashes, and oaks. Here, a tangle of gorse bushes. And there, a village of crumbling, thatched-roof huts. It was a landscape, crisply defined. It was a landscape I recognized.

Gwynedd! The place that in Ector's time would be called Wales. But was I viewing it in Ector's time—or in my own, long before?

A lone figure appeared, wandering out of the trees. It was a boy, moving awkwardly, his long black hair a nest of leaves and grasses. He stooped to examine a small yellow flower, rimmed with lavender and blue. Carefully, he picked it, and blew gently on its petals to make them flutter. Suddenly, watching him, my fingers tightened around my staff. I knew what time I was seeing. For I knew this boy.

I was watching myself.

Amazed, I viewed my own life from years before. The image in the mist, while hazy around the edges, was as sharp as could be. As sharp as the pain of those days. The boy glanced uncertainly at one particular hut at the edge of the village, and I knew that

he was wondering whether to share the flower he had
found with the woman who shared that hut with him.
The woman who claimed to be his mother, though
she refused to tell him any more about his past. Or
her own.

Suddenly the boy stiffened. Very slowly, he turned
away from the hut—and toward me. His eyes, glimmering like black moons, pondered me, even as my
second sight pondered him. Then, all at once, my
view of him drew much closer. I could see none of
his surroundings, not even the flower in his hand:
only his face. I stared at the face, so much younger
and fairer than my own, as if I were looking into a
magical mirror.

All at once, his youthful visage started to change.
The glimmer vanished from his eyes; deep, jagged
scars appeared on his once-smooth cheeks and brow.
His nose, meanwhile, hooked downward, as his bony
chin lengthened. Yet nothing about him changed so
dramatically as his expression: Terrified, he grasped
his own cheeks, clawing at them.

"Go back!" he shouted, his voice so very much
like my own. "You are just a boy, and you are
wounded—forever blinded. You will find only pain if
you stay here. Go back while you can!"

"But I can't go back," I cried, swaying on my staff.
"I need help—and if I don't find it soon, I will die."

"Not here," he shrieked. "Here you will surely—
oh, the flames! Coming back. They will burn you
again!"

Instinctively, my own hands flew to my face. Like
the boy before me, I clutched the deep scars that rut-

ted my flesh. Even if I could have grown a beard thick enough to cover them, I knew that I would always feel them, just as I would always feel the terror of that day.

Just then I heard another voice call my name. Trying to keep my balance, I spun around to find a new form emerging from the veils of mist. Vaporous threads parted, revealing another face I knew well—the face of my own mother.

"Emrys," she pleaded, her sapphire blue eyes probing me. "Heed my warning, my son! You will only be hurt—burned again—if you stray too far from Fincayra."

Weakly, I swatted at the coil of mist wrapping itself around my arm. "I must leave, though, to be healed."

"No, my son." She shook her head, her golden hair brushing the encircling clouds. "You have the power to do it yourself. Don't you know that by now?"

"Mother, no. This is too serious."

She smiled lovingly. "Ah, but you are a healer, my son. Yes, that is what you are, and always shall be. A healer with remarkable gifts." Through the mists, she beckoned to me. "Come home to me now. This way. I will guide you, as I did long ago."

Confused, I looked back at the terrified face of the boy. "Don't follow her," he urged. "That way will only lead to pain, more pain."

All of a sudden, another face appeared—this time in the clouds above me. I felt its dark shadow fall upon me, enveloping the smaller shadow that quivered at my feet. Cautiously, I looked up, squinting into the bright swirls of mist.

"Merlin," growled the face of a man, his face as hard as chiseled stone. "It is I, your father, who calls to you—who would command you, if only you would obey."

With great effort, I lifted myself a little higher against my staff, and thrust out my chin. "You have never been able to command me."

"To your lasting detriment!" roared the man, his mouth fixed in a permanent frown. "For you have listened too long to others, those who would tell you that you are destined to be a wizard."

"He is a healer," snapped my mother. "And a great one."

"Wizard, healer, all the same," thundered my father in reply. His head tilted forward, revealing the gold circlet on his brow. "You are none of those! Hear me, son of Stangmar! You are destined to do only one thing—the same thing your father before you has done."

Sagging a little lower, I asked, "And what is that?"

"To fail." His words echoed in the surrounding clouds. Grim though he remained, for just an instant his face reflected deep sorrow, and still deeper remorse. "You come from bad stock, my son. Nothing you can ever do will change that. All your dreams, all your goals, are as impossible to grasp as the mist itself."

For a long moment, I stared up at him. My whole frame felt heavier, both from the weight of my weariness and the weight of his words. My fingers slipped lower on the shaft of wood that supported me.

"Come this way," he declared. "I will teach you what I can, so at least you will be prepared. For if indeed your lot is to fail, you should know—"

"What it takes to be a wizard," finished another voice, this one behind me. I turned myself around, though the mist was wrapping around my legs, squeezing as firmly as the serpents of the marsh. I found myself facing my mentor, Cairpré.

"You are a wizard, my boy." Vapors swam around him, circling his shaggy gray mane. "From that first day you wandered into my den—yes, even then—I could feel your growing power."

"I'm weak now," I countered, panting heavily. "Too weak, almost, to stand."

"Come to me, then," advised the bard. *The light I see shall set you free.* Have I not always guided you well in the past? And I see a wizard, a great mage, in you."

"Even now?"

"Even now, my boy. Why, your wizardry has only begun to flower."

"Don't do it," pleaded the scarred face of the boy. "It will only lead to more suffering."

"Which you can heal," promised my mother. "Come home now, heal yourself first. Then you can return to mending others."

Hesitantly, I started toward her, though the coils of mist made it nearly impossible to lift my legs. Struggling mightily, I took a step. While I could see the

mist was climbing steadily higher, reaching for my
waist, I hadn't enough strength left to tear it away. It
was all I could do to raise my leg for another step.

"You will fail," intoned my father.

"He will not," countered Cairpré. "He is, above
all . . ."

"Young hawk!" interrupted a new voice, one that
lifted my spirits more than any other.

"Hallia," I whispered, turning to her warm brown
eyes. "Help me know . . . what to do."

"Come to me, young hawk," she implored, reaching out to me. "You don't need to be a wizard for me,
nor a healer, nor anything else. Just my companion.
Now come back to me, and all will be well."

"But . . . no," I said hoarsely. "You saw for yourself . . . the bloodnoose."

"Come to me," she urged. "Stand by my side. Soon
we will be kicking our hooves, running together
again."

My head spun, as the mist crept higher on my
body. It pulled on me, weighing me down. Dimly, I
heard another voice calling through the thickening
fog. Distant though it sounded, this voice struck as
fresh as a woodland breeze. I knew it well. Rhia!

"You have great magic, Merlin," she warned, "but
you're in danger of losing it." Her hand, wearing a
bracelet of woven vines, waved vigorously at me.
"Your magic—your power—has always sprung from
the meadows, the trees, the singing streams. Come
back to the land, Merlin, before it's too late. Leave
this mist behind. Come away with me now!"

She was right—yes, I could feel it. I started to follow her, when a deep voice, bellowing sternly, arrested me.

"No, no, a wizard does not run."

It was the voice of my grandfather, Tuatha. Even if I had possessed enough strength to turn toward him, I did not need to see his face to feel the power of his presence.

"I am your future," he proclaimed. "Your destiny lies here, with me."

"He will fail," grumbled my father. "Just as I did."

"No," objected Rhia, "but his power springs from the land."

"To me!" cried Cairpré. "You already have the power of a wizard in your veins—all the power of Tuatha, and more. Come, my boy, and I will help you follow the ways of wizardry."

Confused, I didn't know which way to turn, which voice to believe. Shadows began to gather in the mist, pressing closer, obscuring the faces around me. Tendrils, heavier by the second, wrapped themselves around my chest. My knees felt ready to buckle; my chest ready to collapse. I couldn't move now even if I had tried.

The voices kept calling to me, vying for my attention. Yet with each labored breath I took, the voices grew dimmer, as did the light that had once scattered through the mist. I could hardly hear all the pleas and commands anymore. Swiftly they faded, like my strength, my will to live.

At that instant, another voice, no louder than the rest but more grating, spoke very near to me—almost in my ear. "Just as I predicted, you infantile wizard, you have doomed yourself."

I went rigid, as Nimue's voice clucked softly. "Now I shall be rid of you and your meddling ways forever. And since I am growing bored with waiting, I shall end your meager little life myself." Suddenly I felt cold fingers of mist curling around my neck. "Right here," she said smugly. "Right now."

At the chill of her touch, whatever strength remained in me erupted all at once. I reeled backward, my arms pummeling the encroaching clouds, my legs straining to burst free of their bonds. I could barely see in the blur of clouds—but felt myself falling, tumbling helplessly downward.

Even as I fell, a great weariness flooded over me. I may have evaded Nimue's grasp, but now, surely, I would die anyway. My strangled heart pulsed with regret: I had so much left to do, so much left to learn. And so many faces that I would never see again.

Faintly, I noticed that the mist itself was changing. Was I merely imagining? No, no, it was true. The mist was not merely shifting, forming shapes within shapes as it had so many times before, but . . . dissolving. Yes, that was it. Vanishing from every side.

Could that be light? It might be, though it seemed dim and wavering, coming from somewhere above. Although I couldn't move, I felt something hard forming beneath me—more like stone than mist. Even so, it didn't matter. Wherever I was now, I felt closer to death than ever before. Helpless, I drew a last, ragged breath.

22

ΠΑMΕS

When I awoke, two large eyes, darker than night, peered down at me. I tensed, my body as rigid as the stones beneath my back. Did those eyes belong to Nimue?

No, no, they were not hers—that much I could tell now, even in the dim light of this chamber where I lay on the floor. Set beneath white brows as thick as brambles, the eyes blinked once, very slowly. When they reopened, they seemed deeper than the deepest chasm: mysterious, frightening, and yet strangely familiar somehow. Suddenly they narrowed, squinting at me.

With a start, I rolled away—and bumped right into someone else. This time, slate blue eyes gazed down at me. At once, I recognized them. Ector!

"It's you," I murmured. Though I still felt too weak to sit up, a new strength was slowly seeping into me, filling me as falling rain fills the hollows of upturned leaves. All at once, I remembered the many faces that had confronted me in the mist. I cringed, and asked, "Are you . . . real?"

The boy, a thin shaft of light glinting on his curls, smiled. "I'm real, yes. And so was that bloodnoose."

"Extracted just in time, young lad. Just barely in time."

Feebly, I turned to the voice—and those unfathomably deep eyes. They belonged to an old man, extremely old by the looks of him, who sat cross-legged on the stones. Even in the dim light of the chamber, his flowing hair and beard seemed whiter than white. Almost . . . aflame. His beard, knotted and unruly, fell over his thighs and onto the floor like a luminous cloak.

"Aye, my lad," he continued, his words crackling like snapping branches. "When those inexplicable mists spat you out—" He caught himself mid-sentence, looking suddenly bewildered. "More truly, the mists are indescribable, wouldn't you agree? As well as indefatigable—if, for consistency's sake, we keep with terms using the Latin prefix *in*, one of Ceasar's more lasting contributions. Or I suppose you *could* say the indeterminate mists spat you out, or rather, was it you who spat out the mists? The indigestible mists? No, no, that's folly. How does one spit mist, anyway? Although a fountain does, I suppose, what what?"

Ector started to speak, but the old man shook his

head, setting loose a small yellow butterfly that had perched above his ear. "An English phrase, that that—I mean, what what. Not Celtic in the least, you understand. With no linguistic logic behind it whatsoever! Like so much else about the English: strictly incomprehensible, and at times, incoherent. I picked it up, you see, in my days in the royal courts of Gramarye, what what."

He drew his prominent brows together. "Now then, what was I saying? And . . . was I saying it now? Or then?" His bewildered look deepened. He grasped a fistful of beard hairs, thrust them into his mouth, chewed for a moment, then spat them out. "So tell me now, where were we?"

I cocked my head, wondering more and more about this old babbler.

"We were saying," answered Ector, "that my friend here almost died." Grimly, he observed me. "You were drawing your last breath, young hawk. I'm sure of it. I don't know how he did it, but my master pulled that bloodnoose clean out of you." His eyes glowed with compassion, then narrowed. "It was thicker than a rope, soaked through with blood."

With a shudder, I placed my hand upon my chest. The skin felt tender, as if my rib cage had been roughly chafed. Everything beneath my bones felt tender, as well—though my chest seemed whole again, more whole than it had for a long time.

Ector glanced proudly at the elder fellow, who was busy pulling some beard hairs out of his mouth. "I told you he was a healer."

"You mean," I asked in disbelief, "that *he* is the one who did it?"

The boy nodded.

"This fellow is your master?"

He watched me with a wry grin. "The same fellow you said had the courage of a newborn hare and the wisdom of a jackass."

I cringed. To my relief, the old man, still occupied with his beard, seemed not to have heard Ector's comment. With effort, I propped myself up on my elbows. I could feel my heart beating strongly beneath my ribs. Then, doing my best to look more thankful than surprised, I faced the elder squarely. "You saved my life, and I am grateful."

Casually, he scratched his nose. "Think nothing of it, my lad. I've always had some difficulty with people who try to die on my floor. Positively indecorous, you know—even indecent. Nothing personal, mind you . . . but I'm certain you can understand. Such a beastly mess, what what."

Still unsure about him, I gave a respectful nod. "I, ah, understand."

"Good," he declared, scratching the tip of his long nose. "That is a good deal more than I can say for myself most of the time." He clasped his weathered hands together and looked expectantly at Ector. "Now then." Briefly, another wave of confusion crossed his face. "No, no. Let's just say now. Less . . . disorienting. So then, now. Maggots and mushrooms! Dear me. Just tell me, please, one thing—one very important thing." The bewildered look vanished, replaced by one of great anticipation. "Where, lad, is the key?"

Ector's shoulders drooped. Clearly, if he could have slinked away between the cracks in the stones, he would have done so. His words, though merely a whisper, seemed to shout out loud: "I have failed you, Master."

For a long interlude, the old man didn't move. I thought, at first, that he had not understood. At last I noticed a slight mistiness in his eyes. "You mean . . ."

"I don't have it."

My stomach clenched. I managed to sit all the way up, placing myself between the two of them. "It wasn't his fault," I explained. "If anyone failed you, it wasn't him. It was me."

The elder studied me. He did not stir except to lift, very slowly, one of his tangled brows.

Feeling the weight of his gaze, I turned away. "He . . . he tried to tell me. And I should have listened better."

With his wrinkled hand, he tapped the floor. The sound reverberated in the shadowy chamber, finally dying away. "I see," he said at last. "Don't fret too much, lad. There have been too many times in my life when I should have listened better, for me to blame you now." He heaved a sigh. "Far too many."

His noble words lifted my spirits a notch. Yet, at the same time, the genuine anguish written upon his face made my throat swell.

With one hand, he tugged on the collar of his tunic—deep blue, it seemed, though I couldn't be certain. "Ah, listening. Most difficult of all the arts." He forced a half grin. "The only thing harder, I suppose, is trying to tame one's own shadow."

Sadly, I nodded. "Believe me, I know what you mean."

He straightened himself, making the joints in his back pop. "Well then. Or now. Shouldn't we introduce ourselves?"

He shot a quizzical glance at Ector. "We haven't yet, have we?"

"No, Master." He waved at me. "This is young hawk."

From somewhere in the room, there came a small screech and a flutter. The old man didn't seem to notice, and went back to watching me. The spare light rippled across his features and the stray hairs of his beard. "An odd name, that. What other names are you called?"

I peered at the dark eyes. "Most people just say Merlin."

Again, a screech echoed—much louder this time. The old man grew agitated. "No, my lad. I wanted your name, not mine!"

I stiffened. "It *is* my name."

"Merlin?" He leaned closer, drumming his bony fingers on the floor. "That's impossible. No, inconceivable."

Ector, reaching a hand from under his tattered robes, touched my knee. "Are you . . . really Merlin?"

Taken aback, I declared, "Of course! Why

shouldn't I be? And why did he say *his* name was Merlin?"

"Because it is." Suddenly the boy's face lit up like a torch. "Why, of course. That must be it! He shares your name because he—my own good master—is really *you.*"

"Me?" I asked, dumfounded.

"Your older self."

My jaw dropped.

The old fellow stared at me, aghast.

The boy, meanwhile, eyed us both with wonder. "Don't you see? You're both Merlin, but from different times." He laughed. "I knew there was something strange about you, young hawk. Strangely like my master! I'm sorry I didn't tell you anything, not even my real name. He—I mean you, the older you—told me not to trust anyone I met in the marsh."

My head whirled. "You mean to say your name isn't Ector?"

He ran a hand through his curls. "No. It's my father, you see, whose name is Ector—Sir Ector, of the Forest Sauvage. My real name . . . is Arthur."

Though I had not heard the name before, I felt an unaccountable stirring down inside myself. "And why do you call him—er, me—your master?"

"Because it sounds better than tutor, or teacher. But teach me he does—all sorts of things, some of them rather, well, unusual. Even bizarre." He gave an embarrassed grin. "Why, he's even told me that one day he'll show me how to pull a sword out of a . . . well, you'd never believe it."

I gasped, as an ancient hand clutched my thigh. "Don't say any more," came the elder's stern command. "The lad doesn't know a particle about his future, all that lies ahead." He tilted his head thoughtfully. "In that regard, I suppose, he's rather like you."

23

DANCE OF LIGHT

With surprising agility, the old man rose to his feet. At the same time, he swept his arm through the air, fingers splayed wide. His tunic's sleeve slapped the air; the sound reverberated in the darkened chamber like a clap of thunder. Could that really be myself, I wondered, however many years in the future?

The grand sweep of his arm, however, stopped short: He had caught several fingers in the knots of his beard. Still, that fact—and the fact that he created several more knots while trying to extract his hand—did not seem to bother him. Nor did it do anything to diminish the new illumination in his face.

At last, having untangled himself, he gazed at me. "Now, my lad, before we speak of things future—or is it things past?—let us have a meal, a genuine repast. Shall we? One doesn't often join oneself for dinner, after all."

"Yes, oh yes!" exclaimed Arthur, clapping his hands. "Except for that, well . . ." He waved a hand at me. "That whatever-it-was you gave me under the trees, I haven't eaten for three days."

"Which, to a boy your age feels like three centuries." The elder snapped a pair of bony fingers. "And which, to a man my age, feels like next to nothing. Oh, but it's a lovely way to gain perspective on life, this living on endlessly! Interminably, I should say. Only a fossil could tell you more—if, indeed, a fossil could speak."

"Fossil?"

"Why yes, my lad. You'll learn to think not in terms of life spans, or centuries even, but geologic time. Truly! Periods so vast that even the present era, Cenozoic, started sixty-five *million* years ago." Seeing my puzzled expression, he went on: "Of course, I agree, it can be unnerving, and confusing at times. Especially when you add in the living backward part."

I caught my breath. "The what?"

"Later, my lad, later." He stroked the forested knob of his chin. "We must have a bite to eat. But first, we need some light, what what?"

Once again he waved his arm, this time keeping clear of his beard. Light suddenly flashed, filling the entire chamber. All around us, assorted objects glittered (despite the layers of dust covering many of them)—whether they rested on the stone floor, the high wooden cupboard whose shelves sagged with leather-bound volumes, the lavishly decorated walls, or the ceiling itself. Some of the objects I recognized immediately, such as the strings of drying roots, herbs, and bark shavings—tied in bundles with a sprig of cedar, just as my mother always did to keep her ingredients fresh—that dangled above our heads. Other objects, though, remained utterly obscure: a silver chalice, whose two handles seemed to quiver restlessly; a shallow bowl holding two twirling red arrows; and a ragged manuscript on the oaken table beside us whose pages were busily turning themselves. Even the many rows of bottles and pots, which at first glance seemed unremarkable, bubbled with strange and colorful chemicals that I couldn't possibly identify.

Suddenly my attention turned from the objects within the chamber to the chamber itself. The walls, the ceiling, the nooks—all glowed with a powerful, pulsing radiance. Awestruck, I clambered to my feet, nearly tripping over my staff that lay on the floor. Slowly, I moved closer to the nearest wall. As I pushed aside a silken drapery, decorated with intertwining blue snakes and silver-green leaves, my heart raced. For I had already guessed what lit the drapery from behind.

Crystals. Thousands upon thousands of them. Utterly different from the crystals of the ballymag's underground home, this was an immensely varied array, in more colors, shapes, and sizes than I had ever seen. Gently, I ran my fingers over the facets. Some, sharply angled, pricked my skin; others gently arched, felt as smooth as icicles. Each crystal glowed with color—sometimes several colors at once—and all of them sparkled and shimmered continuously. The walls themselves danced with light and movement, as luminous as rainbows, as ever-changing as waterfalls.

Always, crystals had moved me, kindling a light within me as bright as themselves. Yet here radiated crystals beyond even my greatest imaginings. So many of them surrounded me—each one so deep, so rich, worth a lifetime of pondering. And each one blessed with a light, as well as a mystery, of its own.

"Well now," announced the old man, observing me. "How do you like it?"

He stood by the nearest wall of the chamber, his flowing hair and beard aglow, no less than the crystals. He leaned on a staff, much like my own but far more gnarled and scarred. With a start, I realized that it *was* my own staff, covered with dozens of additional runes, emblems—and what appeared to be teeth marks. Underneath all the new markings, however, I could still recognize the seven symbols of wisdom that I had struggled so hard to gain.

"How do you like it?" he repeated, with a wave of his hand. "A bit cluttered, perhaps, but not altogether uncomfortable."

"It's magnificent." I gave the hint of a grin. "One might even say . . . incomparable."

He gave a slight bow, swishing the folds of the dark blue cape, sparkling with embroidered stars, that overlay his tunic. But far more impressive than the movement of his cape was the movement of the great, dark form behind him: his shadow. Majestically, it swept across the opposite wall, rising almost to the very ceiling. Even more striking to me, the shadow seemed perfectly obedient, bowing precisely in time with the man.

With the wizard. For that, I now knew, was what he truly was—and what I could one day become. I glanced at my own shadow, so much smaller than his. To my chagrin, it was waving its hand at me in a mocking gesture. My eyes narrowed vengefully, but I could do no more. My day would have to wait. Still, I now had hope that the wait, while it could be very long, might someday be rewarded.

"So," declared the wizard, "let the feast begin."

As Arthur nodded eagerly, the old man pressed together the palms of his hands and whispered some secret command. An instant later, a pinewood table— shaped like a circle, of all things—appeared in the middle of the floor. Beside it rested three polished stools. Viewing his new furniture with approval, he pressed his palms again. A bouquet of blue, bell-shaped flowers appeared on one side of the table, with a basket of plump, golden apples on the other. He repeated the motion, producing a sudden burst of aromas. I smelled roasted chicken, mince pie, buttered river trout, steaming hot loaves, and even my childhood favorite, bread pudding. I smelled them, but couldn't see them. For nothing but the smells had arrived.

"Pigs and paddlewheels!" My elder self growled in frustration and pressed his hands together again, this time so forcefully that his shoulders started shaking and his cheeks took on a crimson hue. Seeing no result, he stopped. Then, breathing hard, he snarled, "Sometimes I wonder why I don't just cook things up the traditional way."

Arthur, looking famished, glowered. "You can't cook, that's why."

"Er . . . yes, well, you have a point." He shook himself. "I never was much for tradition anyway." His brows came together. Staring hard at the table, he muttered a few phrases and pressed his palms yet again.

This time food erupted on the slab of pinewood. All the delights I had smelled appeared, along with many more. There were tall flasks of water and wine (plus some dark, foaming brew that I couldn't imagine swallowing). A wooden platter held several loaves of steaming hot bread, all baked in the Slantos style; ambrosia bread was the first one I broke apart. Nut cakes and bowls of vegetable soup, honeyed chestnuts and strawberries with cream, mashed beetroot and cheese wrapped in dill, baked turnips and assorted greens—all crowded the table. Immediately, Arthur and I leaped to the stools and fell upon the feast.

The old man watched us approvingly for a while, then pulled up his own stool. He reached for the flask of foaming liquid, poured himself a mug, and—to my amazement—drank deeply. As he lowered the mug, his gaze met my own. With a knowing look, he offered me a swallow.

"No thank you," I replied, wiping some gravy off my cheek. "It doesn't look, well, right for me."

He took another sip. Foam clung to his whiskers as he tilted the mug. "*Ahhh.* Are you certain, my lad? I like it ever so much."

I shook my head. "No. But the rest of this feast is extraordinary."

"It's an acquired taste, I suppose, one of those inexplicable phenomena." He laid down the mug, almost toppling the plate of beetroot. "Takes a few centuries of getting used to, that's all."

Arthur, chewing on some cheese while holding a chicken leg in one hand and a large carrot in the other, nodded. "It's your best banquet ever, Master." He tilted his head imploringly. "Could we, perhaps, have a little of that . . . *mmm*, what did you call it? Cold cream?"

The old mage grinned. "Ah, you mean ice cream. Next to helicopters, the most remarkable invention of the twentieth century." He tugged on his ear thoughtfully. "Even so, a helicopter is still nothing compared to a hummingbird! Did you know their little wings can beat the air more than fifty times per second? And that the *Rufous,* while no bigger than the palm of my hand, can migrate over seven thousand miles every year?"

"Errr . . . no," I answered truthfully, having absolutely no idea what he was talking about.

"Well then," he declared. "What about that ice cream?" He winked, and three wooden bowls appeared. A soft, tan sort of pudding filled them, topped with sauce—light brown for us and amber yellow for him. Arthur dropped the chicken leg and plunged straight into his bowl, lifting it to his face. Cautiously,

I touched mine first with my finger. So cold! It seemed more like snow than food. I drew back my hand, frowning uncertainly.

"Coffee flavor," said the elder as he downed a spoonful. "With honeycomb topping on yours." His grin widened. "And a touch of Armenian cognac on mine."

"Armenian . . . what did you say?"

"Cognac, my lad. You'll find out in another millennium. And believe me, it's worth the wait. It's even worth the wretched all-day bus ride to that vineyard."

I frowned. "Bus ride?"

Before he could reply, Arthur lowered his bowl. The honeycomb sauce smeared his chin, cheeks, and nose. He looked ever so much more serene than the frightened boy who had accosted me in the marsh.

"Fumblefeathers!" cried the wizard. "How could I forget? We can't dine without music, what what?"

With a flourish, he pointed at an elegant harp that hung from the wall above a small bed, or nest perhaps, strewn with downy feathers. Instantly, the harp lifted higher on the wall, revealing its glittering strings. But for the oaken sound box, inlaid with bands of ash, its heart-shaped frame was made from living vines, twined securely around each other. Slender leaves from the vines, vibrant green, draped over the harp's edges. As the wizard's fingers snapped, the leaves curled downward—and began to pluck the strings. A soft, drifting melody, as soothing as a splashing stream, filled the crystal cave.

For a moment I watched the plucking leaves, then

turned to the elder who sat across the table. "You made that harp yourself, didn't you?"

"Aye," he answered wistfully, "but only a power far greater can make the music."

Just then a flutter of wings descended on us. A plump white goose landed on the table's edge, not far from the roast chicken. She curled her neck around to face the wizard, her yellow eyes glowering at him. She squawked once, then spoke a single word in her nasal voice: "Disgusting."

Very nearly, I dropped my bowl. "She speaks?"

The old man raised an eyebrow. "Indubitably." He took another spoonful of ice cream, being careful not to miss the sauce. "Now, Mary, you don't have to eat it yourself."

A white wing slapped angrily, splattering some leeks on the floor. "Marigaunce, if you please. There are strangers present."

"Marigaunce it is, then. Didn't I give you that name myself? But, as some bard or other said, what's in a name, what what? Besides, they aren't strangers so much as guests. You already know young Arthur. And this handsome young lad is, in truth, my younger self."

The goose swung her head toward me, stretching her neck to its fullest length. *"Hmmm,"* she muttered. "Handsome isn't the word I would use." Her eyes squinted at me. "I only hope you're less foolish than the old gander over there."

Dismayed, I considered returning the compliment. But the mage spoke first. "Don't mind her, lad. When the last of my owls, nineteenth in his line, finally took the Long Journey to join Dagda, I swore I'd never have another bird. They had lived under my roofs (and, come to think of it, under my hats) for several centuries, but enough is enough. Too many droppings—in the hair, in the soup, in the . . . oh well, you understand. Then Mary came along, barely a fledgling, and a half-starved one at that. And though her manners weren't nearly as developed as her neck, I took pity on her."

"Bah!" spat the goose. "It was I who pitied you, not the other way around."

He scratched the end of his beaklike nose, pondering. "I was wondering, my lad, since you've come all the way here . . ."

"Yes?"

"Would you like a closer look at my—er, your? No, no . . . *our* crystal cave?"

I beamed at him. "Oh yes."

"Good then." He curled his arm around mine. "Let's take a little tour, shall we?"

Together, we strode over to the tall wooden cupboard loaded with books of every thickness and color. The smell of worn leather grew stronger as we approached (as did the sound of harp strings, since the leaf-draped instrument hung on the cupboard's far side). With the tip of his finger, my elder self touched the bindings of several volumes, greeting them like venerable colleagues.

For my part, I stood gaping at the sheer number—and diversity—of books on those shelves. The cupboard itself was three or four times larger than any

I'd seen before, covering a good portion of the wall. The shelves, and the volumes stacked upon them, glowed with the light of the crystals that seeped through the cracks in the wood. Drawing closer, I could tell that the books had not been separated according to subject. On the contrary, they were shelved with no apparent logic: a botany text sat beside a treatise of Aristotle; a pictorial history of a place called the Ganges River lay in between two volumes titled *Astrophysics: The Long View.* There were books on sea voyages, rare birds, cloud formations, someone named Leonardo da Vinci, healing herbs—and one, called *The Wind in the Willows,* that must have been about weather patterns along riverbeds. Many more books displayed titles in languages that I couldn't comprehend; of those, most left me with the feeling that I couldn't understand them even if the tongues had been familiar.

And yet . . . it was clear that *he* understood them. A quiet thrill passed through me as I watched the white-bearded man beside me perusing the shelves. Might I really know so much one day?

"How," I asked, "do you keep track of them all?"

He turned to me, combing his beard with one hand. "Keeping track of what books are here is easy, my lad. It's keeping track of all the books—all the subjects—I know nothing about that's difficult."

"But you have so many," I pressed, waving at all the volumes. "And they're all mixed up, besides."

A hint of a grin lifted the corner of his mouth. "That is because, my lad, the universe *itself* is all mixed up. The only divisions in the sphere of knowledge are put there by us, you see, not by the cosmos. Physics, poetry, biology, philosophy—they're all facets of the same crystal. Why, in another millennium, scientists will realize that the very same questions they are asking about subatomic particles also apply to the very origins of galaxies! That will surprise more than a few of them, what what?"

Seeing my bewildered gaze, he bent toward me. "Don't worry, lad. It's truly the way of things. The universe will always continue to surprise us, no matter how clever we may think we are. That's its nature, just as the nature of people is to keep trying to comprehend it."

I frowned, unsure how to take his words. "So we can't ever really understand the universe?"

His grin broadened. "Not completely."

"Then what *can* we do?"

"We can wonder at it." A light, brighter than the walls around us, kindled in his eyes. "No matter how old you get, my lad, never lose your sense of wonder."

He reached for a thin tube, fashioned from some sort of metal, that rested on the edge of a nearby shelf. "Here. Whenever my awareness of surprise runs low, I try this."

I turned the tube over in my hands. "What do I do?"

"Why, peer through it, of course." He tapped one end. "This side faces you."

Hesitantly, I trained my second sight down the tube. Suddenly I jumped back, knocking into the cupboard and dropping the instrument on the stone floor. "A giant goose! I saw—"

"Mary, that's all."

The goose, glaring at me from the banquet table where Arthur continued to eat, hissed loudly.

The wizard bent, bones creaking, to retrieve the tube. "It's called a telescope. Brings far things much closer." His expression clouded slightly. "Except for those things you might wish most to bring."

I watched him as he stretched his arms outward in the way I so often did myself, trying to relieve that elusive pain between the shoulder blades, that burden of every Fincayran. After a moment, I ventured to ask, "Just because our ancestors lost their wings so long ago, must we always feel that pain? Or do we have to find some way to regain our wings before we can be free of it?"

As if he hadn't heard me, he stepped deeper into the cave.

When I caught up with him, he stood pondering a plant box that hung from a curling lavender crystal. At once, I recognized the plant it contained: eelgrass, the reed most precious to Hallia's clan. Observing the dark green shoots, I could almost feel their rough texture on my tongue. And I could almost hear Hallia's brother, Eremon, when he had explained to me, for the first time, the deer people's many uses for those reeds. They served as thread for baskets and curtains; as kindling, soaked in hazelnut oil, for winter fires; and as a symbol of the clan's connection to the web of worlds—a newborn's first blanket, and a departed friend's funeral shawl. My mouth went dry as I remembered watching Hallia wrap such a shawl of vibrant green around Eremon's own lifeless form.

All of a sudden I noticed a small, thin shape lying

amidst the reeds. It was a lock of hair. Even in the lavender glow of the crystal, its auburn hues shone clearly.

"That's . . . ," I said, my throat constricted. "That's from Hallia."

"Yes," replied the elder, his voice wistful.

I turned to him, searching his face. "What happens to her?"

He gave no reply.

"Please," I beseeched. "You don't have to tell me about the lost wings. Or about whether I ever get to see again through my own eyes. Or anything else I might ask you! But do tell me this: Does something terrible happen to her? To us?"

The old man looked not at me, but at the lock of hair. Behind us, the harp strings' tempo slowed, while their melody seemed more melancholy than before. "Not exactly," he said at last. Slowly, he turned toward me. "If I say any more, it might, well, disturb things. For you, as well as for her. Just savor all your moments together."

"Moments?" I repeated, my voice hoarse.

"All life is but a stream of moments, my lad, each one containing its own choices, its own marvels, its own mysteries. And, I fear, its own perils. But this much I have learned: It sometimes happens that what seems, in one moment, a curse, could turn out in the end to be a blessing."

Tenderly, I touched a shaft of eelgrass. "Or the reverse?"

He nodded. "Or the reverse. And one never knows until the moment has passed."

Reaching for a hefty, twin-bladed ax, he raised it slightly off the stone floor before it fell back with a thud. "Take this terrifying piece of weaponry, for example. Looks most assuredly like an instrument of death, does it not?"

"Of course," I replied. "That's what a battle-ax is for."

His eyebrows lifted like rising clouds. "Well then, it should interest you to know that this battle-ax saved—or will save, I should say—your very life. Indisputably! Mine, too, as I think about it. And in a most unexpected way."

Before I could ask him to elaborate, he ran his fingers over the silver hilt of my sword. "Just as this sword will save the life of young Arthur over there— oh yes, many times."

I glanced over my shoulder at the boy, watching him drain his remaining soup and tear off a slab of nut cake. "I knew, down deep in my bones, that he was the one."

"The very one." Gently, he patted my shoulder. "And you will guide him, as best you can, whether his quest is to find the legendary Grail—something as wondrous as peering into the eyes of seven white wolves—or to find his own true self."

My throat more parched than ever, I tried to swallow. "Does he ever find this Grail?"

"No," answered the mage. "But the quest succeeded nonetheless."

"That doesn't make sense."

He wove his fingers into his beard. "Ah, but it does, truly. As does his even greater quest, to usher forth a whole new concept of justice and law—inspired by high ideals, but doomed to fail in its time. For the effort alone spawned a triumph, frail but nonetheless alive. A triumph that might yet outlast the tragedy." With a mixture of sadness and affection, he watched the boy, who was stuffing more nut cake into his mouth. "That is why, in times to come, he will be called the greatest of all the kings of Gramarye, the King Once and Future."

I shook my head. "How can Arthur fail, but still triumph in the end?"

"I didn't say that he would, lad. Just that he might." His eyes glistened, reflecting the glow of the crystalline walls. "Just as you and I might."

My heart felt suddenly heavy. I stood there, silent, wanting to know more yet afraid to ask.

He drew a slow, ponderous breath. "You see, I sent young Arthur back to that marsh for a simple reason. It was the only way—the only hope—of saving me. You. Us."

24

MERLIN'S ISLE

The aged man—my elder self—ran his sleeve across his brow. Wearily, he confessed, "This will require a bit of explanation, I'm afraid. Shall we sit down?"

Without waiting for my response, he wriggled his fingers in a strange manner. Immediately, the floor behind us erupted, spraying chips of stone across the floor of the cave. I leaped aside, though the wizard didn't even budge. When I turned around, I saw that a fully grown beech tree had surged through the floor, its branches arching from one wall to the other, touching the crystals at either end.

Awestruck, I studied the tree whose sturdy roots now clasped the broken stones. Unlike any tree I'd known before, its trunk rose only a short distance above the roots before bending sharply to the side.

Then, after a short horizontal distance, the trunk lifted upward again, stretching its leafy boughs to the ceiling. Heaving a sigh, my old companion sat himself upon the horizontal section and leaned back against a pair of branches. His feet swung slightly above the floor.

"Ah," he mused, "I have always loved to sit in trees."

"So have I," I replied, "but normally not indoors."

Ignoring my comment, he laid his hand upon the smooth, gray bark. "And beech trees, somehow, always make me feel more peaceful." His voice dropped a little lower, as did the harp music that continued to fill the chamber. "Such things are more and more helpful these days."

"Tell me," I said, stepping nearer. "What has happened to you—to us?"

"In time, lad, though first you should have a seat yourself." His brow knitted. "There's really not room for two of these chairs, however. A matter of floor space, what what? Ah, there's the solution!" He pointed to the empty stools beside Arthur, who was busily devouring another chicken leg, oblivious to anything but the repast before him. "Fetch one of those, would you?"

I started to move when, to my utter astonishment, something else went to fetch the stool. The wizard's shadow! The great form, as tall and broad as the tree itself, slid across the crystal cave's wall and over the floor to the banquet table. Without a sound, it lifted the stool, carried it through the air, and placed it by my side—right on top, I was pleased to note, of my own squirming shadow.

As the immense shadow returned to its position, nestled among the branches next to its master, the wizard gave a nod of approval. "Thanks, old friend."

Old friend, I thought. That part of my own future will surely be different! And yet . . . I glanced down at my own little shadow, struggling to free itself from the chair, and wondered. Could it be possible? Though I felt certain that the answer was no, I grasped the stool and slid it to one side, just far enough that it no longer pinned the shadow. As expected, I received no gesture of thanks—only an impudent kick.

That elder, I realized, was observing me. "How do you get your shadow to behave so well?" I asked. "I'd love to trade mine for one like yours."

He shook his head, making his flowing white hair shimmer in the crystals' glow. "It's part of you, my lad, just as the night is part of the day."

"I wish it weren't," I grumbled, seating myself on the stool. "Now tell me, please. What caused you to send Arthur back to that marsh? The way he described it, you were imprisoned, very likely to die! Yet here you are, in your own crystal cave."

Somberly, he gazed at me. "All of that is true, indisputably true."

"But this place, so full of marvels—"

"Is also my prison," he declared. Sliding his hand over the smooth trunk, he drew a deep breath. "It's that sorceress Nimue, I fear. She lured me—tricked me—into revealing some of my most powerful spells. Then, using the very power of this chamber to enhance her own, she turned those spells against me, sealing me into this place forever."

The final word fell upon me like a stone. "So you're completely trapped?"

His eyelids closed. "I am."

"That Nimue!" I cried. "What torture it must be for you."

"All the more so because of the important work that remains to be done beyond these walls."

For a long moment, his words hung in the air. Then, reopening his eyes, he noticed something above his head. With a curious expression, he raised one hand toward an object, slender and brown, dangling from one of the limbs. A cocoon! Despite his troubles, the wizard seemed rapt in concentration. As the cocoon quivered slightly at his touch, he nodded, and the grimness seemed to lift a little from his face.

He lowered his hand, then turned back to me. "She did forget about one thing, though, one quite important thing. The Mirror! I can still use its pathways, the very Mists of Time, to bring others to me, or send them elsewhere. Even if I can't travel through it myself, it offers me a window, you see, on the world outside." The sober expression returned. "And, for at least a moment, it gave me a chance to escape."

A shudder ran through my whole body. "The key."

"Yes. It is—er, was—the only thing strong enough to break Nimue's spell." He blew some stray beard hairs off his lips. "I recalled that it had been hidden in the swamp. So I sent Arthur to find it, to bring it back. When the sorceress learned of that, she realized she had to find it first. So she, too, entered the mists. No doubt she turned the marshlands upside down searching. Why, she even lured you in there to assist her—changing our history in the process."

"So you, at my age, didn't spend that time in the Haunted Marsh?"

"Heavens no, my lad." He grimaced. "She really made a beastly mess of things."

"I'm the one who made the mess!" I could hardly contain my anger. "Now I understand. She tricked me, just as she tricked you. She knew that the key could only be used once. And even though she expected me to use it to stop the bloodnoose, not to free the marsh ghouls, she still got what she most wanted."

My throat made a sound—part growl, part sob. "By using the key in the past, I sealed your fate, my own fate, in the future. Nimue said so when she left: *You have doomed yourself.* That's what she told me! And she was right. More right than I could ever have guessed."

"At least," said the old man, "you stood up to her."

Bitterly, I hung my head. "What good did that do? It was just what she needed to prevail." I regarded him sharply. "And what good does it do for you to teach Arthur all those high ideals—when you already know that his kingdom is going to fail in the end? That he'll never live to see them prevail?"

Squeezing a branch of the beech tree, the wizard gazed at me. At last, he spoke, his voice full of tenderness. "What good? I cannot tell. Nor can anyone."

I shrugged. "Just as I thought. More good intentions worth a handful of dust."

"Hear me out," he declared, his eyes gleaming anew. "There is still this: A kingdom that is banished from the land may yet find a home in the heart." His back straightened, and he seemed to grow larger as I watched. "And a life—whether wizard or king, poet or gardener, seamstress or smith—is measured not by its length, but by the worth of its deeds, and the power of its dreams."

Absently, I scanned the glittering facets surrounding us. "Dreams can't make you free."

His hand, so deeply wrinkled, reached over and clasped my forearm. "Ah, dear lad, but they can." He looked not at me but through me, at something far distant. "Most surely, they can."

I studied his face: the dark eyes, almost laughing while at the same time almost crying; the wide mouth, so old and yet so young; the wrinkled brow, marked by ideas and experiences I couldn't begin to fathom; and, of course, the great beard—tangled in places, luminous throughout. Yet for all that face made me want to hope, I still felt defeated.

"Know this as well, young wizard," he said kindly. "Everything I have taught and will teach my pupil Arthur boils down to this: Find your true self, your true image, and you shall tap into the greater good— the higher power that breathes life into all things. Most assuredly! And while you may not prevail in your own time and place, your efforts will flow outward as ripples on a pond. Powered by that greater good, they may touch faraway shores, altering their destinies long after you have gone."

"But destiny can't be changed," I protested. "Because of my folly, you—and therefore I—will be trapped in this cave forever."

The old man considered my words for a moment before speaking. "You have a destiny, lad. That much is true. But you also have choices. Yes—and choices are nothing less than the power of creation. Through them, you can create your own life, your own future, your own destiny."

I merely looked at him in disbelief.

Pensively, he rubbed a few leaves between his thumb and forefinger. At the same time, the harpstrings seemed to pluck slightly more rapidly, their notes echoing from the walls with a lighter lilt.

"By your choices," he continued, "you might even create an entirely new world, one that will spring into being from the ruins of the old." He smiled to himself in a secretive way, as if he knew much more than he was revealing. "There is a poet called Tennyson, from a time yet to come, who describes such a world: Avalon is its name. That is a land, he says,

Where falls not hail, or rain, or any snow,
Nor ever wind blows loudly; but it lies
Deep-meadow'd, happy, fair with orchard-lawns
And bowery hollows crown'd with summer sea."

The words fell upon me like a warm summer rain, yet still I could not bring myself to believe him. "I can't even move my own scrawny shadow, no matter how hard I try. So how can my choices make any real difference to the outside world?"

"Well," said the mage with a sigh, scanning the boughs that supported him. "With regard to your shadow, you might stop trying and simply start being."

"Being? Being what?"

"And with regard to your choices," he went on, "you have already affected the world because of them. Indelibly, I might add. Think of it, lad! In your brief time on Fincayra—what has it been? Three years?—you have roused the hidden giants, found a new way of seeing, toppled an entire castle, answered an oracle's riddle, defeated those wicked beasts who devour magic, taken your sister's spirit into yourself, healed a wounded dragon, and so much more. And that is but the beginning! You have (if I recall correctly) become a deer, a stone, a feathered hawk, a tree, a puff of wind—and even a fish."

He paused, glancing over at Arthur, who was finishing one fruit pie and moving on to another. "A fish," he muttered to himself. "Yes, yes, that might be just the right thing for him at this stage."

His bright eyes swung back to me. "You have choices, my lad. And with choices, power. Inestimable power."

Despite myself, I felt a faint glimmer of renewal somewhere down inside. Had I really done all those things? Though I knew that Nimue's treachery had defeated me, forever it seemed, I still found myself feeling curiously different. Stronger, somehow. I shifted my weight, sitting a bit more erect on the stool.

Then a wave of doubts washed over me. "I may have done those things on Fincayra. But . . . what about here? This place called Gramarye? This is the land you wanted to save—but now cannot."

As the old mage regarded me, the crystals lining the walls and ceiling seemed to grow a little brighter. "Whatever happens to me, or to you, my lad, we will have forever changed this place, this island, just as you have forever changed that island that is now your home. Most certainly! I have even heard some people cease to call it Gramarye—or even that modern term, Britain—at all, preferring instead to say Merlin's Isle."

Almost imperceptibly, he smiled. "You doubt me? Then hear these words, penned by a poet named White who will not even be born for more than a thousand years:

> *She is not any common earth*
> *Water or wood or air,*
> *But Merlin's Isle of Gramarye*
> *Where you and I will fare."*

He pointed a knobby finger toward the far end of the cave. From within its depths, a small clay cup came floating toward him. Carefully, he plucked it from the air, reached inside, and pulled out a tiny sphere. Though the sphere was dark brown, it gleamed with an eerie sheen that seemed to pulse like a living heart. It was, I knew at once, a seed.

"The wonders of this seed," pronounced the wizard, "are both too subtle and too immense to name, though in years to come many a bard will try."

Slowly, he rolled it between his fingers. "Its history, too, is immense, so I will share but a little with you now. This seed was discovered in ancient Logres, at the bottom of a deep tarn, possibly by Rheged of Sagremor; transported in secret by an unknown Druid elder to the Isle of Ineen, where it stayed many years; stolen by the stern queen Unwen of the realm of Powyss; lost eventually; found; lost again; and found again by a young page after the terrible battle of Camlann right here in Gramarye."

He smiled briefly, but whether it was smile of pleasure or of sadness, I couldn't tell. "Ah, lad," he continued, rolling the little sphere in his palm. "I could say so much more—yet nothing is more important than this: This seed carries the power to grow into something magnificent. Truly magnificent."

I leaned closer on the stool. "Can't you tell me what that will be?"

"No, I cannot."

I frowned at him. "And you will say nothing, either, about the lost wings?"

He shook his white head. "I will, however, say one thing more about this seed. If you succeed in finding just the right place for the planting, it will, one day, come to bear fruit more remarkable than you can guess. And yet it will take, even in the finest of soils, many centuries just to begin to sprout."

He handed me the seed, pressing my fingers over it. I could feel, through my palm, a hint of motion, a

vague beating against my skin. Gently, I placed it inside my leather pouch.

Then, lifting my face, I looked upon my elder self.
"If, as you say, it will take centuries to sprout, and
time before that to find where it should be planted,
then . . ."

"Yes?"

"Then I had better begin soon, don't you think?"

As he nodded, the stars embroidering his cape
seemed to sparkle. "As soon as you like, my lad."

He plucked a crumpled leaf out of his beard and
cast it aside. "Remember this about seeds—and also
about wizards. They can transform the world, oh yes.
But only to the degree, and in the way, that the bearer
of those seeds is himself transformed."

His eyebrows bunched together. "And there is one
thing more you should know." He bent his head
close to mine, dropping his voice to a mere whisper.
"For all her plotting, for all her treachery, Nimue did
not count on this turn of events: We have met, you
and I! And since we have met, we have been
warned."

"I don't understand."

He moistened his lips. "You have a very long life
ahead of you, my lad. Not even considering the years
you'll add when you learn to live backward! That gives
you the one weapon that could yet triumph somehow
over Nimue—over any spell, no matter how powerful. It's a weapon that can dissolve any knot, destroy
any monument, burn away any realm . . . or build a
new one out of the ashes."

I glanced at the battle-ax leaning against the wall,

glinting in the shifting light. "What weapon do you mean?"

"Time." He tapped the tree trunk beneath him. "Time gives you—us—a chance. Nothing more, yet nothing less. My fate, you see, may not be yours! You still have freedom of choice, as did I. But now you know some things I did not. So perhaps, just perhaps, you will choose more wisely than I did—and avoid Nimue's traps, no matter how alluring, when the time finally comes."

Feeling a flicker of hope, I took his outstretched hand. My fingers, so much smoother and rounder, wrapped around his own. Our hands seemed very different, and yet very much the same. I felt the vibrant passion, along with the uncertainty, of youth—and the deep wisdom, and different uncertainty, of years. I felt the weight of tragedy, and the anguish of loss, that awaited me.

And I felt something more, as well: the barest breath of a chance.

The mage's grip suddenly tightened. His head jerked, then stayed fixed, as if he were listening to a faraway voice, hoping to catch a few words or phrases. At length, he released my hand. "It is time, sad to say, for you to leave."

I studied his troubled brow. "What's wrong?"

"Hallia," he whispered. "She is in danger." He winced, rubbing his temple. "Grave danger."

I leaped off my stool. "Send me back, then."

"I will try," he answered, sliding down from his perch. "But it's not as simple as that. To succeed, I will need your help. For to get there in time, you must go back into the Mirror's living mists, and confront whatever you may find there."

My legs felt as rooted to the floor as the beech tree. "The mists? I . . . I can't go back there. Those faces—you don't know what they're like."

"Ah, but I do." He beckoned to my staff, which flew to my side. Hesitantly, I grasped its shaft, striking its base on the stone floor. At the same time, my shadow reached for the shadow of the staff—then seemed to change its mind and pulled away.

"Those faces," warned the wizard, "will be no less terrifying this time. More so, perhaps. Only you, though, can find your way through them. Only you." His gaze bored into me. "It's nothing that you—that is, we—can't handle, lad."

Anxiously, I swallowed. "I like the sound of *we* better."

His own hand squeezed the gnarled top of my staff. "So shall it be, always."

I gave a nod. "Always."

Removing his hand, he flicked a finger against my pouch. "Remember the seed, now."

"I will."

"And as for those rumors about lost wings . . ."

"Yes?"

His eye seemed to twitch. "You never can tell about those beastly rumors. So much speculation, what what."

I ground my teeth. "Are you sure you can't say something?"

"No, my lad. For the same reason you didn't tell Arthur about his sword. He'll find out, in the proper

way, soon enough." He released a grunt that might
have been a laugh. "As will you:"

"Oh, but you can't—"

"Can't what?"

"Leave me wondering!"

The bushy brows lifted. "About what?"

For a few seconds I glared at him, while he gazed
innocently back at me. Then, with a grand flourish,
he waved at the banquet table. It completely disappeared, food and all, leaving the goose to fall to the
floor with a squawk. Arthur, however, fared better:
He merely bit into the air where, an instant before, a
juicy plum had been. Stepping over the goose, the
boy strode over to us, a satisfied grin on his face. He
paused briefly to admire the beech tree, stroking one
of its roots, before joining us. Seeing me holding my
staff, he wiped some plum juice from his chin.

"You are leaving?" he asked.

"I am," I replied. "I must go to help Hallia."

He stiffened. "Then I will come with you," he declared resolutely.

"No, no," I replied, placing my hand upon his
shoulder. "Your work is here." I scrutinized him for a
moment. "And your work, I am certain, will bring
many moments of greatness."

His jaw tightened. "Will I ever meet you again,
young hawk?"

I shook my head. "Not for a very, very long time."
Then, tilting my head toward his master, I added,
"From my own perspective, that is. From yours,
why—you already have."

He grinned once more, the light playing on his

golden curls. "I suppose that's true." He extended his hand to me. "Though we didn't meet for long, I am glad, very glad, we did."

My hand clasped his. "Yes, my friend. Well met." I cocked my head at the old mage, who was watching us closely. "Take care of him, now. Whether he deserves it or not."

Though he seemed perplexed momentarily, the boy bobbed his head. "I will, I promise."

All of a sudden, thick mist started swirling about me. Swiftly it blotted out the crystalline walls and ceiling of the cave. I watched the last flickering of the facets, knowing that I would not view them again for the span of several lifetimes. An instant later, the beech tree vanished, followed by Arthur himself. Soon only the dark, blurry shape of the elder wizard remained. He lifted his hand, waving to me across so much mist, so much time. Then, abruptly, he disappeared.

25

ϮѴΠΠELS

Rigid I stood, like a pillar of stone in the middle of a swelling sea—a sea of mist. Clouds, darkening swiftly, pressed close, so close that for an instant I feared they would smother me. Yet somehow I continued to breathe. And also to watch, with growing trepidation, the endlessly churning billows that surrounded me.

As before, the swirling vapors formed intricate patterns—worlds within worlds—that stretched without limit in every direction. But unlike before, those patterns were utterly unrecognizable: not just as places or settings that I knew, but as any sort of places *at all*. No valleys, no forests, no villages emerged from the folds of mist. No hints of secret dreams or hidden fears tugged at my memory. No shape or feeling that I could in any way recall sprang forth.

Only mist.

And one thing more: my fear, swelling like a burgeoning cloud within myself. I feared for Hallia, in danger from some unknown source. Could I reach her in time? Even if I could, would I be able to help? And I feared for myself, as well—in ways as profoundly unrecognizable as the mist itself. Even my shadow, cowering at my feet, seemed overcome by fright.

In time, the clouds began to gather in a different kind of pattern. I watched, the drumbeat of terror growing louder in my head, as the vapors before me coalesced into a circle—a hole, tunneling deep into the darkness beyond where I stood. Then, to my left, another hole appeared. Yet another hole opened above my head; two more to my right; several more in front of me. Within moments, I was surrounded by a honeycomb of tunnels that dropped endlessly away.

All at once, a movement stirred within one of the tunnels. An edge of light glinted on a shadowy form that emerged slowly into view. It was, I saw with a shudder, a face. My face! There were the eyes, darker than the tunnel itself; the hair, all askew; the scars, rutting my cheeks and brow. The face, a perfect image of my own, gazed at me intently.

Then, within other tunnels, more faces started to appear. One after another they hardened out of the vapors—all staring at me, all waiting, it seemed, for something to happen. And all the faces were my own. On every side, above me as well as below, I saw the image of myself. Watching in silence, the faces confronted me, each one identical to the rest. Now I looked out not on a limitless sea of mist, but on a many-faceted crystal, with each facet a mirror that reflected myself back to me.

Suddenly one of the faces spoke, its voice precisely my own: "Come, young wizard. Enter my tunnel, for it is the only path that will lead you home."

Before I could reply, another face called from above: "You are not a wizard, but a good son. And this is the pathway you seek! Are you not the brave boy who saved his mother's life on a rocky shore many years ago? Come, follow me now—before your time runs out."

Another face objected: "Heed not their words! I know who you truly are: not a wizard, nor a son, but a spirit of nature—brother of the streams and sky, fields and forest. Come with me now. Home lies this way!"

"Tell the truth," sneered another face. "You have aspired to be all those things and more. But you have failed at all of them, and down inside you know you forever will. For you are a bungler, whose frailties will always corrupt your best intentions. Tell me now, do I speak the truth?"

Regretfully, I nodded.

"Then you must follow me," the face demanded. "Only the true path will take you home. Hurry now, while you still have time!"

"No," objected the face who had spoken first. "You are a wizard, and someday you will be a great one. You know that now! Come this way."

"Beneath that," came the counter, "you are still a bungler. Come now. Follow the deeper truth! Don't be fooled by your own vanity, your own wishful thinking."

Other faces cried out to me—all in my own voice. One appealed to me as a healer, a mender of torn sinews and sliced tissues; another called to me as an explorer, a lone adventurer who had built a raft of driftwood and found the uncharted route to Fincayra long ago; still another hailed me as a champion, a rescuer of those in need. The chorus rose, pounding in my ears. I was, to different faces, a sower of seeds; a master of many languages; a passionate young man who longed to spend endless days beside Hallia; a trickster, who savored any chance to surprise; and many more things besides.

As the voices swelled, so did my confusion—and my certainty that whatever chance I might have to save Hallia was rapidly slipping away. If only one of the tunnels could take me back, I must somehow decide which one to follow. And I must decide soon.

To my horror, the tunnels themselves started to move—to glide higher or lower in the surrounding vapors, to slip sideways, or to dance erratically. Swiftly, the faces' motions accelerated. At the same time, they pleaded, cajoled, and commanded more desperately. I could hardly keep track of which face was saying what, let alone choose the right one.

Amidst the swelling cacophony, I heard another voice, from somewhere deep in my memory: the voice of my elder self. *Only you can find the way,* he had said. *Only you.* But which way was I to find? Which way—and which me?

The faces danced more wildly. Now many of them were only a blur of motion and sound. *You might,* urged the voice of the old mage, *simply start being.* Being what, though? My mind raced. What had he told me that he hoped, above all, to impart to young Arthur? *Find your true self,* he had said. Yes—and with it, *your true image. Then you shall tap into the greater good, the higher power that breathes life into all things.*

My true self. My true image. But which one, of all the images swarming around me, was true? Perhaps some or all of them were partly true—but which one was the right choice? The right reflection?

The tunnels, and the faces within them, began to recede, pulling back into the curls of mist. Even as the cries grew more shrill, they began to fade slowly away. I could hardly hear some of them now; others I could still hear, but barely see for the encroaching vapors. Only a few seconds, at most, remained before all of them vanished.

The right reflection. What was a reflection, anyway? An image, a shape, thrust back at my vision. But was I out there, the face in the mirror—or was that something else, something other than me? The nature of mirrors, after all, was not to show the actual form. The true self. Just as my shadow, shrunken and disobedient, was not the true me, no reflected image could be my true self.

And yet . . . my shadow was different, at least in

one respect. It was, for better or worse, tied to me, just as my elder self's own shadow was tied to him. Unlike a face in a mirror, which would vanish if the mirror were taken away, my shadow was part of my being, a lifelong companion. Yes, as much as I hated to admit it, my shadow belonged to me, and I to it.

In a flash, I understood. The mirror I needed to find, the face I needed to see, was not one of the reflections circling around me now. Nor was it outside of me at all. Rather, it was somewhere within me—in the deepest marsh, the darkest place, of my own being. In a place where daylight never reached, a place where body and shadow merged into one.

The faces, and their voices, suddenly disappeared. A wave of mist toppled over me, enveloping me completely. Down, down, down, it bore me, into a vaporous tunnel of its own. Deeper into the folds of mist I fell, powerless to stop my descent. As the air around me darkened, I knew only that my choice had been made. And that wherever I was falling, my shadow was falling with me.

26
A TEST OF LOYALTIES

The darkness thickened, hardening into cold, crushing weight that pressed upon me from all sides. My bones, my every vein, cried out in torment. Then, all at once, the pressure released. The light returned. A sudden shattering—and then something smacked beside my head. A split second later, a wooden spear bounced off the stone pillar behind me, its shaft slapping my temple. Disoriented, I stumbled forward, almost falling into a reeking pool.

The marsh! I had returned. Rubbing my head, I glanced at the archway and the Mirror it contained. Clouds of mist swirled beneath the shifting surface, just as they had for uncounted ages.

"Hallia!" I cried. "Where—" Before I knew what was happening, a three-fingered hand grabbed me by the throat and threw me backward. I landed, splattering bogwater in every direction.

Rolling over in the mire, I found myself staring up at a muscular assailant. His thin eyes glinted from under his pointed helmet, while a breastplate covered most of his chest. Perspiration ran in streams down the gray-green skin of his arms. A warrior goblin! Where, I wondered, could he have come from? The warrior goblins who had survived the collapse of the Shrouded Castle now lived in hiding, scattered in the remotest corners of the land. They wouldn't show themselves—unless, I realized with dismay, someone had offered to protect them in exchange for their services. Someone truly wicked.

"Here's another," rasped the goblin, kicking me hard in the ribs as he raised his broadsword.

Clutching my side, I couldn't draw my own sword. I spun, barely dodging his blade as it plunged into the mud. Before he could lift it again, I seized the base of my staff and swung. The handle smashed into his head, knocking off his helmet. He roared, tumbling into the marsh grass, where he lay motionless.

Dazed, I struggled to my feet, pressing my hand against my throbbing ribs. All of a sudden, I caught the smell. Sweet, overpoweringly sweet, it filled my lungs even as it assaulted them. I shuddered, as if a terrible vise were closing on me. For I recognized the scent at once: the scent of rose blossoms.

"Well, well, so you've decided to show yourself at last." Nimue's cold, humorless voice struck harder than the goblin's kick.

"Where are you?" I called into the swamp vapors encircling the arch. "Where is Hallia?"

The disembodied voice continued without pause. "You gave me such a fright, you infant wizard. I had started to worry that you had tried to follow that foolish servant boy into the Mirror."

I almost responded—then caught myself.

"You would have shortened your life immeasurably, *hmmm?* And thereby robbed me of the pleasure of doing so myself." She gave a long, low growl. "That Mirror, one day, will also feel my wrath! For while I survived my own voyage through its misty corridors in coming here, I can still feel the scars. And I have no desire at all to reopen them—until the rest of my powers, which you so callously wrested away from me, are restored. Nay, enhanced! So I have decided to remain on your lovely little island for a while, to gather my strength, plus a few precious trinkets. *Hmmm,* yes, such as your staff."

Still peering into the vapors, I squeezed the wooden shaft all the harder.

Nimue chortled to herself. "All of that, though, is beside the point. The fact is, I do so enjoy solving problems. Especially several centuries in advance. So I think that I shall solve *you,* little wizard. Here and now."

With that, she materialized out of the air before me. Her white robe, immaculate as ever, billowed about her; while her lightless eyes scrutinized me. Flanking her, with swords drawn, stood eight or nine warrior goblins. And at her feet, flopped in the mud, lay a young woman's still form.

"Hallia!" I cried. "What have you done to her?"

Nimue puckered her lips, imitating a kiss. "Ever the soft heart." She plucked a small burr off her sleeve. "Worry not, she remains alive. For now, at least. I was saving her final throes of agony for you to witness." She nodded to the nearest warrior goblin. "Remove her head, *hmmm?* I want a ragged, unclean cut."

"No!"

The goblin, wheezing in laughter, clasped his sword with both hands. His burly arms flexed. In one sharp motion, he lifted the blade high over his head. Then, with all his might, he brought it down on Hallia.

In that instant, a new power surged down my arms. I had no idea what it was, nor where it came from, only that it flew through me with the speed of a diving hawk—and that it seemed to flow from every part of me, body and soul, working in unison as they had never done before. Without any time to think, I raised both of my arms, pointing one at the warrior goblin and one at Nimue.

A sudden sizzling rent the air. Bolts of blue lightening shot out from my fingers. One struck the warrior goblin in the chest just before his weapon made contact. His breastplate ripped apart; with a burst of blue light, he and his sword flew backward. The other bolt of lightning blasted toward the sorceress—and stopped abruptly at her outstretched hand. For a split second she held it in place. Then she carelessly waved her palm in my direction. The bolt flashed back through the air, straight at me. I ducked as it passed just over my head, slicing the corner off one of the rough-hewn pillars. The vines rimming the stone withered into ashes.

Nimue eyed me, seeming only mildly perturbed. "Is that the best you can do, puny one? *Hmmm,* such a pity. You won't be getting the time you need to learn how to do better."

Incensed, I rushed toward her, brandishing my staff. She merely puffed a single breath. A massive wall of air crashed into me, hurling me into a thicket of moss-draped brambles. I skidded through the branches, colliding with the trunk of a dead willow at the edge of a pool. Broken limbs rained down on me as I slumped into the bog.

Weakly, I raised my head. Nimue waved at a pair of warrior goblins and barked her command: "Dispense with the deer woman, however you choose." She strode toward me, smirking. "But leave this one to me."

I saw a pair of swords lifting. All at once, Nimue's head and flowing black hair obscured my view. Her smile widened steadily as she approached. Groping, I braced myself against the tree, forcing my wobbly legs to stand. Without warning, my boots slid out from under me and I splashed again into the pool.

"Poor fellow," she cooed, now only a few paces distant. "Allow me to end your discomfort."

I managed to kneel in the muck. Thick ooze slid down my neck and arms. But I held my voice firm. "You'll never win. Never."

Her eyes narrowed cruelly. Slowly, she raised one arm. Her finger, curved slightly, pointed at my chest. "Ah, my little wizard, you are wrong, very wrong. I have already won." A cackle bubbled up from her throat. "And isn't it a lovely irony, *hmmm,* that I have won by mastering the very spells that you—in your older form—taught me?"

Her finger straightened. "Your time has—"

Slam. An enormous shape, larger than a boulder, dropped out of the sky. It struck the ground right behind Nimue, sending an explosion of mud and debris in all directions. With a shriek, she tumbled headlong into me. A wave of grime washed over us both.

Pulling my head from the mire, I glimpsed Nimue, dripping with the dark juices of the swamp. She cursed viciously as she fought to extract herself. Suddenly I saw the gargantuan head that hovered over us. A triangular eye, glowing orange, stared down at me. Purple and scarlet scales covered the entire face—except for the long blue ear that protruded like a wind-blown banner.

"Gwynnia!" Wrapping my arm around her immense nose, I pressed my face against her own. Then I pointed toward the warrior goblins, many of whom had also been knocked off their feet. "Now get Hallia! Over there."

With a thunderous snarl, she whirled about. Her tail snapped like a whip before smashing into the warrior goblin nearest to Hallia's motionless form. The goblin sailed straight at the Mirror. All at once, its surface flattened, gleaming darkly. Like a bottomless hole in the terrain of time, it swallowed the goblin completely. Even before the sound of shattering died away, the surface contorted again, churning with clouds as before.

The dragon's gangly neck, meanwhile, stretched over to Hallia. Whimpering, Gwynnia nudged her friend's body with the tip of her nose, while her leathery wings fluttered anxiously against her back. But Hallia did not move, or make any sound.

I stumbled out of the pool. Retrieving my staff, I glanced back at Nimue. She was yanking at clumps of mud and sticks that had stuck to her hair, and pulling out her own hair in the bargain. Seeing me, she shrieked in rage and swung her arm wildly. A blazing ball, searing the air like molten lava, appeared in her hand. With the cry, "Death by fire, you upstart wizard!" she reared back and hurled it at me.

The scars on my cheeks stung from the heat as the fireball whizzed toward me. I had only enough time to raise my staff, sending into it whatever power I could muster in the hope that it might shield me. At the moment of impact, jagged fingers of lightning erupted from the staff's head. They collided with the flaming ball, deflecting it into a nearby mound of peat. A roaring wall of fire flew upward, consuming all the reeds, moss, and broken roots on the spot.

Gwynnia, sensing no movement from Hallia, bellowed in anguish. Her tongue, as slender as one of her claws and dark purple in color, gently lapped the face of her friend. Hallia's arm seemed to stir, then fell back. Whether it had lifted on its own accord, I couldn't tell.

"Warriors!" shouted Nimue. She strode from the

pool, still pulling at her tangled hair. "Kill them all. Now, I say!"

Roaring angrily, the goblins descended on us. Wielding heavy spears, swords, and axes, several of them charged at Gwynnia. Two more threw themselves at me. It was all I could do to stay out of reach of their deadly blades, while trying to edge closer to Hallia. On one side, I saw Gwynnia's tail lashing the air, trying to protect our fallen companion from the attackers. On the other side, Nimue prepared to throw another blazing fireball at me.

Swords slashed just over my head; spears plunged into the muck by my boots. Now I was backed against the scorched pillar of the archway. For a split second I considered diving into the mists and saving myself—yet I couldn't leave Hallia behind. As Nimue's laughter rose above the din, a huge warrior goblin wearing a red armband above his elbow confronted me. He gave a harsh, wheezing grunt and swung both of his battle-axes at my head.

Instead of ducking, I did the one thing he least expected: I braced my foot against the pillar and sprung at him. My chest rammed into his shoulder, breaking off an armor plate. One of his axes struck the pillar. Sparks flew into the air. His second ax buried itself in another warrior's back. Meanwhile, I rolled helplessly through the marsh grass.

Finally, I came to a stop. Though my head was spinning, I realized that I was almost underneath the dragon's tail. The shadow of its barbed tip passed over me as she swung at one of our assailants. I didn't watch more of her battling, however, for my attention turned to the limp form nearby. I crawled to Hallia's side and lifted her head toward my own.

"Hallia . . ."

Feebly, she opened her eyes. My heart leaped to see those deep pools of brown, and the fire within them, once again. But the fire burned weakly, faltering. A few seconds later, her eyes closed once again. I poured all the strength I could summon down my arms, through my hands, and into her. Flow, my power! Bring her back to me!

I waited for her to stir, to draw even one halting breath, but nothing happened. Desperately, I shook her by the shoulders. Still nothing. She lay there, as still as my own frozen heart.

Suddenly she quivered, gasping for air. Her eyes reopened. "Young hawk," she said hoarsely. "You're back."

Even as I started to reply, Nimue's voice shook the swamp. "Die, all of you!"

Hallia, seeing the sorceress take aim with her blazing fireball, clutched my arm. At the same time, I caught sight of a dreadful look on Gwynnia's face: a look of fear. Surrounded by warrior goblins, she was no longer able to hold them at bay. They pressed closer by the second. Their weapons hammered against the scales of her back, slashed at her eyes, and probed at her heaving belly. In a few more seconds, she would surely fall.

Nimue's arm uncoiled. The fireball, glowing bright, flew out of her hand. Spitting flames, it bore down on us. Closer and closer it came. Having no staff this time to ward off the blow, I tried to shield Hallia's body with my own.

At that instant, something shot out of the vapors. It sliced through the air, leaving a thin trail of darkness. When it collided with the ball of flames, right before our faces, there was a sudden *woomppf*—and the fire-ball vanished.

Nimue, her mouth agape, glared at the spot. Her warrior goblins, too, sensed something was wrong. Though they still brandished their weapons, they faltered, looking worriedly at one another. Two of them stepped back, moving away from the dragon. At that moment, dozens of figures emerged from the surrounding swamp, encircling us with their shadowy forms.

Marsh ghouls! Most of them could be seen only as vague, shimmering shapes, or as flickering eyes that floated in the vapors. Yet they couldn't be missed. Many of them held hefty bows nocked with coal-black arrows. Arrows that could pierce through the day.

The immense goblin with the red armbands growled fiercely. He stepped toward the nearest marsh ghouls, swinging a battle-ax over his head. Instantly three arrows, trailing ribbons of darkness, plunged through his chest. He fell face first into the muck, and did not move again.

Quaking with rage, Nimue strode toward the line of marksmen. On silent command, a large number of them shifted, aiming their arrows straight at her. She went rigid, glowering at them. Fighting to contain her wrath, she adjusted her silver-threaded shawl about her shoulders. At last, she said in a strained voice, "Now, now, my old friends. You wouldn't think of bringing harm to me, would you?"

In answer, the marsh ghouls drew back their bow-strings. Nimue's face, already pale, went whiter still. After a tense moment, she addressed them again, abandoning any pretense of alliance.

"You really think I am so easily defeated?" she ranted, clenching both of her fists. "You will pay for this treachery, ah yes, with many lifetimes' worth of pain! Just wait until my powers are fully restored to me! Those chains you wore before will seem a delight compared to what torments I shall heap on you."

A few of the marsh ghouls seemed to waver; two or three of them lowered their bows. But the rest remained in place, their arrows nocked, facing the sorceress squarely. What no one had noticed, though, was that during her diatribe, she had slowly raised her hand, pointing it at the spot where Hallia and I sat on the ground. All of a sudden I noticed a reddish glow appearing at the tip of her outstretched finger.

"Beware!" I shouted. "She's going to attack us!"

"Too late, you nursling wizard," she spat back without turning from the line of marsh ghouls. "Now, my former allies, we shall test your loyalties. Shall we, *hmmm?* Hear my terms, for I shall offer them only once: Drop your weapons now, and I shall harm you no further. You have my word on that. My only prize will be the lives of these two assassins who have done me so much harm."

She paused, allowing her words to register. "Or, in

your stubbornness, you can choose to attack me. But if you do, I warn you, I shall have just enough time before your arrows strike to send a blast of fire at your wizard friend and his maiden." Her fingertip seemed to smolder, sizzling in the air. "Perhaps I will not be so fortunate as to kill them both. But at least one of them, I can promise, will surely die."

As Hallia and I sat motionless, a low murmur arose from the assembled marsh ghouls. I cast around in my mind for anything, anything at all, I could do. But any attempt to move, let alone to attack, would certainly cause Nimue to release her pent-up flames, incinerating Hallia and myself. I could tell that Gwynnia, too, had arrived at the same terrible conclusion. Although her eyes brimmed with torment, she remained utterly still, even holding her wings tight against her back.

At length, the marsh ghouls again fell silent. Their luminous eyes glinted through the threads of mist that wove about their shifting forms. Though I was sure that the sorceress, like myself, had expected that they would choose to retreat and save themselves, they did not budge. Clearly, they had decided to test her resolve—and to try to save my life and Hallia's in the process.

Nimue's face twisted. Her finger sizzled all the more, sending upward a thin trail of smoke. My hand squeezed Hallia's as my mind raced to find some way to escape.

A slight quiver of motion by my side caught my attention. My shadow! In that instant, I sent it a silent command: *If you never heed me again, you must do so now! Go now—stop her if you can.*

The shadow seemed to hesitate, shrinking itself down to a fraction of its size. Then, like a pouncing wolf, it leaped away from me and hurled itself at the sorceress, slamming straight into her abdomen.

Nimue shrieked, lurching backward. The searing blast of flames shot from her finger, expending itself harmlessly on the swamp vapors above her head. Before she could gather herself, I lunged at her myself, plowing into her with all my strength. She flew backward, ramming into one of the stone pillars. Fingers of mist broke out of the Mirror's surface, groping at her. She swatted at them, stumbling sideways. The surface suddenly snapped into a rigid, black sheet. For a brief instant, waving her arms to keep her balance, she stared at her own dark reflection, and at something else beyond.

"No!" she cried, even as she fell into the Mirror. She vanished into its depths, her final shriek fading into the sound of shattering, which in turn faded into silence.

As her sweet aroma diminished, no one moved for a long moment. Then, all at once, a resounding cheer went up—first from Hallia and myself, then from Gwynnia (who also battered the ground with her tail, spraying mud in all directions), and finally from the marsh ghouls, whose voices rose in eerie, heaving moans.

When the cries at last died away, the remaining warrior goblins dropped their weapons. Slowly, very slowly, the marsh ghouls' circle parted. Hesitantly at first, the warrior goblins moved toward the opening. A moment later they broke into a run and scattered in the swamp, their heavy boots pounding through the mud.

The marsh ghouls stood, shimmering darkly, for another few seconds. Then, as quietly as they had arrived, they melted into the vapors, vanishing from sight. Only the empty trails of their arrows remained, scrawled upon the air by the ancient archway.

I held Hallia close. The swamp seemed strangely calm. Together, we listened to the sound of our own breathing, and Gwynnia's, not fully believing we remained alive.

Then out of the quiet arose a new sound. It came from somewhere nearby. Although it lasted only a second or two, it seemed almost like a voice. Almost . . . like a cat giving a single, satisfied meow.

27

†HEIR OWN S†ORY

As I sat on the ground beside Hallia, swamp vapors encircled us, much as the marsh ghouls had only moments before. Suddenly I felt a strong nudge against my back. I turned to see Gwynnia, her fiery eyes trained on us.

With a quivering hand, Hallia reached up to stroke the dragon's enormous nose. "You did well, my friend. Though you can't yet breathe fire, you fought like a true dragon. Yes—even your namesake, mother of all the dragon race, would have been proud."

Gwynnia, as if embarrassed, shook her head, making the rows of tiny purple scales beneath her eyes glitter like amethyst jewels. It also made her floppy ear slap against her shoulder, splattering us with mud. Laughing, Hallia pulled a glob off her chin. Without warning, she turned and threw it at my head. It smacked me on the temple.

"That," she declared, "is for being late."

Before I could protest, she pulled my face to hers. Those doelike eyes studied me for an instant. Then she planted a soft kiss on my lips. "And that's for coming back to me."

Sputtering with surprise, I pulled away. "You . . . well, I—er . . . uh, that's . . ."

"There," she said with finality. "You remember that there was something I wanted to tell you? Well, now I have."

My babbling ceased, and I grinned.

Suddenly pensive, she scanned the surrounding bog, watching the coils of rising vapors. Her fingers ran over the mud at our side, touching the scattered ashes that were the only remnant of Nimue's fireball. "Somehow, young hawk, I knew you would come back in time to help. But the marsh ghouls? That surprised me."

I nodded. "Surprised Nimue, too."

"I've never heard of them doing anything to help another creature." She began to comb her tangled locks with her fingers. "Certainly not a man or woman. Even my own people, famous for their forgiveness, have little to spare for marsh ghouls. All of our stories about them—every last one—ends in terror."

Giving up on her mud-crusted hair, she stopped combing and peered at me thoughtfully. "It's possible, I suppose, you did the right thing after all with my father's key. Maybe it will have some effect that reaches beyond today. Maybe it will even change the marsh ghouls, at least a little."

"Perhaps," I replied. "It's hard to know."

I turned to the stone arch, pondering the Mirror within it. Beneath my shifting reflection, clouds of mist knotted, swirled, and congealed, forming numberless shapes and passageways. Slowly, as I watched, my own image disappeared, replaced by something else. It was, I realized, a face, though quite different from my own. It belonged to a man, whose flowing beard melted back into the mist: a face very old, very wise, full of sorrow and torment and centuries of longing—and, at the same time, a touch of hope. Even as I gazed at the face, it seemed, for an instant, to gaze back at me. Then, like a wind-blown cloud, it faded away.

My hand moved to my leather pouch. Reaching inside, I touched a seed, small and round, that seemed to pulse like a living heart. A seed that might, one day, sprout into something marvelous to behold.

Turning back to Hallia, I mused, "You could be right about the marsh ghouls. People tell lots of stories about them, and always will. But the marsh ghouls still have time to write their own story." I drew a deep breath. "With their own choices, their own ending."

She pointed toward the archway. "Someday will you tell me all the things you saw in there?"

"Not all of them, no. But I will tell you one, the most important thing." I took her hand. "It was a mirror. A mirror that needs no light at all."

Hearing the phrase, her whole face brightened. "And what did you see in that mirror?"

"Oh, many things, and among them, a wizard. Yes, the wizard I'll one day become. Not because it's my destiny, mind you, but because it's *me*." I tapped my chest. "The same me, made from the same flesh and bones, that you see right here."

Sensing some motion on the ground, I turned to see my shadow. It seemed to be watching me, shaking its head with determination. I started to scowl, then caught myself. Slowly, I gave a nod. "Made from the same shadow, as well."

The dark form ceased shaking—for the moment, at least.

All of a sudden, we heard a thump from the nearest mound of peat. A sucking sound ensued, and a ragged flap of turf lifted from the puddle at its edge. From under the flap appeared a head that was round, whiskered—and unmistakable.

The ballymag started to say something, then gasped at the sight of the dragon. For a long moment he watched us, tugging anxiously on his whiskers. At last he spoke, his voice thoroughly gruff. "Humans-filthy, always needhaving scrubamuck."

Hallia's eyes shone, as radiant as the liquid light in which we had once bathed. "That," she replied, "would be mooshlovely."